Facing the Sea

Essays in Swedish Maritime Studies

Edited by
Simon Ekström & Leos Müller

NORDIC ACADEMIC PRESS

The publication of *Facing the Sea* has been made possible
through a generous grant from Riksbankens Jubileumsfond.

Nordic Academic Press
Lund
www.nordicacademicpress.se

Typesetting: Anders Gutehall, Visuell Arkeologi
Cover design: Lönegård & Co
Cover image: Thomas Ambrosius' map of 1564.
Photo: GStA PK, XX. HA, AK Allgemeine Kartensammlung
des Historischen Staatsarchivs Königsberg, B Nr. 10001
Print: Livonia Print, Riga 2021
ISBN 978-91-89361-03-4

Contents

Preface

The foundation of a Centre for Maritime Studies in Stockholm in 2010 was inspired by a vision. Not by a rigid plan for maritime history, but by an open-minded hope for maritime studies of all kinds. Museums and universities are both knowledge institutions, with their differences and similarities. The Swedish National Maritime and Transport Museums (SMTM) and Stockholm University decided on a long-term collaboration between the cultural heritage sector and academic research in the humanities and the result was CEMAS – the Centre for Maritime Studies – funded jointly by the SMTM and Stockholm University.

CEMAS may not be large in size, but it has consistently demonstrated a dynamic breadth of creativity. Its ethos, while grounded in flexibility and open-mindedness, acknowledges that one must always play to one's strengths and not risk being a jack of all trades, master of none. Its members are forward-looking and have successfully initiated or participated in special exhibitions and peer-reviewed external research funding. In the autumn of 2020 the director of CEMAS, Leos Müller, and his colleagues landed a substantial six-year research grant for the research programme *The lost navy: Sweden's 'blue' heritage, c.1450–1850*.

CEMAS makes it possible for individuals to grow as professionals, which in return is of immediate benefit to CEMAS. It pursues all aspects of maritime studies: maritime history, maritime ethnology, and maritime archaeology. It is committed to the preservation and development of maritime and transport history and to increasing public knowledge.

This book presents the multifaceted research done at CEMAS and its close collaborations with the cultural heritage sector. It is also an expression of gratitude to CEMAS's former chairperson, Professor Karl-

Olof Hammarkvist, or to all of us in the field, Olle. Olle would be the first to credit CEMAS's many successes to the hard work of committed, skilled people at the museums and the university, yet it is important to remember the blessings of having a good helmsman. Yes, in this case a helmsman more than a commander. A boundless source of support, wisdom, and common sense; engaged and engaging, always interested in what is going on, and proud of the results: such a person is Olle. It has been a privilege for CEMAS and its crew to have him at the helm for over seven years.

Göran Blomqvist
Chairperson, CEMAS

Introduction

Simon Ekström & Leos Müller

This collection of essays is written by scholars associated with the Centre for Maritime Studies (CEMAS) at Stockholm University. Our aim with this book is to give an insight into the centre's research, to illuminate its breadth, and to present the highlights of what has been done in recent years. *Facing the Sea* is CEMAS's second essay collection. The first appeared in 2017 and, with essays in Swedish, it primarily targeted a Swedish readership. With *Facing the Sea* we look to reach a readership outside Sweden.

CEMAS is a unique collaboration between Swedish academia in the shape of Stockholm University and the heritage sector, represented by the Swedish National Maritime and Transport Museums, which include three leading Swedish maritime museums: the world-famous Vasa Museum, the Maritime Museum in Stockholm, and the Naval Museum in Karlskrona. The researchers at Stockholm University are drawn from three disciplines: history, ethnology, and underwater archaeology. CEMAS was founded in 2010, since when it has produced excellent research across the field of maritime studies, contributed to the maritime museums' exhibitions, organized conferences and seminars, and provided expertise for the heritage sector.

What links these essays is that they are all in some way about the sea: a CEMAS smorgasbord of sea-related topics. Although beyond that there are no common subjects, it is nevertheless possible to trace several common themes, mirroring current issues or fashions in research interests, and involving borders or borderlands: between death and life, between legal and illegal, and, of course, between land and sea.

Death at sea, from different perspectives, is present in four essays. Hanna Jansson's essay is about recent burials at sea. Based on interviews, she provides a sensitive mapping of the relatively new habit of scattering ashes at sea. The popularity of the practice is related to the increasing variability of people's views on death and burial. In Sweden, as Jansson's conversations with relatives and officials show, it is specifically linked to the deceased person's own relationship to the sea and life on the coast. Spreading the ashes of our loved ones at sea means they are always close to us, always within reach. Another interesting observation Jansson makes is that the practice of scattering at sea can give rise to private sites of memory in a maritime landscape as the mourners attribute new meanings to it.

Death at sea is something very different in Simon Ekström's essay. Here, successful Swedish salvage projects that have ended up in the public eye are analysed to see how both the ships and their salvage have been incorporated into collective memory. Using examples ranging from a steamer that went down in 1895 to the localization in 2003 of a long-lost military aircraft, the discussion provides essential keys for understanding why some vessels and their salvage are still very much present in museums, literature, and popular culture while others are largely forgotten. Among the circumstances that affect their retention in collective memory are the loss of human lives, the time elapsed between the sinking and the salvage, and the national pride associated with the salvage process.

One of the salvaged ships mentioned in Ekström's essay is *Vasa*, the royal warship that sank on its maiden voyage in 1628, and which is today on display in the Vasa Museum. In Anna Maria Forssberg's essay, *Vasa* appears in a different light, with a renewed perspective on the topic of death at sea. In many respects *Vasa* is as much a well-researched historical artefact as a maritime object. We know a great deal about it; about its architecture, its shipbuilding material, its guns, its rich sculptures. But we still know remarkably little about the people trapped on board when it went down. Forssberg summarizes what is now known about these men and women from archaeological work and archival sources, and points to further questions and findings. What more can we discover about the people who died on *Vasa* in August 1628, and what does it say about Sweden at that time?

Mirja Arnshav only touches on the theme of death at sea in passing, but its threat is present in her essay even so. Her theme is the 'Great Escape' across the Baltic at the end of the Second World War, when about 30,000 people from Estonia and Latvia crossed the sea to Sweden, fleeing the approaching Red Army. Many used small open boats, risking their lives. The refugees most often fled as whole families, including children. Arnshav traces the children's emotional experiences of their escape with help of surviving material culture such as their toys. At the same time, she shows how the maritime museums' ideas of what is considered proper maritime heritage often excludes such objects from collections and exhibitions.

The awkward boundary between lawful and unlawful at sea is the underlying theme of Ida Hughes Tidlund's and Leos Müller's essays. Hughes Tidlund uses the example of the Åland Islands, the Baltic archipelago between Sweden and Finland, to study the practicalities of an established borderland. Politically, the Åland Islands belong to Finland, but linguistically and culturally they are Swedish: a typical borderland, in other words, and as such a hotbed of smuggling, which is the subject of the essay. Hughes Tidlund approaches the issue through the life stories of three Åland smugglers, illustrating how the legality of smuggling was seen as negotiable by the people involved, whether the smugglers themselves or the authorities and coastguard. Small-scale smuggling might be illegal, but it was thought morally acceptable on both sides, and common. Like Hanna Jansson's analysis of scattering ashes at sea, Hughes Tidlund has based her study on interview material, although with the addition of published and archive sources.

In his essay, Leos Müller investigates the seizing of Swedish merchant vessels by the British in the American Revolutionary War (1776–1783). The war began as a colonial revolt against the British Empire, but soon turned into a war between Britain and the alliance of American rebels, France, and other countries. Sweden was neutral and profited from trade with all the belligerents and on shipping their goods. The British refused to recognize the flag of neutrality, arguing it was unacceptable support of the enemy, and they seized numerous Swedish ships. The legality of Swedish shipping was a source of tension between Sweden and Britain, but nevertheless neutrality persisted. Müller's study is based on the Prize Papers, a large collection of records from ships seized by the British navy and privateers, used by the British High Court of Admiralty to rule on whether ships had been legally captured – in this case, Swedish ships.

Fredrik Kämpe's essay, too, examines British–Swedish encounters at sea. His subject is the honour of the naval ensign in the longue durée, from the symbolic significance of naval flags and the importance of military honour in the early modern period to the twentieth century. Military honour was a key component of naval identity. It forced naval commanders and officers to react in a specified fashion that seems destructive and meaningless to modern eyes, but was the only acceptable way at the time. Kämpe provides several examples of how Swedish naval commanders met the challenges of British naval superiority, when to fight often meant loss of life and the destruction of ships, but to surrender meant loss of military honour, a court martial once home, and hypothetically a death sentence. He illustrates how the Swedes created room to manoeuvre by using pragmatic solutions to avoid armed conflict while simultaneously not risking the flag's honour. Kämpe shows how little, whether in practice or in the officers' minds, the perception of honour in the navy changed between the Great Northern War and the Second World War.

Compared to the shifting borderlands between legality and illegality, the distinction between land and sea seems far more stable. Henrik Arnstad and Abigail Parkes' and Niklas Eriksson's essays consider the early exercise of naval power. Henrik Arnstad and Abigail Parkes look at archery in European naval warfare, which had a long history stretching back to antiquity. The archers on board were used for a wide range of tasks and were equipped with specially prepared arrowheads. The introduction of firearms did not mean the archers were dismissed. In fact, there is strong evidence bows were used in the sixteenth century and even as late as the seventeenth. The authors combine the written record with images and substantial archaeological evidence, for example from the English *Mary Rose* which sank in 1545, and consider sixteenth-century naval warfare between Denmark and Sweden in the Baltic Sea.

Niklas Eriksson investigates how Stockholm's maritime landscape dictated the approaches to the capital and Lake Mälaren, and how state formation related to the landscape. Stockholm, like other ports and capitals such as London, is some distance from the open sea, primarily to protect it from enemies and the weather. Eriksson shows how the rise of the early modern state was mirrored in the development of fortifications, customs checkpoints, and harbours on the sea routes into Stockholm. His focus is the sixteenth and seventeenth centuries, but Eriksson also looks back at the history of the sea route into central Sweden and the old Lake Mälaren settlements of Birka and Sigtuna in Viking times.

The essay by Andreas Linderoth of the Swedish Naval Museum considers the intriguing relationship between Swedish national identity and the sea. Sweden's geography is shaped by the sea – modern Sweden has one of the longest coasts in Europe and several large, varied archipelagos – all its major cities are coastal, and foreign trade goes mainly by sea. Nevertheless, the sea is almost invisible in the modern Swedish national identity. Like other European nations, Sweden's national identity is a recent product of the nineteenth and twentieth centuries. Linderoth looks at the magazine *Vår Flotta* (Our Fleet) published in the early twentieth century by a Swedish naval association to see what its contents say about the role of the sea in the mediated image of a national identity. His conclusion is that not only did the sea figure in the magazine, but a stronger Swedish presence in the maritime sector was a fateful question for the Swedish nation, as without it Sweden risked disaster. The sea played prominent part in shaping, or forcing, Swedes to become true Swedes.

With their linking themes, all the essays are in dialogue with one another as the authors engage with the same sea-related matters. While we have chosen to present the contributions in chronological order, beginning with Niklas Eriksson and ending with Hanna Jansson, readers will find they can be read in any order they wish.

This book is dedicated to Karl-Olof Hammarkvist, who was chair of the CEMAS steering board for many years and a maritime enthusiast all of his life. We cannot imagine the CEMAS of today without Olle's engagement and help.

Finally, we would like to express our gratitude to Riksbankens Jubileumsfond for making it possible to publish this book, our publisher Nordic Academic Press, and our copy editor Charlotte Merton.

CHAPTER I

The architecture of the early modern sea routes into Stockholm

Niklas Eriksson

A sea route is more than a simple path between obstacles formed by Nature. Harbour installations, fortifications, customs offices, and umpteen other expressions of material culture formed the architecture of the sea routes – an architecture that underwent a significant remake in the fifteenth and sixteenth centuries. This essay looks at how the Swedish state took control of the natural landscape along the sea routes into Stockholm and transformed them.

Perhaps the most obvious starting point for archaeologists studying landscape is to map the topography, ancient monuments, and other elements. However, as scholars have noted, a map view is insufficient and even anachronistic when considering how humans experienced landscape in the past. The human experience of a landscape should be gauged using the human body, as the state of being is always located somewhere in the world, in a building or in a landscape, or, as we will see, aboard a ship. Humans live on the ground and the human experience of a landscape differs from a map view, as the map describes the world from above – a total picture of a specific part of the world.[1]

When understanding the human experience of a landscape, it is crucial to assess people's ability to move through it. Each human experience of a landscape will consist of one specific view, meaning that to travel along a path, a road, or a sea route can be described as a sequence of views that evoke specific experiences, notions, and emotions. Driving along a winding road and suddenly coming up on a speed camera round a bend can leave drivers with a sense of being monitored. Medieval travellers approaching a castle could not know if they were being observed from the battlements. Discuss the ability to move through a landscape and it is thus necessary to include ships or boats. All watercraft could be said to be extensions of the human body, as their characteristics – size, draft, manoeuvrability – have a decisive impact on the ability to move. There is a difference when approaching an archipelago in a kayak or sailing a first-rate warship.

This essay shows where and how a traveller bound for Stockholm experienced entering the control of the Swedish state. I will show this by reviewing the development of late medieval and early modern ships and land fortifications, but also the places where this architecture of power appeared along the sea route. I will argue the changing preconditions for monitoring and defence along the sea route were connected to the introduction of the new heavy artillery. More effective guns could not only cause devastation from a greater distance, they also required far larger platforms from which to fire. The heavy artillery thus gave rise to a new architecture, both on land and at sea, in three phases roughly coinciding with the Late Middle Ages, the Vasa Era (1521–1611), and the Swedish Empire (1611–1721).

In Sweden, the move to rebuild simple medieval castles as palaces equipped with characteristic round artillery towers came under the Vasa dynasty. This is why these buildings are commonly called *Vasaborgar* (lit. Vasa castles) in the literature.[2] As will be seen, purpose-built warships – the floating gun-platforms introduced at the same time – shared some stylistic features with the castles. This is why one might call them Vasa ships. However, before embarking on the question of how this new architecture reshaped people's experiences of the landscape when moving through it towards Stockholm, it is necessary to say something about natural topography and the city's position.

Where is Stockholm?

The natural topography provides the physical prerequisites for sailing through an archipelago. Arrangements for the control and monitoring of vessels and people are usually placed in narrow straits. Hence the city of Stockholm's position. The earliest settlement, on a small island today known as Gamla Stan (Old Town), provided good seaborne communications with the Baltic Sea on the one side and Lake Mälaren on the other.

Prehistoric Mälaren was a bay of the Baltic Sea. When entering it there were two passages to choose from, either from south, through the rift at present-day Södertälje, or from east, by sailing by present-day Stockholm. Post-glacial land uplift closed the passage at Södertälje by the first century AD, making the passage at present-day Stockholm more strategically important when heading to the religious centre at Uppsala, the administrative centre at Adelsö, or the commercial centre at Birka.[3] Towards the end of the tenth century, Sigtuna was established as the Christian and administrative centre of the Mälaren region, but just as with Birka it was necessary to sail past present-day Stockholm to get there.

The Icelandic Sagas and other sources mention how the sea route to Birka and Sigtuna was blocked at a place called Stocksund. Most scholars agree this place was synonymous with present-day Norrström on the northern side of Stockholm's Gamla Stan.[4] Archaeological excavations in the area in 1978–1981 revealed a great many piles, thought to be the remains of this blockage, which were dated to the period 970–1010.[5] The arrangement at Stocksund was most likely limited to the pile blockage at first, and it was not until the mid thirteenth century that written accounts mentioned buildings on land.[6] The strategic and spatial relationship between Stockholm and the central places in Mälaren is revealed by the Chronicle of Duke Erik, written in around 1320, which described how Sigtuna was razed by heathens from Karelia in 1187. In order to stop them, Birger Jarl 'þen wise man' founded Stockholm.[7]

The archaeological traces and the written sources together reveal how Stockholm grew into a significant commercial city with far-reaching networks under a strong Hanseatic influence, overtaking Sigtuna as the most prominent urban centre and international metropolis. That the city which developed into Sweden's capital was built where it controlled the sea route is a fairly well-known story. Yet there is a logical follow-up question which is rarely addressed. Where were the sailing routes that led to Stockholm controlled?

Medieval sea routes

Whereas the sea routes to the Iron Age and early medieval metropolises in the Mälaren Valley could be controlled at present-day Södertälje and Stockholm, and Sigtuna also at Almarestäket, the sea routes into Stockholm were far more complex to monitor. The archipelago outside Stockholm formed a wall towards the open sea, but it was a wall with cracks and openings through which boats and ships could slip through.

The oldest written description of a sea route in the Baltic Sea area is in a document dated to the fourteenth century, but which most likely was compiled in the 1230s. It is known as the 'itinerary' of Danish King Valdemar II or just these days King Valdemar's *segelled* or sea route. It is a laconic text in Latin that mentions 101 place names on the Baltic coast from Utlängan in Blekinge to Reval (Tallinn). It has no topographical information and it would be impossible to navigate from it.[8] The place names are mentioned with no hierarchy; rather, it is a compilation of harbours along routes that would be used in coming centuries. There were two to choose from when sailing from Stockholm to the open sea: either past Vaxholm or through Baggensstäket, a strait known as Harstäket in medieval and some early modern sources, and sometimes Södra stäket (lit. southern strait), as opposed to Almarestäket which was also called Norra stäket (lit. northern strait) (Fig. 1.1). In the Middle Ages both the Vaxholm and Baggensstäket routes were frequently used, and the strategic passage at Baggensstäket played a crucial role in several conflicts, not least under the Kalmar Union. For example, in 1436 Erik Nilsson Puke blocked this route to stop his fellow nobleman Karl Knutsson Bonde from reaching the sea, and from the Engelbrekt Chronicle's description of events it was evident the strait had been blocked before.[9]

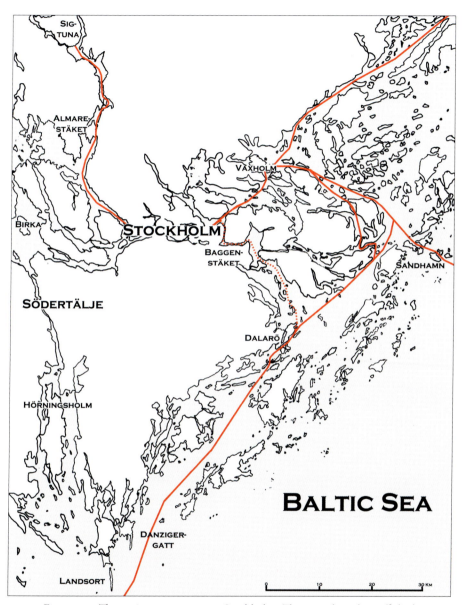

Figure 1.1. The main sea routes into Stockholm. The most heavily trafficked route entered the archipelago from south through Danziger gatt and made a U-turn left to round Vaxholm. Smaller vessels could use Baggensstäket, which is marked with a dotted line. Note also how Stockholm forms a lock for the sea routes into Lake Mälaren and Sigtuna. Map: Niklas Eriksson.

Towards the end of the Middle Ages, Baggensstäket dwindled in importance. This was partly due to the effects of post-glacial land uplift, which made the route shallower and narrower, but also due to ships' increasing size and draft. Large ships had to use the northern passage past Vaxholm, which was longer, especially if they had approached from the south. They were forced 'to sail around the entire compass before one reached in or out through the skerries', as a visiting Dutch diplomat said of the route in the early seventeenth century.[10]

Medieval floating castles

Before the mid sixteenth century saw the introduction of artillery, fortifications along the sea routes into Stockholm appear to have consisted of barriers in the water with smaller fortifications on land. This was efficient enough if ships were armed with longbows or crossbows, or the relatively light and inefficient wrought-iron, breach-loaded cannons.

The ships used by the Hanseatic League, the Danish kings, or other contractors in the conflicts under the Kalmar Union often served a dual purpose. Warships were simply large merchant ships equipped under specific circumstances with light artillery and manned with knights. Queen Margareta (1389–1412) and subsequent Union kings owned a few large ships, and had to borrow ships from loyal ship-owning elites whenever a naval force was required. If the ships survived the conflict they were returned to their owners to be used as merchantmen again.[11] A ship well suited to these dual purposes was lost in the Dalarö roadstead in the archipelago south of Stockholm at the turn of the sixteenth century. The Bellevue wreck, so called because it lay off the old Hotel Bellevue, was discovered by recreational divers in 1964. A recent archaeological study shows it was an unusually large clinker-built ship, probably nearly 30 metres from stem to stern. Judging by its location in one of the most convenient harbours bordering on the open sea, it was departing from or approaching Stockholm when it sank (Fig. 1.2).

As Arnstad and Parkes show elsewhere in this volume, sea battles fought before the introduction of heavy shipboard artillery ended in close combat and the enemies fighting with lighter weapons. For any

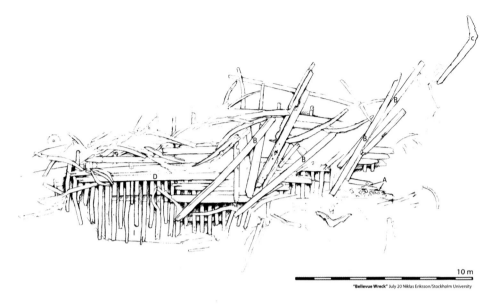

Figure 1.2. Site plan of the Bellevue wreck on the seabed off Dalarö, with the bow pointing to the left. (A) Bricks from the galley (kitchen). (B) Deck beams. (C) Deck-knee. (D) Inner planking. Illustration: Niklas Eriksson.

vessel, size and most notably height was an advantage. High castles were thus erected on the bows and sterns of the largest merchantmen, so they could defend themselves against pirates and so they were ready to be used as fighting ships. The bow of the Bellevue wreck was salvaged in the 1960s and careful investigation revealed it originally had a forecastle, a fighting platform jutting out from the bow where soldiers were stationed ready to board the enemy.[12]

In the grand narrative of late medieval shipbuilding in northern Europe, cogs and hulks were the leading ship types. Several other types – crayers, 'bardese', and others – also appear in written sources, but cogs and hulks are among the most common, which is why they have received the greatest attention. This research began long before the advent of maritime archaeology, and scholars built their arguments on what the different types looked like from written documents and images, and especially medieval town seals (Fig. 1.3). In 1956, Paul Hensius argued

21

Figure 1.3. The seal of Elbing (left), first mentioned in 1367, has a straight-bowed ship of the type said to be a cog. The ship on the seal of Gdansk (right), first mentioned in 1400, has a long, curved bow and is frequently used to illustrate the hulk. Note the fore- and sterncastles with crenellations. Reproduced from Herbert Ewe, *Schiffe auf Siegeln* (1972), 122, reproduced by permission of NAME, 128, drawing by Gerda Nützmann, reproduced by permission of Hinstorff Verlag GmbH.

that a group of ships found in medieval images that were single-masted, straight-bowed, high-sided, and clinker-built should be regarded as cogs, and since the discovery of the Bremen cog in 1962, several other finds that share its constructional characteristics have been identified and labelled cogs or 'cog-like'.[13] For example, it has been suggested that two wrecks – one from the Helgeandsholmen excavation in Stockholm and the other found in shallow water at Jungfruskär in the archipelago – represent the type.[14] However, as it is far from certain how medieval writers defined these ships, some prefer to call them 'archaeological cogs'.[15]

The hulk, though, is often said to have gradually replaced the cog, even though written sources indicate that hulks and cogs existed simultaneously, and on occasion both terms were applied to the same vessel.[16] As with the cog, scholars long tried to determine the characteristics of the hulk from town seals and other images. It has been said that a plank keel is the defining element, a pronounced, almost 'banana-shaped' hull built up of strakes of planking laid in reverse clinker, sometimes even called 'hulc-type planking'.[17] Written sources that mention hulks are numerous, but archaeologists still await the discovery of a wreck which will do for the hulk what the Bremen ship did for the cog – the many medieval wrecks already discovered and surveyed seem to lack this characteristic look.[18]

In the past four decades, several scholars have come up with an alternative solution to the 'hulk question' by suggesting that it was the large, clinker-built ships designed to carry bulky loads that were hulks, as they were referred to as such in their day. It is certainly very tempting to sort the Bellevue wreck into this category.

The Bellevue wreck, which could have transported heavy goods between the Baltic Sea and the rest of the known world, but could also be used for war, offers an interesting comparison to another almost contemporary wreck, *Gribshunden* (lit. 'Griffin Hound') or *Griffin*, which sank in 1495. The wreck is one of the oldest gun-carrying ships discovered in the Baltic Sea. *Gribshunden* belonged to King Hans, who when it sank was king of Denmark–Norway and who later became king of Sweden. *Gribshunden* was one of his own ships; the rest of his navy consisted of large ships assembled from the ship-owning elites. Neither the Bellevue wreck nor *Gribshunden* has been excavated, but the tentative results show their principal dimensions were much the same. Even if they were among the largest ships of their day, they were still small next to the purpose-built, sailing artillery platforms – the Vasa ships – introduced a few decades after *Gribshunden* sank. Both *Gribshunden* and the Bellevue wreck were likely too large to sail through Baggensstäket and would have to take the longer sea route that passed Vaxholm.

Vaxholm, from blockhouse to stone tower

The heavy seaborne traffic passed Vaxholm, so it was there the most important, most impressive constructions to protect, control, and monitor the ships sailing towards Stockholm were first erected. It was at Vaxholm that arrivals first encountered the Swedish state aboard ship. In the early sixteenth century the Vaxholm area developed into the gateway to Stockholm, although the eponymous town was not founded until the 1650s. Where the name comes from is not known for certain, but one reading is that 'vax' derives from the Swedish 'vaka', 'to watch', and the island Vaxön is believed to have been part of a beacon system for coastal defence.

The oldest written sources to mention permanent defences at Vaxholm date from 1510, when Svante Nilsson Sture ordered it be fortified. The year before the Danes had burnt the nearby island of Värmdön and they were expected to return. Repeated Danish attacks a decade later again revealed the need for some form of outer defence in the archipelago, but it was not until 1544 it was decided that defences and a fortress should be built at Vaxholm.[19] According to the decision, the arrangement consisted of a blockhouse and an iron chain that stretched across the strait. The decision also mentioned *galejor* – small galleys – which would patrol the area. The archipelago around Vaxholm consists of several islands with alternative passages between them. Obstructing the passages in order to force ships to pass close by the blockhouse was an extensive and costly endeavour. The main challenge was Oxdjupet, the passage between Rindön and the largest island, Värmdön, which was 30 metres deep in its natural unregulated state. In the winter of

1548 rubble was dragged out and dumped through holes cut in the ice, and the nearby strait of Stegesundet was blocked by a boom.[20] That is the extent of our knowledge of the considerable work done to control the waterways by the mid sixteenth century. The fortress at Vaxholm has since been enlarged and still forms an important point in Sweden's coastal defences. All archaeological traces in the landscape or the seabed have been erased by later fortifications, while the underwater topography is still a military secret and to a large extent inaccessible for marine archaeological surveys.

The late medieval system for controlling the sea routes into Stockholm concentrated on blocking them in order to delay enemy ships or to attack them while they were stuck. The blockhouse was a small wooden fortress, and probably a relatively light construction. The key architecture on land and at sea changed dramatically in the sixteenth century with the introduction of heavy artillery, and with it the development of the sea routes.

The Vasa Era was when Sweden's medieval castles were rebuilt as palaces, ornamented to proclaim the divine power of its newly Protestant monarchs. The majority of the Vasa castles – Kalmar, Åbo, Örebro, Nyköping, Vadstena, and Tre Kronor in Stockholm – were in urban settings. Together with the great churches, the castles embodied divine and earthly power in their dimensions and ability to rise above all the surrounding buildings. Of all these castles, though, only Kalmar Castle is visible from the open sea; the others are all on navigable waters, but in a topography that hides them behind serried ranks of archipelago. Friend or foe, whoever sailed in towards the cities of early modern Sweden would have travelled between several thousand islands with grazing cattle and peasants' cottages before encountering the magnificent buildings that announced the presence of the Swedish state. As the Spanish captain Francisco de Eraso wrote to Philip II as he travelled along the coast towards Stockholm in 1578, the islands belonged to the Swedish king, but only peasants live here.[21]

The old Vaxholm fortress is usually thought of as the large, round, stone tower known from the earliest images. It was built, demolished, and rebuilt several times over the centuries, but it remains uncertain

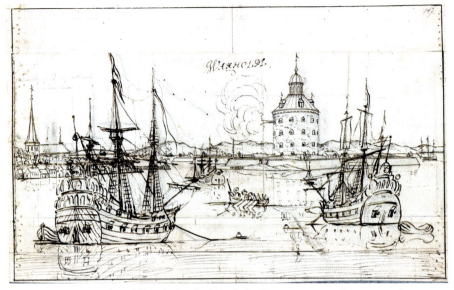

Figure 1.4. Erik Dahlbergh sketched Vaxholm Fortress in 1668 for a copperplate engraving for his monumental *Suecia antiqua et hodierna*. The two ships are moored inside the fortress. Ships bound for Stockholm used the narrow strait to the left of the tower. Dahlbergh has included the boom used to close the passage. Photo: Kungliga biblioteket, Stockholm.

when the first foundations were laid. Some argue the work began in the reign of Gustav I (1523–1560). In 1550 they mention a 'rundel' and later a tower with walls over four metres thick.[22] In any case, the first tower was finished and in use in the 1560s.

The fortress's medieval, breach-loaded, wrought-iron guns were replaced by muzzle-loaded, cast-bronze guns. They were more solid and could be loaded with more gunpowder, they could fire at a greater distance, and they could cause greater devastation. Whereas an iron gun was sensitive to corrosion, the lifespan of a bronze gun could be several hundred years. They could go down with a sinking ship and yet be salvaged to be used again. Damaged, they could be melted down and recast. The catch was that bronze guns were expensive, and only a well-developed state administration could raise the money to finance a large number of them. The decision to arm the tower at Vaxholm with artillery was taken in 1552 and the armament was strengthened in 1559.[23]

One of the clearest sketches of the old tower was by Erik Dahlbergh in 1668 (Fig. 1.4). Just below the eaves of the roof there is an edging reminiscent of the decoration on the round towers of contemporary castles. It is almost as if one of the corner towers of Gripsholm or Örebro, or perhaps the keep of the royal castle of Tre Kronor in Stockholm, had been transported to a skerry in the archipelago. A traveller acquainted with the architecture of the Vasa castles would no doubt have seen the Vaxholm tower's associations. The number of stone buildings erected along the sea route was limited in the sixteenth century – many fortifications still consisted of structures built of wood, gravel, and soil – so a tall tower was an unusual sight and would have been a striking landmark for those approaching Stockholm from the sea. Manoeuvring a large, heavily laden ship through the Stegsundet strait which was only 140 metres wide, passing under the stone tower and its deep, dark gunports must have been an extraordinary experience.

The Northern Seven Years War

In 1563 the Northern Seven Years War broke out. The background was Denmark's longstanding anger at Sweden for breaking loose from the Kalmar Union, but also Swedish expansion on the Eastern side of the Baltic, which affected Denmark's trade with Russia and the Gulf of Finland. As a consequence Poland joined the conflict, as did Lübeck, who allied with Denmark.[24] It has been described as 'the first big war', as it was the first of a long series of wars fought to control trade in the Baltic in the centuries to come.[25] It was bloody and prolonged, and fought at sea and on land. When the barrier, boom and checkpoint was first set up at Vaxholm it was only manned when war seemed likely. At the outbreak of the Seven Years War a constant guard (*ständig vakt*) was mounted at Vaxholm, and it was ordered that 'all ships coming from foreign places would give notice'. The guard numbered only seven men in the first year, but was increased to twelve thereafter. Whenever a foreign ship approached Vaxholm its presence was to be reported to Stockholm Castle before it reached the capital. As noted by Allan Cyrus, the message must have been sent the fastest way, either by rowing boat or on horseback.[26]

The system of obstacles and chains in the straits between the islands around Vaxholm and the massive stone tower glowering down on ships taking the sea route seem part of a vast system. They were permanent constructions, anchored on the ground or the seabed, but only part of the imposing architecture of the sea route, a significant portion of which consisted of ships, an ever-present if constantly changing setting. The situation was evident in King Gustav I's decision to have the stronghold at Vaxholm in 1544 and that 'the galleys should patrol once in a while', and Erik Dahlbergh's sketch serves as illustration (Fig. 1.4). In a travel description from 1561 Henrik Norman noted seeing two royal *håpar*, barges that belonged to the court, which at night 'were moored next to a blockhouse, which all ships bound for Stockholm must pass'.[27]

A spy's map from 1564

The Prussian Secret State Archives in Berlin have a remarkable map that shows southern Sweden with specific focus on the routes to and from Gripsholm Castle, and how they were controlled (Fig. 1.5). The history of the map is both fascinating and spectacular. It was produced in 1564 in the thick of the political conflicts, intrigues, and scheming driven in no small part by the enmity between the sons of King Gustav I. The posthumous reputation of the eldest, Erik XIV, focuses on his mental health and his paranoia about conspiracies against him at home and abroad. His fears were largely justified, but this is not the place for a detailed consideration of cause and effect in Erik's troubled soul.

Gustav I's death left Erik king, while his brothers were made dukes of various regions of the Swedish kingdom. Erik's suspicions were primarily directed towards his brother Johan, who was Duke of Finland. From his seat at Åbo Castle, on the eastern side of the Baltic Sea, Johan made increasingly important foreign contacts on his own, especially with Catholic Poland, something that worried Erik. When Johan married the Polish princess Katarina Jagellonica, Erik had enough. In August 1563, in desperate attempt to control events, Erik had Johan and Katarina

Figure 1.5. Thomas Ambrosius' map of 1564 for the rescue of Duke Johan and
Katarina Jagellonica from Gripsholm Castle (centre), showing escape routes and
possible obstacles, and thus the most significant architecture on land and at sea
– Vasa castles and Vasa ships. North is to the right. Photo: GStA PK, XX. HA,
AK Allgemeine Kartensammlung des Historischen Staatsarchivs Königsberg,
B Nr. 10001.

seized and imprisoned in Gripsholm Castle. The Polish king, Katarina's father, was already worried about King Erik's expansive policy, which was having an increasingly detrimental effect on trade in the Baltic. In October 1563, Poland joined forces with Denmark. It was about this time the peculiar map in the Berlin archive was made. The purpose was to compile the information needed to free Johan and Katarina. The map thus summarizes the critical passages that any expedition would need to deal with as they fled Gripsholm Castle for freedom abroad.

The briefest of glances reveals that as a topographic map it leaves something to be desired (compare Fig. 1.1). North is to the right and the proportions are incorrect. The thousands of islands have been left out and the coastal contours are simplified and wholly schematic. On the other hand, the cartographer has made a point of depicting several buildings carefully – the buildings that would no doubt be noticed when using the sea routes it described. In a cursorily drawn landscape, the more important strongholds and castles appear correctly done. As noted by late cultural geographer Bertil Hedenstierna, the detailed description of the castles reveals that the mapmaker was someone with good local knowledge. One person who had the opportunity to observe the buildings and the topography was Thomas Ambrosius, a Prussian ambassador who was obviously also a spy. He compiled the map from his observations in Sweden and sent it to Duke Albert of Prussia, who was part of the conspiracy to release the couple.[28]

The map has inscriptions that give the distances involved. Someone, whether Ambrosius himself or an informant, had travelled the main roads in southern Sweden and measured the distances. As Hedenstierna noted, the measurements corresponded well with the actual distances, but the distances for the land routes were more accurate than those for the sea routes, which are overestimates.

On an island in the middle of the map Gripsholm Castle is depicted with its characteristic towers. The bridge that links it to the mainland is shown, as are the surrounding guardhouses and gatehouses, which would have been crucial to a rescue attempt. From the castle, several waterways that led out to the open sea are shown. The route that was the main shipping artery is shown as a narrow passage passing under the eye of Vaxholm fortress, drawn as a stone building with crenellations and the familiar tower. In the critical passage is a large ship that can be fired on by one of the heavy cannons that protrude through the tower's gunports.

The alternative route through Baggensstäket is depicted as even narrower, which reflects actual conditions. The size and character of this passage is illustrated by two small, single-masted vessels in the channel. On the strait is a large building labelled 'Jacob Bagges hof' or estate. Jacob Bagge was King Erik's admiral and held the estate in fief; it was from him that Baggensstäket took its new name. Smuggling Duke Johan and Princess Katarina past King Erik's admiral must have seemed a bad idea, even if the house was drawn not as heavily fortified as the stronghold at Vaxholm.

The map also indicates the passage through Södertälje, which would have been the shortest escape route. Had they chosen this route they could have travelled out of sight of the capital; the drawback was having to go ashore in Södertälje and travel a short distance on foot. One building clearly thought to be of some importance was Hörningsholm Castle. Ambrosius has captured the castle's distinctive location on top of a high, steep cliff, overlooking the approaches to Södertälje. The waters around Hörningsholm had been controlled for centuries – archaeological investigations of the seabed of nearby Pålsundet reveal there was an extensive system of piles in the Viking Age.[29]

There were fortifications at Hörningsholm by the end of the Middle Ages and around 1500 it was mentioned as 'hørningxholm' for the first time.[30] Given the extraordinary location, however, there seem likely to have been prehistoric settlements before then, as is also indicated by several prehistoric graves just south of the castle. The present castle is eighteenth century, but has many remnants of the medieval building, for example a large round tower. According to a seventeenth-century source, the tower was erected in around 1560; it was certainly there to be included in the Ambrosius map. Hörningsholm thus seems to have been something to be reckoned with by the putative rescuers, but it is not evident whether it was thought an obstacle or an asset. As Hedenstierna said, the castle was owned by Svante Sture the Younger and the impris-

oned Duke Johan's aunt Märta Lejonhuvud. To say the Sture family
had a complicated relationship with Erik XIV is an understatement.
Three years after the map was drawn, it would cost Svante Sture and
two of his sons their lives in the events known as the Sture murders.[31]

The escape plan was never put into effect, and Johan and Katarina
remained in house arrest in Gripsholm Castle for four years. Whether
this was because the routes in and out of Sweden were too well guarded
is not known. Ambrosius' map survives, though, as unique testimony
to the places in the landscape and the arrangements made by the mid
sixteenth century for controlling the movement of ships and people.
It showed with all necessary clarity that all routes had checkpoints of
various kinds. Vaxholm fortress on the main sea route into the capital
was depicted as the largest building on the map – hardly surprising as
the passage it guarded was so important to all the big ships that arrived
in Stockholm by sea.

Vasa castles, Vasa ships

Ambrosius' map gives a sense of how by the mid sixteenth century the
architecture of power towered up along the sea route. Even though it
is schematic, it captures how buildings such as Storkyrkan and Tre
Kronor in Stockholm and Vaxholm in the archipelago dominated their
surroundings. The same is implied for the buildings of some of the most
influential families, such as the Bagges at Baggensstäket and the Stures
at Hörningsholm.

An interesting aspect of the map is that it shows almost as many
boats and ships as it does castles and other buildings on land. In the
waters either side of the barriers erected by the state, Ambrosius has
drawn several large purpose-built warships, ships that were novelties
by the standards of the day. At the same time as the construction of the
Vaxholm tower and the rebuilding of Tre Kronor or Gripsholm, Sweden
was establishing a standing navy. The medieval navy had consisted of
ships borrowed from the ship-owning elite for a specific conflict: this
was a navy as an event rather than an institution. In contrast to the large
merchantmen equipped for the medieval wars, the new state-owned

navy of the sixteenth century had purpose-built warships.[32] Among the perhaps most conspicuous features with these new ships were that they were carvel built, so the hull planks are laid flush instead of overlapping as on clinker-built hulls.[33] The planking could be made much thicker, so a carvel-built ship was more robust and heavily built, both to withstand but most notably to carry artillery. The introduction of cast bronze cannons changed not only the nature of warfare on land and at sea; it changed the architecture of war.

Acquiring the new warships was expensive and required a well-developed state administration. A substantial portion of the funding was derived from the Reformation and the dissolution of Sweden's monasteries. It is interesting to see how the very materials were reused: to take a well-known example, Mariefred Charterhouse was demolished and the bricks reused for Gripsholm Castle, while several church bells were melted down and recast as cannons.[34]

Medieval sea battles are sometimes described as land battles fought at sea, where the fighting vessels sail up to one another and the battle was fought at close quarters using longbows, crossbows, swords, and pikes. With the introduction of artillery, battles were fought at a greater distance. Boarding and close combat were still part of war at sea in the Napoleonic Wars, but became less decisive as guns became more effective and had greater range.

Buildings can endure for centuries – many medieval and early modern buildings are still in daily use – but ships have a very limited lifespan. There are only limited sources that describe the architecture of late medieval and early modern ships: the written sources are not clear even regarding the overall dimensions of these ships, and no constructional drawings survive (indeed, it is doubtful they existed in Sweden at this time). Luckily, though, the archaeological record provides some information.

The same year as Ambrosius made the map, two of King Erik XIV's most prestigious floating Vasa castles were lost at sea. The second-largest ship was *Elefanten* (The Elephant), which sank in shallow water just north of Kalmar. The ship was excavated by the pioneering maritime archaeologist Carl Ekman in the 1930s. The better known of the ships

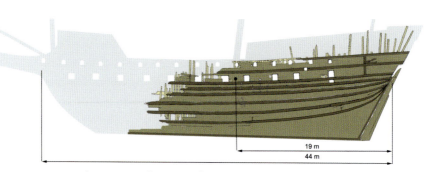

Figure 1.6. In design, Vasa ships were floating Vasa castles – gun platforms. A reconstruction of the port side of *Mars*, which sank in a sea battle off Öland in 1564 when its bow exploded. Illustration: Niklas Eriksson.

was named for the Roman god of war: *Mars* sailed under the command of Admiral Jacob Bagge, he whose house Ambrosius had drawn on Baggensstäket. In a battle against the combined Danish–Lübeckian navy, fire broke out aboard *Mars*. Admiral Bagge struck the colours and left the burning ship to the enemy, and when the fire reached the gunpowder magazine the bow exploded. In 2011, the wreck of *Mars* was relocated at 75 metres depth and has been the subject of archaeological surveys. About two-thirds of the large, heavily built oak hull is preserved (Fig. 1.6). Though partially collapsed, it is still possible to piece it together for an idea of what the ship originally looked like. In the sixteenth century, fighting ships increased significantly in size. The Bellevue wreck and *Gribshunden*, mentioned above, were among the largest in the Baltic at the turn of the sixteenth century and measured some 30 metres from stem to stern; *Mars* is calculated to have been around 44 metres.[35] *Mars* was probably not so much longer than other contemporary warships, but was probably one of the first to carry the most recent cast-bronze cannons on two relatively full gun decks, and it also had a large number of smaller cannons on the fore- and sterncastles and in the masts – in all around 107 pieces.[36]

An exciting detail on *Mars* is that the upper edge of the gunport openings on the second gun deck is rounded, echoing the arched gunports of contemporary castles. Kalmar, Gripsholm, Örebro, Nyköping: all had these characteristic gunports, as did the Vaxholm tower.[37] In the same way as the medieval cogs and hulks had had crenellated fore- and sterncastles, sometimes even painted to imitate masonry, *Mars* was an expression of stone-built architecture afloat.

Whenever *Mars*, *Elefanten*, *Hector*, *Morianen*, or one of the other Swedish royal ships used one of the sea routes or was moored in a roadstead in one of the archipelago's natural harbours, there was no doubt that the Swedish state was present.[38]

The next step, the Swedish Empire

In 1615 a Dutch diplomat called Antonis Goeteeris visited Stockholm. He had been in Russia and Finland and entered the archipelago from the North. The first building on Swedish land he mentioned was the customs house on Vaxholm on the Stegsundet strait, opposite the round tower. A nearly contemporary sailing description published in Amsterdam and in translation in England noted that 'Upon Waxholm standeth the Kings castle, there all the ships are visited wether they go up or down the chanell there by it, is paled too se neare, that they can shut it with a boam.'[39] Goeteeris stayed in Stockholm for some weeks and then set off for the Netherlands. His voyage from Vaxholm to Älvsnabben in the southern archipelago took almost a fortnight. The journey gave Goeteeris plenty of time to register the agricultural landscape on the islands that slowly passed by. What is striking from his description, as from contemporary printed sailing descriptions such as Willem Blaeu's *The sea-mirror* of 1625, is that the Swedish state was not much in evidence in the archipelago.

Several documents reveal how the Swedish navy used several natural harbours in the archipelago when on a war footing, and that warships occasionally anchored at Älvsnabben, Nyhamn, Djurhamn, Dalarö, and elsewhere. However, beyond Vaxholm there were no permanent installations and facilities for the state to monitor the sea routes. The situation described in Ambrosius' map in 1564 still pertained 70 years later. But then came a sea change.

The Swedish Empire is generally characterized as a period of war and conquest. Yet it was also when Sweden saw the creation of a more powerful state administration. In 1636 a system of *stapelstäder* or staple ports was set up, whereby only selected towns could trade with foreign countries. There had been attempts in this direction for a long time: it was thought concentrating foreign trade in this way would make it simpler to control – and tax.[40]

The Stockholm archipelago beyond Vaxholm, with its hidden natural harbours, was difficult to control, which led to smuggling and unregulated trade. It might be an exaggeration to call it a no-go area, but there were problems getting all goods checked by customs officers and duly taxed. The solution for Stockholm and for all staple ports was to establish *inloppsstationer*, customs houses at points of entry to the archipelagos. The customs houses were placed on the sea routes, as far out in the archipelagos as possible, with the exception of Kalmar, for the simple reason that Kalmar has no archipelago. This measure saw the state move its area of control further out towards the sea. From 1636 onwards, any ship heading for Stockholm met the long arm of Swedish government out at Dalarö, not at Vaxholm.

From the mid seventeenth century on, the roadstead at Dalarö was protected by the large and impressive Dalarö Fortress, built along the same lines as Vaxholm. Its massive grey stone tower was visible far out at sea, an important landmark for all approaching the Stockholm archipelago from the south: the gateway to the Swedish Empire.

Conclusions

The Swedish state continually extended its reach towards the open sea, increasing the area it monitored and governed in the country's archipelagos. This development was driven by several societal processes, but may be summarized as falling into three phases.

The first phase began when Stockholm was established as a trading town at the spot where seaborne traffic into Lake Mälaren was regulated by a series of obstacles. High and late medieval ships, which were combined trading and fighting vessels, could be stopped and detained at locations such as Baggensstäket and to some extent at Vaxholm.

The second phase was the Vasa Era archipelago. Stockholm was a city of increasing importance, while innovations such as artillery put new demands on the architecture of the sea route into the capital. The fortifications at Vaxholm were built, centred on a massive stone tower armed with novel, muzzle-loaded bronze guns. The tower stood sentinel over everyone who approached Stockholm by that sea route, and was the gateway to Stockholm in the sixteenth and early seventeenth centuries. The tower was visible from a great distance. Aboard an approaching ship, you could not tell if you were being watched from inside the tower, or if the bronze guns would open fire. Submission to the Swedish state was more than likely, passing through the organized landscape on the sea route past Vaxholm.

The third phase was the Swedish Empire archipelago, when ships approaching Stockholm could not tell if they were already being monitored as they entered the Danziger gatt in the southern archipelago. As soon as they saw the massive tower of Dalarö fortress, which is placed so it is always in full sun and visible from a great distance, there was a chance they were being watched.

Sweden's development from a medieval fiscal–military state into a modern state is thus visible in many forms of material culture, from cast-bronze cannons to castle architecture and shipbuilding. What I have addressed in this essay is the fact that this development also had an impact on the arranged landscape along Sweden's key sea routes.

Notes

1 See, for example, Christopher Tilley, *A Phenomenology of Landscape: Places, Paths and Monuments* (Oxford 1994); Matthew Johnson, *Behind the Castle Gate: From the Middle Ages to the Renaissance* (London 2002).

2 Fredric Bedoire, *Den svenska arkitekturens historia 1000–1800* (Stockholm 2015).

3 David Damell, 'Nya fakta om Södertäljeleden', *Fornvännen* 68/1(1973), 23–5; Anders Ödman, *Stockholms tre borgar: från vikingatida spärrfäste till medeltida kastellborg* (Lund 1987), 127.

4 Snorre Sturluson, *Norges konungasagor: Andra delen* (Lund 1922); Per Vikstrand, 'Namnet Stockholm', in Susanne Thedéen & Torun Zachrisson (eds.), *Stockholm före Stockholm: Från äldsta tid fram till 1300* (Stockholm 2016), 192.

5 Ödman 1987, 82, 116; see also Christian Lovén, *Borgar och befästningar i det medeltida Sverige* (2nd edn, Stockholm 1999), 88–9.

6 Snorre Sturlasson mentions a castle, but most scholars argue that he relies on accounts contemporary with himself, which means the thirteenth century (Lovén 1999, 85).

7 Sven-Bertil Jansson, *Erikskrönikan* (Stockholm 1985), 9–12.

8 Gerhard Flink (ed.), *Kung Valdemars segelled* (Stockholm 1995).

9 Gustaf Edvard Klemming (ed.), *Svenska medeltidens rimkrönikor, ii: Nya eller Karlskrönikan: Början av unionsstriderna samt Karl Knutssons regering, 1389–1452* (Stockholm 1866), 107.

10 Antonis Goeteeris, *En holländsk beskicknings resor i Ryssland, Finland och Sverige 1615–1616: Trenne reseberättelser* (Stockholm 1917), 187.

11 The fleets of the Kalmar Union are described by Jørgen Barfod, *Flådens fødsel* (Copenhagen 1990) and the ships by Jan Bill, 'Castles at Sea: The Warship of the High Middle Ages', in Anne Nørgård Jørgensen (ed.), *Maritime warfare in northern Europe: Technology, organisation, logistics and administration 500 BC–1500 AD* (Copenhagen 2002), 47–56.

12 Niklas Eriksson, 'The Bellevue Wreck: A recent study of a large, late medieval shipwreck in Dalarö harbour, Sweden: a possible hulk?', *International Journal of Nautical Archaeology* (in press 2021).

13 Paul Hensius, *Das Schiff der hansischen Frühzeit* (Cologne 1956); Tim Weski, 'The Ijsselmeer type: some thoughts on Hanseatic cogs', *International Journal of Nautical Archaeology* 28/4 (1999), 360–79 with references and response by Ole Crumlin-Pedersen, 'To be or not to be a cog: the Bremen Cog in perspective', *International Journal of Nautical Archaeology* 29/2 (2000), 230–46.

14 Jonathan Adams & Johan Rönnby, 'Kuggmaren 1: the first cog in the Stockholm archipelago, Sweden', *International Journal of Nautical Archaeology* 31/2 (2007), 172–81.

15 Jan Bill, 'Scandinavian warships and naval power in the thirteenth and fourteenth centuries', in John Hattendorf & Richard Unger (eds.), *War at Sea in the Middle Ages and the Renaissance* (Suffolk 2003), 37–9.

16 For example, Detlev Ellmers, 'The Cog as Cargo Carrier', in Robert Gardiner (ed.), *Cogs, Caravels and Galleons: The Sailing Ship 1000–1650* (London 1994), 29–46; Reinhard Paulsen, *Schifffahrt, Hanse und Europa im Mittelalter: Schiffe am Beispiel Hamburgs, europäische Entwicklungslinien und die Forschung in Deutschland* (Cologne 2016), 187–96.

17 Basil Greenhill, 'The mysterious hulc', *Mariner's Mirror* 86/1 (2000), 3–18; Jonathan Adams, *A Maritime Archaeology of Ships: Innovation and Social Change in Late Medieval and Early Modern Europe* (Oxford 2013), 99–110.

18 Klara Fiedler, *Large clinker built cargo vessels from the late medieval period in Northern and Western Europe: The Mönchgut 92 wreck in context* (Esbjerg 2016).

19 Axel Zettersten, *Svenska flottans historia: åren 1522–1634* (Stockholm 1890), 265; Allan Cyrus, *Vaxholms fästning: anteckningar om fästningens och dess garnisons historia* (Stockholm 1947), 5–6; Lars Ericson, '"Att förmena fienderna inloppet": Om försvaret av Stockholms vattenvägar', in Kerstin Abukhanfusa (ed.), *Vattenstäder: Sankt Petersburg–Stockholm* (Stockholm 1998), 243–55.

20 Göran Dahlbäck, 'Vaxholmen och dess fästning i de äldsta källorna', *Meddelanden från Föreningen Vaxholms Fästnings Musei Vänner* 19 (1979), 44–50.

21 Emil Hildebrand, 'Johan III och Filip II: Depescher från det spanska sändebudet till Sverige kapten Francisco de Eraso 1578–1579', *Historisk Tidskrift* 6 (1881), 1–50.

22 Cyrus 1947, 7; Zettersten 1890, 265.

23 Jonas Hedberg, *Kungl. Artilleriet: Medeltid och äldre vasatid* (Stockholm 1975), 274.

24 Lars-Olov Larsson, *Arvet efter Gustav Vasa* (Stockholm 2005), 77–106.

25 Alexej Smirnov, *Det första stora kriget* (Stockholm 2009).

26 Zettersten 1890, 266; Cyrus 1947, 9.

27 Hildebrand 1881, 265; for 'håpar', see Zettersten 1890, 325.

28 Bertil Hedenstierna, 'Ambrosius Thoms' South-Sweden, 1564', *Imago Mundi* 9/1(1952), 65–8.

29 Rune Edberg, Marcus Lindström & Johan Rönnby, *Pålsundet: Arkeologiska studier av en sörmländsk kustmiljö* (Stockholm 2001).

30 Quoted in Lovén 1999, 317.

31 Larsson 2005, 127–40.

32 See Jan Glete, *Swedish Naval Administration 1521–1721: Resource Flows and Organisational Capabilities* (Leiden 2010), 1–50, 80–5.

33 For an overview, see Adams 2013.

34 Carl-Johan Clemedson, *Kartusianklostret Mariefred vid Gripsholm* (Nyköping 1989).

35 Niklas Eriksson, 'How large was Mars? An investigation of the dimensions of a legendary Swedish warship, 1563–64', *Mariner's Mirror* 105 (2019), 260–74.

36 Glete 2010, 534 n. 49.

37 Bengt Thordeman, 'Hörningsholms byggnadshistoria', *Tidskrift för Konstvetenskap* (1921), 61–78; Lovén 1999, 317–19.

38 Eriksson 2019; Niklas Eriksson & Johan Rönnby, 'Mars (1564): the initial archaeological investigations of a great 16th-century Swedish warship', *International Journal of Nautical Archaeology* 46 (2017), 92–107.

39 Willem Janszoon Blaeu, *The sea-mirrour containing, a briefe instruction in the art of navigation; and a description of the seas and coasts of the easterne, northerne, and vvesterne navigation; collected and compiled together out of the discoueries of many skilfull and expert sea-men, by William Iohnson Blaeuw and translated out of Dutch into English, by Richard Hynmers: The Second part Fourth book ... Containing the description of the Seacoastes of the East side of Enngland and Scotland* (Amsterdam 1625), 102.

40 See, for example, Åke Sandström, *Mellan Torneå och Amsterdam: En undersökning av Stockholms roll som förmedlare av varor i regional- och utrikeshandel 1600–1650* (Stockholm 1990).

CHAPTER 2

Maritime military archery
Bowmen on European warships, 1000–1600
Henrik Arnstad & Abigail Christine Parkes

There is a considerable research gap in both maritime and military history concerning the naval use of bowmen. For over three millennia – spanning from the ancient Egyptians until around the year AD 1600 – archery was a key component in maritime combat. This essay highlights the importance, flexibility, and impact of naval archery with special attention given to European waters in the late Middle Ages and the early modern period.

At the sea battle off Buchow on 4 June 1565, a Danish fleet under the command of Herluf Trolle, 'Admiral and Inspector of the Fleet', attacked the Swedish navy in the southern Baltic Sea. Trolle attempted to board a small Swedish warship, *Troilus*, almost capsizing it as the much larger Danish flagship crashed into the leeward side. *Troilus'* mizzenmast broke and fell overboard as water gushed into the ship's gunports, seemingly outmatched, but according to the sources the Swedes refused to give up:

> *Troilus*, however, did not lose courage, but with 12 guns and 70 archers stopped the enemy from coming aboard. Trolle became angry and shouted in disdain to Captain Nils Schenk on *Troilus* that he should surrender. Trolle, being dressed in a blue breastplate with the Brunswick hat and feathers, was easily recognized by Schenk, who with an arrow took revenge for the insult and gave Trolle a deadly wound.[1]

Figure 2.1. Naval longbowmen attacking enemy infantry, crossbowmen, spearmen, and stone-throwers and the rigging of an enemy ship. This late medieval image illustrates the excellent tactical flexibility of maritime archery. The Pageants of Richard Beauchamp, Earl of Warwick, 'HOWE Erie Kichard, in his commyng into Englond, wanne ij. greet Carykkes in the See' (1485). Cotton MS Julius E IV/3 fol. 18v, by permission of the British Library.

Eventually the Danish fleet retreated, having lost over 700 men, among them eventually Trolle, who died of his wounds on 25 June 1565 (Fig. 2.1).

For over three millennia, military archery was a key component of naval warfare. Trolle's fate demonstrates the continuing importance of maritime bowmen, well after the end of the Middle Ages into the early modern period. In the sixteenth century, naval bowmen were still as tactically flexible, efficient and deadly as they had been for over 3,000 years. Furthermore, we can see that, even though the longbow is famously associated with the English army, this weapon was neither exclusive to England nor to land warfare.[2] Naval archery was a transnational weapon system, and bowmen may in fact have been even more effective at sea than on land. Additionally, archery had a profound impact on naval combat and ship design, with stern- and forecastles being added originally as platforms for bowmen. The bow was the original ship artillery.[3]

Naval archery was used for thousands of years across the globe, and for example was well developed in South-East Asia, yet despite that fact very few studies exist regarding this segment of warfare. We will thus address the considerable research gap in both naval and military history by focusing on naval archery in European waters in the period AD 1000–1600, the period when the organized use of naval archery reached its peak and then declined in use by end of the sixteenth century.

We will use the terms 'naval archery', 'maritime military archery', or simply 'maritime archery' to describe the use of bowmen in armed conflict at sea, and the related use of crossbowmen, since they were often the archers' adversaries. Historically, maritime archery was not limited to ship-to-ship combat, being also employed in amphibious warfare, and in naval logistics operations. In some cases, archers were also employed by civilians as 'hired guns', protecting merchant ships.

Specific literature on maritime archery is very sparse, with a few notable exceptions such as *The Military Archer at Sea* by the archery expert Hugh Soar, and 'The Long-bow and the Tudor Navy Royal' by the naval historian Justin Reay.[4] Additionally, the deployment of archers at the Battle of Sluys (1340) has been studied by the historian Kelly DeVries.[5] Otherwise, maritime archery is discussed as a side note in two general research fields: (1) the history of naval warfare, and (2) the history of military archery:

1. Naval warfare studies sometimes take time to discuss maritime archery, one example being Charles Stanton's *Medieval Maritime Warfare*; however, the use of archers on warships is commonly reduced to a prelude to the 'real' battle, as in Susan Rose's *Medieval Naval Warfare 1000–1500*, where she writes the 'opening phase of the battle was fought with missiles' and similar.[6]

2. Military archery studies, meanwhile, are always focused on land warfare – and especially the triumphs of the English longbow in the fourteenth and fifteenth centuries – and the maritime use of bowmen is usually overlooked. One of the few exceptions is *War Bows* by the archery expert Mike Loades, which includes several passages on the subject.[7]

The beginning of naval archery

The bow and arrow was perhaps the first man-made machine, dating back some 50,000 years.[8] Combining archery with maritime activities (fishing, hunting, and armed conflict) on rivers and lakes and at sea also seems to have been an early step for humanity.

In ancient Egypt, the New Kingdom (1570–1069 BCE) saw the birth of organized military units of naval archers, alongside the creation of a state navy.[9] The deployment of naval archery gave the Egyptians a decisive advantage in Mediterranean wars against the Sea Peoples.[10] Spectacular murals at the Temple of Rameses III in Luxor show the divine ruler using a bow to defeat his seafaring enemies at the Battle of the Delta in 1178 BCE, indicating the importance of the weapon to the Egyptians (Fig. 2.2). Indeed, maritime archers were adopted by all major Mediterranean navies in antiquity, the most important being those of the Phoenicians, Greeks, and Romans. The ram was the main weapon on their war galleys and triremes, while bowmen provided close-in fire, alongside large swivel-mounted crossbows called ballistas. Later Roman warships also had one or two wooden turrets for archers.[11]

Figure 2.2. Pharaoh Ramses III defeating the Sea Peoples with his warbow, from the north wall of the Medinet Habu temple in Luxor. Photo: Wikimedia Commons.

Mediterranean naval warfare in antiquity and the post-Roman early Middle Ages was dominated by amphibious operations conducted close to the coast, due to the difficulties galley fleets had in operating on the open sea. Purely naval engagements on any scale were rare. Ship-to-ship combat was an unpredictable, messy affair and usually avoided.[12] Nevertheless, when sea battles did occur, archery was a key component, especially once ramming fell out of fashion. Changing naval tactics benefited from the use of archers, as they were flexible and able to adapt to new fighting techniques.

In the Baltic region, finds on the Nydam Boat show that warships were armed with bows by the fourth century AD. During excavations of the Nydam Bog in the south of Denmark an intact oak boat was found and with it 40 longbows and over 100 arrows.[13] The use of archery was well documented for the Viking Age (793–1066) too, both in archaeological finds and the sagas; one saga described how 'the arrow storm pours forth its rain'.[14] The best-known discovery is the yew longbow

(191 cm) found during excavations at Hedeby, a Viking Age trading settlement on the Jutland peninsula. Excavations of the Viking town of Birka, on a small island close to what is now Stockholm, have also revealed plenty of military archery material.[15] At this time, the Atlantic waters of the North Sea saw ship construction take a different direction to the Mediterranean patterns, as higher seas favoured durability. Viking navies used clinker-built longships, which provided platforms for archers.

Naval archery in the High Middle Ages

In the High Middle Ages, as trade routes in the Mediterranean expanded and grew in economic importance, tensions developed regarding control of maritime networks. For example, in the eleventh century, Norman naval expansion in the central Mediterranean resulted in military conflict with the Venetian navy. At the Battle of Corfu in 1084, the changes in the tactical use of maritime archers were evident. The Venetians deployed taller bireme galleasses against the lower Norman galleys, enabling archers to shoot down into enemy ships. A contemporary source, William of Apua, wrote that the victorious Venetians 'showered arrows from on high on their enemies'.[16] The effect of archery on warship construction was plain, with vessels built higher to increase the efficiency of naval archers.

This development in ship design also proved useful when warships were attacking land targets. A drawing of the Siege of Damietta (1218–1219) in the Fifth Crusade shows a crusader ship charging a coastal fortress, with bowmen and slingsmen standing on tall scaffolding at the aft, shooting at the defenders.[17] This rickety construction may be a predecessor of the elevated fighting platforms or 'castles' soon to emerge on medieval warships, making archery tactically even more efficient. Other sources also show archers shooting from fighting tops (crow's nests) high in the rigging, alongside slingsmen, stone-throwers and spearmen (Fig. 2.3).

In the thirteenth century, naval archers and crossbowmen grew in importance, sometimes surpassing the significance of hand-to-hand combat during boarding. One example was the Battle of Malta in 1283,

Figure 2.3. Crusader warship attacking the Damietta chain tower during the Siege of Damietta in 1218–1219. The bowmen on both sides are using short recurve bows. Matthew Paris, *Chronica maiora II* (*c.*1240–53). MS 016II fol. 59v, by permission of the Parker Library, Corpus Christi College, Cambridge.

when a Provencal fleet was defeated by murderous barrages of bolts shot by 'Balistarii Catalani' (Catalan crossbowmen). The battle was described in the *Crònica* of Ramon Muntaner:

> The play made by the spears and darts that the Catalans threw was such that their opponents had no defence against them. And of the crossbowmen I need not speak, for they were on the foredeck and so hardened that they fired no shot that did not maim or kill the man it struck.[18]

After that, the melee resembled more of 'a mopping-up operation' than a battle, according to Stanton.[19] Successful barrages of missiles were increasingly necessary to ensure the success of melee fighting when boarding (Fig. 2.4).

In the High Middle Ages, the cog ship type became common in northern European waters. Often, they were not specialist warships, but merchantmen converted for armed conflict by installing an elevated

47

Figure 2.4. Fighting cogs in the fourteenth century. The ship on the left has two longbowmen standing on a sterncastle, an excellent platform for maritime archery. The archers are shooting broadhead arrows. Decretals of Gregory IX (*c.*1300–1340). Royal MS 10 E IV, fol. 19, by permission of the British Library.

sterncastle (and later also a forecastle). The high freeboards also made the cog tactically suited to naval archery, and the combination of the two became a highly effective weapon system in medieval naval warfare. In 1217 the cog proved itself in combat, when an English taskforce defeated a French fleet at the Battle of Sandwich.[20] This battle was also an early example of a mobile engagement in the open seas, as opposed to static fights between linked ships, close to land.

Specialist arrows

As well as the usual armour-piercing arrowheads used in land warfare, there were specialist arrows, which may have been particularly effective in naval warfare. This included fire arrows, arrows equipped with limebags, pig bladders filled with oil, and specially shaped heads for cutting through ropes and sails.

The use of lime in naval warfare in the thirteenth century has been studied by the historian William Sayers. The chronicler Bernat Desclot said of the Battle of Malta in 1283 that 'the battle was widespread and fierce, with spears and stones, and with lime and crossbow'.[21] At the Battle of Sandwich in 1217, the English struck their enemy with a 'fusillade of missiles', including pots of quicklime.[22] Another thirteenth-century source mentions that the Ottomans too used it in naval warfare – 'as the Turks threw lime at their foes'.[23] At the end of the thirteenth century, Jean Priorat, giving advice on naval combat, mentioned both archery and lime:

> Also, shields and bucklers should be stronger and larger to deflect the blows of stones and many different kinds of materials that they throw and cast and with which they kill those who are poorly protected, also quarrels and arrows, shot from long-bows and crossbows, and javelins and iron-tipped spears, pots of lime and great pieces of metal, and sickles and many other things that are both fatal and dangerous.[24]

But why would lime be used in naval warfare? Giles of Rome provided the answer in his *De regimine principum* (1280): lime was used to blind the enemy.

> An eighth recommendation for naval warfare is that there be a large number of pots filled with ground quicklime, which are to be thrown from aloft into the enemies' ships. When the pots are thrown with force and shatter on impact, the powder rises in the air (as has been noted above in reference to land war) and enters the enemies' eyes and irritates them so greatly that, nearly blinded, they cannot see.[25]

What Sayers does not mention is archers shooting limebags at the enemy, using heavy war bows. A contemporary drawing shows a limebag being shot with a bow at the Battle of Sandwich in 1217. The bows used to shoot these bags must have been powerful, to be able to deliver such a heavy payload over a considerable distance (Fig. 2.5).[26]

Alternately, pig bladders filled with oil could be secured over the head of an arrow, in the same way as a limebag. Once the arrows hit the enemy ship, the oil would leak out onto the decks and make them slippery, making it more difficult for soldiers to manoeuvre and launch their counter-fire.

One mainstay of the bowman was the fire arrow. Fire arrows could make naval archery potentially ship-killing, especially after the intro-

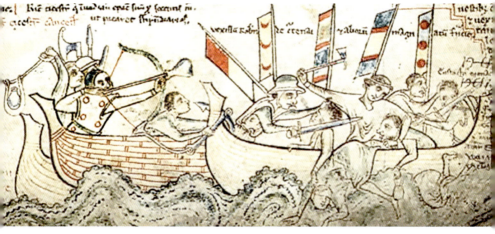

Figure 2.5. The Battle of Sandwich, 24 August 1217. The bowman to the left is shooting a limebag with his recurve warbow. Matthew Paris, *Chronica maiora II* (c.1240–53). MS 016II fol. 55, by permission of the Parker Library, Corpus Christi College, Cambridge.

duction of cannons, when gunpowder was stored on board. They could also destroy sails and rigging. Fire arrows had existed for centuries and had been used by many navies by the time an Ottoman fleet used them at the Siege of Constantinople in 1453. Hermodoros Michael Kritovoulos (c.1410–c.1470) wrote about the Ottoman naval attack on enemy ships during the siege:

> Then he furiously attacked the center of the fleet. Of the heavy infantry on the decks, some carried fire in their hands with the purpose of setting fire to the ships. Others hurled flaming arrows.[27]

Fire arrows were also used in Scandinavian waters. Their effectiveness as a weapon system was proven by their continuing use by the navies of northern Europe well into the early modern period. In 1565, the Swedish king Erik XIV instructed his admiral Klas Horn to equip the royal warships with 'fire arrows that can be shot with bows'.[28]

Several designs of arrowhead have been suggested to be for fire arrows. Generally, they fall into two groups: a cage type and a bag type.[29] The cage-type fire arrow involved, as the name suggests, a sort

Figure 2.6. Replicas of standard late medieval arrowheads. From the left, a needle bodkin (for penetrating chain mail), a war bodkin (for penetrating plate armour), a cage-type fire arrowhead, and a crescent arrowhead. Photo: Henrik Arnstad.

of cage built into the arrowhead, filled with an incendiary device. Bag-type arrowheads were long and thin so a bag of flammable substance could be secured over the top. The cage type would have been easier to prepare on board ship, but experiments have shown they may extinguish in flight. The ready-made bag type was more reliable and could be coated to make them waterproof, meaning they could be stored on a ship without the risk of damp ruining them.[30] Fire arrows also had an iron point, enabling them to penetrate the wooden sides of a ship, which could cause significant damage to a ship's structure and potentially sink it. Studies by Mark Stretton show the general effectiveness of fire arrows in setting both damp material and thick wood ablaze and reaching distances of up to 180 metres.[31]

Additionally, some have suggested that crescent-headed arrows were specially designed to cut rigging and tear sails.[32] Were this true, it would have added to the tactical flexibility and effectiveness of the archer at sea by impacting the manoeuvrability of enemy ships. Stretton's tests to investigate these ideas, while successful – the arrowheads were able to cut through hemp rope and sailcloth – show it was only possible over limited distances and at certain angles.[33] It is difficult to see how this could have been achieved in real life, on a constantly moving ship. However, Stretton's tests confirm that bows could be used for this purpose, and perhaps in the hands of a highly skilled archer who could shoot many arrows per minute, the potential for inflicting damage was high enough for it to be worthwhile (Fig. 2.6).

Rise of the English longbow

The legendary English longbow, sometimes called the English warbow, became an important part of England's fighting forces in the thirteenth century and remained so until around 1600.[34] The weapon is most famous because of the legends of Robin Hood and its use by the English armies in land battles against France in the late medieval period. At this time, the longbow gained credit for many English victories, particularly in the Anglo-French Hundred Years War (1337–1453). The sudden popularity of the weapon in England has led to a belief that it was in some way special – more powerful than those that came before it. In the nineteenth century, this gave rise to the theory that an inferior, shorter bow preceded the longbow; however, as we now know, the invention of the longbow pre-dated its medieval popularity, the evidence is less clear.[35] A typical English warbow was heavy, with a draw weight of 70–200 pounds (30–90 kg) and most commonly 90–130 pounds (40–60 kg).[36] It seems reasonable to suggest that English warbows had higher draw weights than earlier longbows; however, this is more likely this was because of people's level of practice, not that an intrinsically better design made the medieval English longbow somehow a superior weapon. Moreover, how much the draw weight actually increased is yet to be determined, as no direct comparison has been made between bow draw weights from prehistory to medieval.

The English late medieval state used all means at its disposal, including legislation and proto-nationalist propaganda, to produce a steady supply of longbowmen, intended for both the army and the navy. A skilled, strong, well-trained bowman could shoot an impressive 10–15 arrows per minute, while the equally impressive maximum range was 200–300 metres. In the hands of massed archers in battle, the English longbow has been described as a medieval machine gun, starting the infantry revolution and contributing to the end of the medieval period.[37]

On European battlefields, the longbow and crossbow (and the gunpowder firearm) spelt the end of the dominance of the heavily armoured mounted knight, and the rise of the foot soldier.[38] This change in the composition of European armies also allowed for an increase in size: equipping an armoured knight was far more expensive than equipping archers, crossbowmen, or pikemen, and thus a larger army could be mustered for a lower cost.

To maximize the efficacy of archers, the English state enforced the training of archers by law, making a substantial part of the male population military bowmen.[39] Men had to train with the longbow from the age of seven, and there were penalties for fathers who failed to supply their sons with archery equipment. The price of the longbows was kept artificially low by the Crown to keep them affordable for the yeoman classes. Compulsory, lifelong practice would allow men to draw bows of higher and higher draw weights over their lives. This impressive state project lasted well into the late sixteenth century, which saw renewed – and enforced – legislation on the matter. For example, in the county of Essex in 1573–4, fifty-nine men were charged by the authorities for failing to practise archery.[40]

An important question remains, though. If the longbow was the outstanding weapon of its time, why did not more states (primarily France) use it to the same extent as the English in their armies and navies? The answer seems to have been political stability. The period saw some European states move away from medieval feudalism towards early modern territorial states, and research suggests that what was important to England, employing the longbow, was the country's relative stability.[41] The corollary of massing large numbers of peasants as well-trained archers for the Crown's purposes was there was a large number of deadly bowmen among the populace available for uprisings and revolts. Tapping the full potential of the longbow by training large numbers of men to draw very heavy bows necessarily posed a significant risk to the Crown. As such, the monarchy had to be in a relatively stable position for the risk not to outweigh the benefit. This was on top of the fact that the passing and enforcing of laws to mandate longbow training also required a degree of control over the population. The reason countries such as France and Spain did not employ longbowmen to the same extent as England was that their monarchies did not consider themselves secure enough. The foreign (primarily Genoese) mercenary crossbowmen they turned to were militarily inferior to longbowmen both on land and at sea but were unlikely to join in a revolt.

On English warships in the High Middle Ages, longbows came with other types of artillery. The hi-tech naval artillery of the fourteenth century was the gunpowder cannon – the English 760-ton carrack, *Holyghost*, had seven cannons, for example.[42] However, these guns were still mainly small breech-loaders, intended as anti-personnel weapons. They could not yet be compared to the efficiency of the longbow regarding range, accuracy, and firing rate. A bowman could shoot six times faster than an arquebusier and five times faster than a crossbowman, while adjusting their aim to account for the movement of the vessel they were on. Against that, there was a significant delay between firing a gunpowder weapon and the charge going off.[43] Reay writes:

> A skilled archer on land could place his missile within an inch – to 'the breadth of a shilling' was a common boast; once he got his sea-legs, accommodating the lift of the sea and judging the effect of wind on ship and missile, this level of accuracy would ensure that he could, for example, hit the face of a human target with reasonable certainty.[44]

Loades writes about the schooling of bowmen for war at sea:

> Naval archers were an extremely important element in the defence forces of the nation. As well as needing to be able to rake the decks of enemy ships from a distance, naval archers also had to be able to shoot at targets high in the rigging. When ships grappled together, men in the crow's nests – archers, javelin-men and men with large rocks – would assail the enemy decks with missiles; those on the decks sought to pick off those aloft.[45]

The English devised a training method for this type of naval archery combat, called popinjay shooting.[46] It entailed shooting at targets, usually in the form of birds, which were set up on tall masts (usually on land so the arrows could easily be retrieved). These extensive, elaborate training methods employed by the English state indicate how important naval archery was.

In the Hundred Years War, England and France were emerging naval powers of regional significance.[47] But they had different objectives regarding naval operations. England's strategic aim was to transport troops and supplies to the theatres of war on the continent, favouring larger vessels such as the cog. The extensive English tactical use of naval archery lent itself to the castles of cogs and carracks. France's strategic aim, meanwhile, was to hamper English military movements, and thus favoured quick, smaller vessels such as oared galleys. For naval combat, French tactics relied on men-at-arms and crossbowmen. The English thus had an advantage over the French, as its merchant fleet had plenty of cogs, which could easily be converted into warships by installing castles, both fore and aft, making them excellent fighting platforms for bowmen.

The Battle of Sluys

The English longbow gained its place in history in the Hundred Years War. However, it did not first prove itself in the famous battles of Crécy in 1346 or Agincourt in 1415. Instead, it was at the naval battle of Sluys in Flanders, in 1340 (Fig. 2.7). The battle has been studied by the historian Kelly DeVries:

> Most historians of the Hundred Years War see the battle of Sluys, fought on June 24, 1340, as the first major onslaught of this late medieval conflict between France and England. A victory for the English, this naval battle allowed Edward III to land on the continent, to gather his Low Countries' allies to him, and to besiege the town of Tournai. … The most often recognized tactical cause for the English victory is the English inclusion of archers on board their ships leading to the longbow's first great victory in the Hundred Years War.[48]

Planning to engage a French fleet, the English set sail from Ipswich on 22 June 1340 with about 150 ships carrying 600 men-at-arms and 7,000

Figure 2.7. The Battle of Sluys on 24 June 1340. Jean Froissart, *Chroniques* (fourteenth century). MS Fr. 2643 fol. 72, by permission of the Bibliotheque Nationale de France.

bowmen – proportions which indicate the relative importance of naval archery as part of the English war effort.

Encountering the French fleet outside Sluys on 24 June, the English found that the enemy had linked their ships together in three 'battles' (lines). Unlike the English, the mainstay of the French forces consisted of melee infantry supported by Genoese crossbowmen. The English arranged their ships in groups of three – two ships filled with archers flanking a ship with infantry – and to the rear, according to a French source, a 'flanking squadron made up entirely of archers, which was to give support wherever needed'.[49] When the English fleet attacked, they unleashed their first 'shower' of arrows. The longbows, with their superior range and rate of fire, shot five projectiles for every Genoese crossbow bolt. 'Screened by the hail of arrows from their archers, the English crews were easily able to grapple with individual French vessels', according to Stanton.[50] Several English sources acknowledged the archers were crucial, according to DeVries – 'Wherefore, God favouring them, the French and Normans were conquered harshly by the English archers'.[51]

The French writer Jean Froissart (c. 1337–c. 1405) wrote about the battle in his *Chroniques*. He was appalled by the violence inflicted by the English longbowmen and Genoese crossbowmen:

> This battle which I describe for you was very foul and very horrible; battles and attacks on the sea are longer and larger than those on land, because one is unable to flee, or to retreat. … And the archers and the arbalestriers [crossbowmen] commenced to draw their bows one against the other diversely and rapidly, and the men-at-arms approached and fought hand to hand harshly and hardily. But the English proved so good and so brave.[52]

The battle turned into a massacre, as the panicking men aboard the French ships could not flee, as Froissart remarks. Estimates put the dead at between 25,000 and 30,000 French soldiers and Genoese crossbowmen. Many were thrown overboard to drown, unable to swim in their armour. Thomas Burton's *Chronica monasterii de Melsa* (1396) ridiculed them: 'If God had given the fish the power of speech after they had devoured so many of the dead, they would have spoken fluent French.'[53]

Longbows on *Mary Rose*

The Tudor period (1485–1603) has previously been considered the end of the longbow's career, its usage in decline as gunpowder weapons overtook it in efficiency. However, particularly in terms of its use at sea, this does not appear to be accurate. Historical records show that Henry VIII (1509–1547) was a keen sport archer and passed laws to continue the

Figure 2.8. *Mary Rose* in the Anthony Roll in the 1540s. Pepys 2991, by permission of the Pepys Library, Magdalene College, Cambridge.

tradition of training all young men to be proficient longbow archers. He had the highest quality European yew wood imported for his armies and paid bowyers handsomely for making the staves into bows.[54]

In terms of naval archery, records such as the Anthony Roll of 1545 show that all the ships in the Henrician fleet were equipped with a large number of bows and arrows. The most famous of them was *Mary Rose* (Fig. 2.8). Completed in April 1512, *Mary Rose* had a 33-year long career as Henry's flagship, seeing its first battle on 10 August that year.[55] Unusually among his contemporaries, Henry VIII's policy was to maintain his fleet outside of combat, and *Mary Rose* underwent repairs in 1527 and a major rebuild in 1536 to allow the addition of more cannons.[56] It capsized and sank nine years later on 19 July 1545, the extra guns the likely culprit.[57] However, it also carried 250 bows and 9,600 arrows, showing the continued importance of naval archery even as cannon usage increased.

The discovery, excavation, and salvage of *Mary Rose* in the 1970s and early 1980s gave a whole new understanding of life aboard a Tudor warship. Among the thousands of unique artefacts recovered were 172 English longbows, most of which are complete and appear as new, and not only comprise the largest collection of longbows in the world, but the only collection of longbows from the medieval and early modern period. They therefore present a unique opportunity to learn about the weapon in general but also about the use of the longbow at sea. However, since an initial study by the Mary Rose Trust, the bows have not been revisited, and many questions about them remain unanswered (Fig. 2.9).

At first glance, the *Mary Rose* longbows appear fairly uniform. However, closer inspection reveals there is a great deal of variation. The lengths of the complete longbows range from 1,740 mm to 2,113 mm and four shapes of cross-section have been identified. A small group of bows have a grip area in the centre, marked by a change in cross-section. Approximately half the bows have markings, but these are in many forms. Bows were found on all decks of the ship, both loose and in chests on the Orlop and Upper decks.[58] These differences have given rise to many theories about the reasons for the variations and how the bows were used at sea, which fall into two distinct groups: one that the bows were standardized; the other that there were different groups of archers with different roles aboard the ship.

Much of the evidence speaks against the idea that the bows were standardized, yet while they appear different physically, it is possible their function was the same by having the same draw weight. Wood is not homogenous, even within the same species, and variations in the wood create variations in its mechanical properties, so for all the *Mary Rose* bows to have the same draw weight, slightly different shapes would have been required. For bows, one of the key properties was density; a stave with a high density would need to be made into a shorter bow than a lower-density stave to achieve the same draw weight in the finished weapon. If the bows were standardized by draw weight it would mean any man aboard the ship could pick up and use any weapon.

The opposing idea is that different groups of longbows aboard the ship had different roles, and the variations in the collection represent this. For example, seven bows in the collection have been categorized as 'handled'; it has been suggested that they were designed to shoot fire arrows. The handle is a section at the centre of the bow, where it changes in cross-section from flat-sided to a more rounded, traditional D shape. This change in cross-section could allow the bow to accommodate a binding that would prevent it from being burnt when drawing a lit fire arrow. It is certainly the case that these bows are also some of the largest and sturdiest in the collection, with high predicted draw weights.[59] Fire arrows, as Stretton notes in his tests, are on the heavier side because of the added weight of the incendiary device.[60] A larger draw weight would be needed to maximize their range. In addition, there were nine arrow-like objects recovered, which are potentially shafts for fire arrows. They have ambiguous features, which make certain identification difficult: the notched taper at the end, for example, is typical of a crossbow bolt, but they are longer than was usual for a crossbow. At the same time, they are shorter than a longbow arrow.[61] However, were they fitted with an extra-long bodkin arrowhead, as tested by Stretton, they could have been fired from a longbow. Other suggestions of alternative roles aboard the ship include archers using other specialist heads (discussed above), and acting as rangefinders for gunners, wind indicators, or sharpshooters to pick off enemy marksmen.

There is also the matter of the meaning of the marks on the bows. Numerous objects on *Mary Rose* were found to have ownership marks, but many of the marks on the bows are not unique enough to indicate ownership, as several bear the same mark. Perhaps they were makers' marks, or indicated something to the archers – where to hold the bow, which way was up, where to nock the arrow, etc. Of course, that still does not explain why some had them and others did not.

As well as the physical variation, there is also the matter of the context, found in a chest or loose, and location where the bows were found. Bows found in different parts of the ship might have had different functions, while it is also possible those found loose were in use or intended to be used on the ship, while those in chests were being

Figure 2.9. Archaeological Supervisor Christopher Dobbs examines a longbow just raised from one of the stored boxes. Courtesy of the Mary Rose Trust.

transported, ready for a land campaign. In this case there might then be a difference between bows designed for use at sea and bows for fighting on land. An alternative suggestion is that the loose bows belonged to a specialist company of archers, while those in chests were for any man on board to pick up as necessary, as they would all have been trained archers to some degree. Yet if that were the case, what was the role of specialist archers aboard the ship?

A statistical analysis of the bows' dimensions suggested a possible link between the draw weight and the shape of the cross-section. For each cross-section, the average length and density of that group of bows was different, which may indicate different draw weights – both length and density being factors in determining the draw weight of a bow.[62] A shape analysis of the cross-sections using geometric morphometrics was done to determine whether the groups of bows were 'true' groups or the result of the human tendency to find patterns in random data, and it found that two of the groups in particular differed significantly from each other and the rest.[63] The next step in investigating whether archers on *Mary Rose* had different roles will be understanding how shape relates to the function of the bow in terms of draw weight and range, which in turn will give a clearer picture of archery tactics.

The longbow finds from *Mary Rose* are important when understanding the longbow as a weapon in general and its use at sea. Yet despite the context of the bows being maritime military archery, this has been forgotten. Data from the bows has been used to inform replicas tested against armour in order to 'prove' the effectiveness of the longbow in battle, while questions about the bows in context of the ship itself are left unanswered. The historical records show that longbows were valuable weapons for Henry VIII's navy. They were not just a relic from the past that can only help us understand the land battles of Agincourt or Crécy.

'Find V', a Scandinavian *Mary Rose*?

Kalmar Castle was of paramount importance to Sweden. Built in the twelfth century in the far south of the country, it was a border stronghold until the seventeenth century, and saw centuries of wars against

Figure 2.10. Broken remains of the 'pointy sticks' found on Find V. Photo: Jenny Nyberg, Statens historiska museer.

Denmark which included extensive naval and amphibious operations. Kalmar Castle, guarding not only a hostile border but also overlooking a strategic strait in the Baltic Sea, played a key role. The fortress saw a great deal of action, especially in the turbulent sixteenth century, when Sweden broke away from the Kalmar Union with Denmark and fought its way to independent statehood.

In 1920–1940, Kalmar Castle underwent extensive restorations and the surrounding bay was drained, exposing a multitude of shipwrecks. A construction draftsman, Harald Åkerlund (1900–1980), organized excavations, becoming a pioneer of Swedish maritime archaeology. The finds were presented in the book *Fartygsfynden i den forna hamnen i Kalmar* (1951, 'Ship-finds in the former harbour of Kalmar').[64] Unknown to Åkerlund, his finds also suggest that archery was part of Scandinavian naval warfare in the 1520s.

The 'most interesting find' during the excavations, according to Åkerlund, was a warship referred to as 'Find V'.[65] Åkerlund's book discussed in detail when Find V may have sunk. A type of shoe found on the ship was common in the period 1525–1550, from which Åkerlund concluded that the ship probably met its fate in the battles fought at Kalmar in 1523–1525. This would make it contemporary with *Mary Rose*. Find V was found close to the castle walls and had been partly destroyed by fire before it sank, probably set alight by the castle's defenders. This would imply the warship was Danish. 'It probably got stuck while attempting to land, and thereafter shot ablaze,' Åkerlund wrote, implying fire arrows were used.[66] He also enthused about a 'couple of interesting finds' on Find V: 'two crossbow arrows made of wood. One of them is broken, the other one is still in one piece.'[67] However, he did not reflect on crossbows' suitability for shooting fire arrows. Another find on the warship puzzled Åkerlund:

> In the ship were furthermore two long, thin, and pointy 'sticks' made of ash. One of them is in one piece and is 73 cm long, pointy at one end and the other end is cut off. Some other parts of similar sticks were found. The author cannot explain the purpose of these.[68]

Mary Rose provides a likely answer to Åkerlund's question about the 'pointy "sticks" made of ash': they were probably remains of arrow shafts (Fig. 2.10).

Over 3,500 longbow arrows were found on *Mary Rose* and they are very similar to the Kalmar finds. The Kalmar sticks are slightly shorter than *Mary Rose* arrow shafts, which measured between 740 mm and 790 mm, but still fell within the typical range for a longbow arrow.[69] Their shorter length suggests that Scandinavian naval bows may have been shorter than the English longbows, resulting in a shorter draw length. However, the Kalmar sticks are thicker in the middle, implying that Scandinavian fletchers were as experienced in arrow-making as their English colleagues, knowing that the middle of the arrow was exposed to greater stresses when released (Fig. 2.11).

The existence of warbows in Scandinavia is further supported by multiple finds of military arrowheads all over Sweden. For example, during excavations of the small Stockholm island of Helgeandsholmen in 1978–1980, some 50 warbow arrowheads were found.[70] Regarding Kalmar specifically, during an excavation in 1992, military arrowheads were found.[71] These were of the needle bodkin type, made for penetrating chainmail. The same type – alongside other types of standardized military arrowheads – can be found all over Europe.

The most interesting thing about the finds in Kalmar is the date, as they place Scandinavian maritime archers in the sixteenth century. The assumption that in the early modern period the military use of bows and arrows was a thing of the past, at least outside England, can thus be

Figure 2.11. Visual evidence that Scandinavian warships carried archers is plenti-
ful, as in this mid-fourteenth-century wall painting of a cog in Skamstrup,
Denmark. The bowman on the ship's sterncastle has a recurve warbow. Photo:
Kurt Villads Jensen, Stockholm University.

dismissed. The Swedish navy equipped its warships with 'fire arrows that
can be shot with bows' in the Northern Seven Years War (1563–1570).[72]
There was the example which opened this essay: the Danish–Swedish
naval battle of 4 June 1565, when Admiral Trolle met his death when
exposed to Swedish warbows (Fig. 2.12). Plainly, the definition of naval
archery must be broadened, both temporally and geographically. Maritime bowmen were deployed on warships for longer than is commonly

Figure 2.12. Admiral Herluf Trolle, the Danish Inspector of the Fleet (1551). Photo: Wikimedia Commons.

recognized – and they continued to constitute a transnational weapon system, not a specifically English one.

The decline of military archery in the 1590s

On 28 August 1595, an English fleet under the command of Francis Drake and John Hawkins set sail from Plymouth, heading to the West Indies to attack the Spanish. The bills of lading for *Defiance*, *Garland*,

Hope, Elizabeth Bonaventure, Adventure, and *Foresight* included 'longe bowes', 'bowe strings', 'longbowe shotte', 'arrows with ffirewourkes' (fire arrows), 'arrowros [*sic*] for longbows' and 'chesstes for bowes and arrows', suggesting Drake and Hawkins understood the value of naval bowmen and intended to put them to good use in the West Indies campaign of 1595–1596.[73] Nevertheless, warbows were soon to disappear from European warships. Over 3,000 years after the Egyptian pharaohs first created organized units of maritime archers, a naval tradition came to an end.

In the 1590s there was a fierce debate in England about whether its military should focus on gunpowder handguns or continue the use of longbows. 'The debate was primarily concerned, on the one hand, with arguments favouring the complete abandonment of the longbow and, on the other, the defence of the bow as fully superior to firearms', according to the historian Thomas Esper.[74] In the hands of bowyers, fletchers, arrowsmiths, and stringers the manufacture of archery materials developed into a major early modern proto-industrial business – with a keen interest in the continuation of the English military use of longbows. The craftsmen and merchants commanded considerable financial resources, allowing them to publish pamphlets and treatises arguing the benefits of the longbow. In 1596, the bowyers and fletchers of England were behind the publication of *A briefe treatise, to proove the necessitie and excellence of the use of archerie*, which announced:

> Archerie to be of farre greater effect then anie other weapon that ever was invented: And that in respect therof onlie, this Realme of England hath been ever feared and honored of all Nations.[75]

The historian Lois G. Schwoerer remarks that a historical mystique of sorts continued to surround the longbow in England, even as it gradually disappeared from the armed forces. 'English people generally believed, as a law put it, that the longbow was God's gift to England', according to Schwoerer.[76] William Shakespeare's play *Henry V* in 1599 was perhaps part of the same pro-longbow propaganda effort, immortalizing the bowmen at Agincourt in 1415. The king names them his 'brothers' in the play: 'We fewe, we happie fewe, we bond of brothers, For he to day that sheads his blood by mine, Shalbe my brother.'[77]

On the pro-handgun side in the debate in the 1590s, the main argument was that using the English longbow, however effective it might have been two centuries earlier, was now an embarrassment to the English armed forces. The origin of this standpoint was the experience of English soldiers who had served in the Netherlands, who, as Esper writes,

> were greatly impressed by what they termed the 'new discipline.' Elizabeth's army was never a standing force, and its organization remained inferior to that of the Spanish. The poorly organized English forces sent to fight the Spaniards soon proved unequal to the superior training, armament, and staff organization of the Iberians.[78]

One English officer, Sir Roger Williams, saw service on both sides of the fighting there. To military men like him, the warbow symbolized a frightening English backwardness in the art of modern warfare: 'God forbid we should try our bows with their muskets and calivers [harquebuses], without the like shot to answer them.'[79] Military officers arguing for the continued use of bowmen were ridiculed as victims of nostalgia – 'king Harry captains'.[80] Also, as argued in 1592 by Humfrey Barwick in his *A breefe discourse, concerning the force and effect of all manuall weapons of fire and the disability of the long bowe or archery*, the new types of harquebuses could fire 40 shots an hour, which he said brought their rate of fire close to that of the longbow.[81]

However, when studying the sources, the sheer embarrassment of the English using bows seems more important to the pro-gun side than the actual relative effectiveness of archers and musketeers. Esper's opinion is that 'the replacement of the longbow by firearms occurred at a time when the former was still a superior weapon'.[82] Be that as it may, when it came to the usefulness of longbows versus the firearms of the 1590s, 'the gun triumphed', as Schwoerer concludes.[83]

The forgotten naval archer

Warbows were not completely forgotten after 1600. Quite the contrary, in fact, as England had pronounced proto-nationalistic sentiments about the longbow. In the seventeenth and eighteenth centuries, the myths about the English national hero and master longbowman Robin Hood became more and more popular. However, at the same time as the forest-dwelling 'prince of thieves' and the army bowmen of Agincourt in 1415 became cornerstones in an early English national identity, the naval archers of England were forgotten.

This continued into the post-1789 era, when modern English nationalism was constructed using memory culture surrounding the longbow. In the nineteenth century, following the enormous success of Walter Scott's novel *Ivanhoe* (1819), longbow archery and Robin Hood developed into a nationalist English mass movement.[84] To be a true native Englishman was synonymous with being a longbow archer, according to the nationalist discourse voiced in *Ivanhoe*.[85] In 1791 the archery expert Thomas Roberts had proclaimed the longbow not to be British but English.[86] Alas, the most obvious difference between the two identities is the role of the sea. The British identity is largely maritime, Britain being 'the British Isles', while English national identity is land-based. In the nineteenth century, Britannia ruled the waves while Robin Hood ruled the Sherwood Forest. The identarian heroes of Britishness were Admiral Horatio Nelson and the quest-driven, ever-travelling Arthur, 'king of the Britons', while English longbow nationalism was contextualized by the forest, far from transnational coastlines and imperial British maritime ventures.[87] It is hardly surprising that, even today, the maritime sixteenth-century longbows of the English (not British) ship *Mary Rose* are contextualized, in both popular and scientific writing, as the land-based medieval warbows of Agincourt. The 130 years that elapsed between the Battle of Agincourt in 1415 and the *Mary Rose* sinking in 1545 were unimportant when it came to obscuring the importance of maritime archery, because the longbow was central to the English land-based national identity. This was not a conscious decision. On the contrary, the decision-making was unaware, showing how strongly modern minds are affected by nationalism, social hegemonic structures, and power discourses.

Maritime history since the 1980s has focused on the introduction of cannons on warships in the late Middle Ages and the early modern period. Warships were transformed into platforms for heavy gunpowder artillery, which was undeniably an important transition of warfare at sea. Nevertheless, the importance of this narrative should not obscure the success of maritime archery. Castles were originally built on warships not to accommodate guns but units of archers, and the first guns did not outcompete trained archers in rate of fire, range, or accuracy. At sea, gunpowder risked getting wet, rendering the gun useless, while fire arrows could even be made to work at sea with the application of a waterproof coating – and may even have been more effective there than on land.

The use of warbows lives on in modern military language. For example in words such as 'marksman' (shooting 'at a mark' being a form of military archery practice developed in the fifteenth century), but also at sea, where the order to 'shoot' is still often used as a firing command.[88] The continued use of archery-related language shows the long-lasting impact maritime archery has had. It is baffling to think that despite this the naval archer has been forgotten. This essay has focused on Europe in the medieval and early modern period, and there are thousands of years of maritime military archery around the world which warrant further study. Bows and arrows were known in six of the seven continents and taking them to sea was similarly widespread.

Notes

1 Carl Gustaf Tornquist, *Utkast till swenska flottans sjö-tåg af Carl Gustaf Tornquist* (Stockholm 1788), 46 an account based on letters from the Northern Seven Years War (1563–1570). We are grateful to Niklas Eriksson for the information about archery at the battle of 1565.

2 The longbow (unlike the shorter bows often used by mounted archers) is typically defined as a bow taller than the person who draws it, so usually 180–200 cm. The length of the limbs allows more energy to be stored in the bow and transferred to the arrow upon release. Yew (*Taxus baccata*) was considered the best wood for longbows, although elm and hazel have been documented. A self-bow is a bow made from a single piece of wood, using the natural properties of the wood to form a spring; a composite bow uses layers of different materials (wood, horn, bone or sinew), glued together to achieve the same effect.

3 The International Longbow Archers Association, www.archery-longbow.com/Longbow/: 'Many still current expressions in the English language come directly from Artillery Shooting or shooting at the Marks. Are you 'up to the Mark'. To 'up the Stakes'. To 'hit the Mark'. To 'make your Mark'. To 'lower your sights'. To 'have Clout'. Even

'on your Marks' is nothing to do with athletics; it meant do you have your eye on the Mark, i.e. are you ready to shoot.'

4 Hugh David Soar, *The Military Archer at Sea* (Bristol 1996); Justin Reay, 'The Longbow and the Tudor Navy Royal', *Britannia Naval Research Association Journal* (2007), www.academia.edu/9079374/The_Long_bow_and_the_Tudor_Navy_Royal.

5 Kelly DeVries, 'God, Leadership, Flemings and Archery: Contemporary Perceptions of Victory and Defeat at the Battle of Sluys, 1340', *American Neptune* 55 (1995); reprinted in id. (ed.), *Guns and Men in Medieval Europe, 1200–1500* (Aldershot 2002).

6 Charles D. Stanton, *Medieval Maritime Warfare* (Barnsley 2015); Susan Rose, *Medieval Naval Warfare 1000–1500* (Oxon 2002), 24. The extensive index includes crossbows, crossbowmen and cannons, but does not list archery, bowmen, or bows.

7 Mike Loades, *War Bows* (Oxford 2019).

8 A bow may be defined as a machine designed to store the low-quality muscle power of the archer, converting it on release into high-quality rapid mechanical movement, see Gad Rausing, *The Bow: Some notes on its origin and development* (Lund 1967), 16; Robert Hardy, *Longbow: A Social and Military History* (Stroud 2006). This very early evidence is based on arrowhead finds. The earliest confirmed bow specimens come from Mesolithic bog sites (15,000–5,000 BP). Some fragmentary wooden pieces found alongside wooden arrow shafts in Stellmoor, Germany, are believed to be the remains of bows, dating to 9000 BCE. Complete elm self-bows have been recovered in Holmegaard, Denmark, dating to around 6000 BCE. Charles Grayson, Mary French & Michael O'Brien, 'A Brief Overview of Traditional Archery', in *Traditional Archery from Six Continents* (University of Missouri Press 2007), 1. The Stone Age 'Ötzi the Iceman', who lived some 5,000 years ago, was equipped with a 183 cm yew self-longbow, similar to the weapon used by European armed forces in the sixteenth century.

9 Finds from tombs – including the famous tomb of Tutankhamen (1341–1323 BCE) – show that Egyptian archers were using sophisticated equipment (Rausing 1967, 77); Jimmy Dunn, 'The Ancient Egyptian Navy', Feb. 2003, www.touregypt.net/feature-stories/navy.htm.

10 Dunn 2003: 'The Sea People, who we are told of on reliefs at Medinet Habu and Karnak, as well as from the text of the Great Harris Papyrus (now in the British Museum), are said to be a loose confederation of people originating in the eastern Mediterranean.'

11 *Encyclopaedia Britannica*, s.v. 'Naval ship' (2017).

12 Stanton 2015, 5.

13 Soar 1996, 5.

14 Soar 1996, 2.

15 Fredrik Lundström, 'Det vikingatida bågskyttet i Birka: Ett exempel på en framstående stridskonst med främmande inslag' (MA diss., Stockholm University 2006).

16 Stanton 2015, 70.

17 Miniature from the thirteenth-century *Chronica maiora* by Matthew Paris (Parker Library, Corpus Christi College, Cambridge).

18 William Sayers, 'The use of quicklime in medieval naval warfare', *Mariner's Mirror* 92/3 (2006), 263.

19 Stanton 2015, 157.

20 Stanton 2015, 236. The battle is also known as the Battle of Dover.

21 Sayers 2006, 262.

22 Stanton 2015, 239.

23 Sayers 2006, 263.

24 Sayers 2006, 265.

25 Sayers 2006, 265.

26 Soar 1996, 8.

27 Hermodoros Michael Kritovoulos, *History of Mehmed the Conqueror*, ed. & tr. Charles T. Riggs (Princeton 1954), 50.

28 Tornquist 1788.

29 Loades 2019, 28.

30 Fire arrows' payload was a mix of gunpowder and alcohol, which would burn intensely for a certain period of time.

31 Mark Stretton, 'Fire Arrows Part 3: How Far can they be Shot?', 28 Oct. 2017, and 'Fire Arrows Part 4: What can they set on fire?', 22 Nov. 2017, markstretton.blogspot.com.

32 Loades 2019, 68.

33 Mark Stretton, 'Practical Tests Part 6: Was The Crescent Head Used to Cut Rope and Sails on Ships?', 20 Feb. 2016, markstretton.blogspot.com.

34 The term warbow refers to the idea that larger, heavier draw weight bows, which could fire arrows further and harder, were used in war. Hunting longbows did not need to be as heavy or long ranged. Edward I (1239–1307) is usually credited with the introduction of massed longbow archers in the English army. Edward is said to have tested the new English tactics against the Scots at the Battle of Falkirk in 1298.

35 There is limited archaeological evidence of the bow in this period, owing to the biological nature of the materials and the inexpensiveness of the weapon, meaning the bow was discarded when broken rather than maintained as a suit of armour might be.

36 Hugh David Soar, *The Crooked Stick: The history of the longbow* (Yardley, 2004), 101.

37 Martin Neuding Skoog, *I rikets tjänst: Krig, stat och samhälle i Sverige 1450–1550* (Stockholm 2018) discusses the introduction of the infantry's new ranged weapon tactics (longbows, crossbows, and muskets) over the course of the century to 1550; also Clifford Rogers, 'The Military Revolutions of the Hundred Years War', *Journal of Military History* 57/2 (1993), 241–78.

38 Clifford Rogers, 'Tactics and the face of battle', in *European Warfare, 1350–1750* (Cambridge 2010), 203–235.

39 Interestingly, 'the minimum property qualification which gave a man the right to vote in Parliamentary elections was set at the low level of 40 shillings of land income per year – the same amount which legally obliged him to own a bow' (Rogers 1993, 254).

40 Lois G. Schwoerer, *Gun Culture in Early Modern England* (Charlottesville 2016), 55.

41 See, for example, Douglas W. Allen & Peter T. Leeson, 'Institutionally Constrained Technology Adoption: Resolving the Longbow Puzzle', *Journal of Law and Economics* 58/3 (2015), 638–715.

42 Stanton 2015, 246.

43 Loades 2019, 61.

44 Reay 2007, 6.

45 Loades 2019, 40.

46 Loades 2019, 40.

47 Stanton 2015, 241.

48 DeVries 1995/2002, 223, 224.

49 Stanton 2015, 264.

50 Stanton 2015, 266.

51 DeVries 1995/2002, 227.

52 DeVries 1995/2002, 223–34.

53 DeVries 1995/2002, 226.

54 Jim Bradbury, *The Medieval Archer* (Woodbridge 1985), 155; Hardy 2006, 201.

55 Brian Lavery, *Mary Rose: King Henry VIII's warship, 1510–45* (Yeovil 2015), 11–19.

56 Peter Marsden, *Sealed by Time* (Portsmouth 2003), 15.

57 The reason why Mary Rose sank will probably never be fully known; see Geoffrey Moorhouse, *Great Harry's Navy* (London 2005) and Margaret Rule, *The Mary Rose* (London 1982).

58 For a full breakdown of the features of the longbows, see Alexzandra Hildred (ed.), *Weapons of Warre* (Portsmouth 2011), ch. 8.

59 Clive Bartlett, Chris Boyton, Steve Jackson, Adam Jackson, Douglas McElvogue, Alexzandra Hildred & Keith Watson, 'The Longbow Assemblage', in Hildred 2011, 602–604.

60 Stretton, 'Fire Arrows Part 3: How Far can they be Shot?', 28 Oct. 2017.

61 Alexzandra Hildred, 'Handgun Bolts, Incendiary Arrows or Top Darts', in Hildred 2011, 700–702.

62 Abigail Parkes, 'Mary Rose Bows: A statistical analysis' (BSc diss., University of Southampton, 2018).

63 Abigail Parkes, 'Mary Rose Bows: A morphometric analysis' (MSc diss., University of Southampton, 2019).

64 Harald Åkerlund, *Fartygsfynden i den forna hamnen i Kalmar* (Uppsala 1951).

65 Åkerlund 1951, 68.

66 Åkerlund 1951, 79.

67 Åkerlund 1951, 78, tr. Henrik Arnstad.

68 Åkerlund 1951, 78, tr. Henrik Arnstad. Jenny Nyberg at the Swedish National Historical Museums tracked down the Kalmar arrow shaft fragments, which today measure at 680 mm – in the original catalogue and on one of the find tags the measurements are given as 735 mm and 900 mm.

69 The length of an English longbow arrow was between 711 mm and 914 mm. John J. Mortimer, 'Tactics, strategy, and battlefield formation during the hundred years war: the role of the longbow in the infantry revolution' (PhD thesis, Indiana University of Pennsylvania 2013), 32.

70 m.facebook.com/medeltidsmuseet/photos/a.155473727815710/2540286809334378.

71 Kalmar County Museum 1992, https://digitaltmuseum.se/021017078357/arkeologisk-undersokning-for-husbyggnation-pilspetsar

72 Tornquist 1788.

73 'Bill of Lading for the Ships Returning from the Drake's Last voyage', 1595–96, available at www.indrakeswake.co.uk/Society/Research/billoflading.htm (Loades 2019, 68).

74 Thomas Esper, 'The Replacement of the Longbow by Firearms in the English Army', *Technology & Culture* 6/3 (1965), 384.

75 R. S., *A briefe treatise, to prooue the necessitie and excellence of the vse of archerie* (London 1596), with a dedication by the 'Companies of Bowyers and Fletchers', available at http://name.umdl.umich.edu/A11250.0001.001.

76 Schwoerer 2016, 54.

77 Shakespeare, *Henry V*, Act IV Scene III (London 1600).

78 Esper 1965, 384.

79 Esper 1965, 385.

80 'King Harry' being Henry V, the victor of Agincourt in 1415.

81 This seems to be a remarkable statement, considering that a longbowman could fire 600–900 arrows in an hour. However, perhaps the true rate of fire was less than this due to physical exhaustion – an issue that did not affect the handgun. Humfrey Barwick, *A breefe discourse, concerning the force and effect of all manuall weapons of fire and the disability of the long bowe or archery, in respect of others of greater force now in vse* (London 1592).

82 Esper 1965, 393.

83 Schwoerer 2016, 58.

84 The notion being the 'Anglo-Saxon' English were superior to the 'Celtic fringe' who populated the rest of the British Isles. Stephanie Barczewski, *Myth and National Identity in Nineteenth-Century Britain: The Legends of King Arthur and Robin Hood* (Oxford 2000), 6 describes the difference between Englishness (nationalism) and Britishness (allegiance to an imperial transnational state) as 'A Briton could be made, but one had to be born English'.

85 The author of *Ivanhoe*, Sir Walter Scott, an Edinburgh-born Scot, included the Lowland Scots in the Anglo-Saxon 'race', claiming that the real border was with the Highland Scots, who were Celtic and thus inferior.

86 Thomas Roberts, *The English Bowman* (Yorkshire, 1791, 1801), 14: 'The bow used by the inhabitants of this island, has always been distinguished by the title of the English longbow. Although the English do not claim the merit of its first invention, yet the wonders it has performed in the hands of our ancestors (who we find at a very early period adopted and fostered this their darling weapon,) very naturally and significantly annexed their name to it. The bow was the singular gift of God to the English nation.'

87 Henrik Arnstad, *The Amazon Archers of England: Longbows, gender and English nationalism 1780–1845* (Stockholm 2019), 54.

88 Reay 2007.

CHAPTER 3

The human factor

The ship *Vasa* and its people

Anna Maria Forssberg

One Sunday afternoon in August 1628 the ship *Vasa* set out on its maiden voyage and foundered in the middle of Stockholm. In 1961 the wreck was salvaged and today is on display in one of the most popular museums in the world. Yet we still know little about the people on board the ship when it sank. The aim of this essay is to consider how written sources, artefacts, and human remains in the collections of the Vasa Museum can be combined to learn more about the *Vasa* people and the society they lived in.

On 23 August 1628, Gabriel Oxenstierna, a member of the Swedish Council of the Realm, wrote to his brother Axel Oxenstierna, Chancellor of the Realm, and told him about the unexpected sinking of the new ship *Vasa* some two weeks earlier. According to the letter, the beautiful ship had set sail in calm weather, but had been capsized by a small gust of wind, sinking with 62 cannon. Around 30 people – seamen and their wives and children 'who wanted to come along to Vaxholm' – were dead. The old captain Hans Jonsson had also drowned, and the Vice Admiral Erik Jönsson and the captain Söfring Hansson had only barely survived, having been a long time underwater (Fig. 3.1).[1]

There were at least two inquests after the sinking, but it was impossible to establish who was to blame. The documents give us the estimated

Figure 3.1. The Vasa Museum. Photo: Anneli Karlsson, Vasa Museum/SMTM.

number of deaths and the names of seven people on board the ship for the fatal journey (one of whom died). But what about the others? According to naval sources, *Vasa* was supposed to carry 133 seamen and 300 soldiers. It has been assumed that the soldiers were going to board later, which meant only seaman and some wives and children were on the ship, but equally there might have been absences, so there is no way now to know how many were on board. Around 150 people is a figure that is sometimes mentioned, but that is merely an assumption.[2] Who were they and what happened to them? After the inquest into *Vasa*'s sinking, the focus shifted swiftly to the attempts to salvage the ship. Nothing more was said about the fate of the crew.

When the ship was rediscovered and salvaged, new finds shed light on the people of *Vasa*. Human remains of around 15 people were found. Objects such as clothes, shoes, hats, pottery, tableware, board games, and tools of various kinds gave new insights to the people who had once sailed the ship. For the archaeologists who excavated the ship, the conservators and curators who took care of the finds, and the staff making and presenting the exhibitions in the new museum, the people on and around *Vasa* have always been of great interest. Yet there has been a tendency for the people to be overshadowed by the ship itself. First came the great undertaking of piecing the ship back together, conserving it, and getting it into the custom-made museum building, and then new challenges when it was discovered the ship was not faring well and new measures were needed to preserve it.[3] Even though there are several interesting publications about the people of *Vasa* and the everyday objects found on the ship, only little research has been done and plenty of questions remain unanswered. As the Vasa Museum has recently launched a research programme about the people of *Vasa* and is also part of the multi-institutional research programme *Den glömda flottan*, 'The lost navy', there will soon be the opportunity to offer some answers. This essay is an inventory of available sources and previous research with which to discuss the new research about the people of *Vasa*. What, then, do we know, how can we find out more, and what can we learn?

Sources contemporaneous with *Vasa*

On 11 August 1628, the day after the accident, the Council of the Realm wrote to King Gustav II Adolf's brother-in-law Johann Kasimir, who was responsible for Sweden's defences, and told him that *Vasa* had foundered. In their letter they said nothing about how many people were on board or how many had drowned; they just stated that the ship had sunk to a depth of 18 fathoms 'with cannon and all'. Most of the letter was spent reporting military preparations and popular discontent.[4]

The next day they wrote to the king and delivered the bad news. Once again they reported that after a short journey the ship and its cannons had sunk to a depth of 18 fathoms. They said the reason for the accident remained unknown, but a hearing was being planned. The people thought responsible had been taken into custody: Söfring Hansson was being held in the castle, Erik Jönsson was near dead after having been 'full of water and badly hit by the hatches', and old Hans Jonsson was dead. The letter thus gives us three names of people actually on board the ship for the accident. The Council added they did not know the number of dead since they had not had the time to muster the crew. Interestingly, the wording of the signed letter sent to the king differs from the transcript in the registry. The first reads 'Whatever other party there might have been is mostly dead [Umb-kompne]', whereas the other reads 'Whatever other party there might have been is mostly escaped [und-kompne].[5] It could also be a scribal error, or perhaps the Council first thought most people had died, but later learnt that most people actually had been rescued. However, because in the seventeenth century the words were synonymous – both could mean to die or to get away – it is not possible to draw any firm conclusions.[6] We cannot know whether the Council believed that most people had been saved or were dead. The focus of the letter was on the big questions: why the ship had sank and how it could be salvaged.

Both Abraham Brahe, a prominent member of the Council of the Realm, and Johannes Bureus, a scholar who had been the king's tutor, wrote short passages about the sinking in their diaries, but said nothing about casualties.[7] Erik Krabbe, a Danish diplomat in Stockholm, described the event in a report home dated 17 August, saying that the ship had capsized despite there being no wind to speak of. He mentioned that the cannon had gone to the bottom, and reported that it was being said that over 50 people had died – including women and children aboard who were only going as far as the archipelago.[8] According to a report sent by the English envoy James Spens the same day, 40 people had drowned and the rest had been saved by boats. He also claimed that

Figure 3.2. Gabriel Oxenstierna's letter to his brother Axel. Photo: Riks-arkivet. →

before leaving for Germany Gustav II Adolf had had a dream about his new ship sinking at that exact spot.[9]

Gabriel Oxenstierna, in his letter a fortnight later to his brother Axel, wrote that around 30 people were dead (Fig. 3.2).[10] This source is usually seen as the most reliable when it comes to the number of casualties. As things stand, then, five letters and two diary entries are the only written data we have about the number of deaths. It is apparent from the Council's letter they were planning to hold a roll call of the seamen, but nothing has been found in the archives to indicate that it went ahead.

Söfring Hansson was questioned briefly the day after the accident. He assured the Council that 'all people were sober' and that he had 'put everyone to his right place and task'. According to him the problem with the ship was that it was too unstable – it could not carry its masts.[11] The same day the master shipbuilder, Hein Jacobsson, was called in for questioning, but the minutes record nothing of his answers.[12] A few days later the Council discussed 'the ship' and 'Skeppsholmen' again, but the minutes do not reveal what was said.[13]

On 21 August two captains, Klerk and Forbus, delivered a written 'caution' – some sort of personal guarantee – for Söfring, *Vasa*'s captain.[14] We do not know whether that meant he had been incarcerated until then and was now set free on bail, or if it was part of a bigger legal process. Some 'proof' from 'Kaggen' (most likely the military commander Lars Kagg) was delivered to the same meeting of the Council, but it is unclear whether that too was connected to the sinking of *Vasa*.[15]

On 5 September an inquest into sinking opened.[16] It was held by a special court, seventeen strong, of whom six were members of the Council. Unfortunately, the only surviving document is a fragmentary transcript.[17] The purpose of the hearing was to find out why *Vasa* sank and who was responsible (questions which have been discussed at length in the literature and are not the focus of the present essay). Around twenty people were heard, including six who had been on board the ship for its maiden voyage. No one admitted any guilt and their explanations varied: some thought there was too little ballast, others that the ship was top-heavy and badly built, or that the hold was not big enough. In fact the answers all highlighted the problems of the ship from different aspects, and revealed the panel was knowledgeable and well aware of the problems.

The number of people interrogated, like the size of the court itself, shows that great importance was attached to the matter, even though proceedings were inconclusive. The account also gives some insight into the division of labour – who was supposed to do what in the ship-yard and on the ship – and rare glimpses of everyday life. Erik Jönsson assured everyone that all the cannon had been properly tied. He also told them he had not had time to eat, but had twice had something to drink 'and then he was alone in the great cabin with his boy, where he took a small piece of meat and bread, and that was all he had eaten that day'. Why this story was deemed relevant is unclear, but the part about the boy is interesting, and we will return to it later. The boatswain Peer Bertilsson was asked whether he had been drunk and he too answered in the negative, saying that he had taken Communion that day.

Nothing was said about the dead and wounded – probably the question was already answered to the court's satisfaction.

Shortly after the accident 'Master Willam' (probably Willem de Besche) and Ian Bulmer were asked to salvage the ship.[18] Numerous attempts were made in the 1630s, but the ship remained on the bottom. The focus shifted to the cannon, but it turned out to be difficult to get them up. Finally Albrecht von Treileben and Andreas Peckell salvaged most of *Vasa*'s cannons in 1663–1665 using a diving bell. For all that time *Vasa* was most likely a living memory for the people who had been on the ship on its maiden voyage and for their families. Most likely this information was also passed on to others. The French diplomat Charles Ogier wrote of observing one of the salvage attempts on 17 April 1635, describing it as a 'man-o'-war that had sunk at the entrance to the port and still remained there.'[19] The Italian Francesco Negri went to see the salvage of the cannon and commented that the ship had 'gone to the bottom with men and all'.[20] At the inquest after the sinking of the flagship *Kronan* in 1676, one witness recalled hearing someone say 'let us make sure what happened to *Vasa* in Stockholm in the days of good King Gustav Adolf does not happen to us'.[21] Yet *Vasa* and its fate gradually drifted into oblivion once its guns were salvaged. It was not entirely forgotten, as we will see, but unknown to most. Yet evidence of the ship's existence was saved in the archives. Building contracts for the ship, lists of personnel, correspondence about its design, and so forth, all waiting to be rediscovered.

Vasa in historiography

In 1642 the Swedish priest Joannes Baazius published his church history *Inventarium ecclesiæ Sveo-Gothorum*, starting in the oldest times and ending in the 1640s. Despite his ecclesiastical theme, Baazius described the sinking of *Vasa*. His narrative started in 1632 with Queen Maria Eleonora wanting to visit her husband in Germany. A merchantman called *Waase* (after the royal dynasty's emblem) was sent ahead, but suddenly sank with people on board. Attempts had been made to salvage the ship, but it was still at the bottom of the sea. *Vasa*'s foundering was described as a bad omen, a premonition of the death of Gustav II Adolf.[22] Baazius' book was published only sixteen years after the sinking and it is somewhat strange that he misdates it by four years. Maria Eleonora had indeed tried to go to Germany, but in 1628 and she was stopped from travelling – and *Vasa* was never part of the plan. She later visited Germany in 1631 and saw her husband several times in 1632. Baazius was working in Jönköping at the time of the sinking, but had powerful connections and attended several Diets. He might have been mistaken, but it is more likely the story he wanted to tell was that of the death of Gustav Adolf and all bad signs that presaged it, and *Vasa* made for a good example.

Baazius' account was picked up by Johannes Schefferus for his history of the Swedish people in 1671 and from there lived on into the eighteenth century.[23] Carl Bechstadius quoted it almost verbatim in his directory of Sweden's nobility descended from naval officers, repeating that it took place in 1632 and portended the death of the king.[24] A couple of years after Bechstadius, Johann Georg Rüdling got the date for the queen's trip right, but maintained that the foundering was a premonition of the Battle of Lützen. According to him the ship sank with all hands and much of value.[25]

No further details were added to the *Vasa* story until the end of the eighteenth century. Writing a book about Swedish naval history, Carl Gustaf Törnquist found both the Council's letter to the king and Abraham Brahe's diary, and was able to date the sinking correctly.[26] But, with the exception of Söfring Hansson, he said nothing about the people on board or the number of casualties. Yet more sources emerged. In a history of Gustav Adolf's reign published in the mid nineteenth century, Abraham Cronholm cited both the Krabbe letter and various letters between the king and Council found in the official correspondence, Riksregistraturet.[27] *Vasa* was now correctly described as a man-o'-war, setting sail for Älvsnabben, a roadstead south of Stockholm in the outer archipelago.

In the summer of 1920 a wreck was discovered by a fisherman off Viksten, outside Nynäshamn in the Stockholm archipelago. By studying the inscriptions on the cannon, the historian Nils Ahnlund identified the wreck as *Riksnyckeln* (Key of the Realm), and while searching for it in the archives he found information about *Vasa*. He published a long article about *Vasa* in the newspaper *Svenska Dagbladet*, describing how the ship went to the bottom with 'standing sails, flags, and all', and how boats came to the rescue from all sides but there was nothing they could do. He claimed most of the crew died, including its two shipmasters, but that the captain, Severin Jute, was saved.[28] He went over possible locations of the sinking and detailed the inquest and the various salvage attempts in the seventeenth century – it was the salvage attempts which were his main concern, in fact, and neither the building and sinking of *Vasa* nor the people on board.

Vasa research after the discovery

Anders Franzén's discovery of *Vasa* in 1956 immediately led to renewed efforts in the archives. Nils Ahnlund seems to have been an enthusiastic supporter and was present when one mast was salvaged, but did not live to see the ship raised in April 1961.[29] Much of the work in the archives was done by Georg Hafström, who published his results in *Tidskrift i Sjöväsendet* in 1957 and 1958. With that, most of the key *Vasa* sources had been discovered and used – sources that would continue to be at the heart of the *Vasa* story. In the years in which the wreck was pieced together and conserved and the new museum was planned and built, several publications appeared. In addition to popular works for the general public there were also specialized studies about the excavation, salvage, and conservation.[30] Hans Soop wrote a doctoral thesis about the *Vasa* sculptures and in a new book series – *Wasastudier* – both artefacts and the various functions of the ship were analysed.[31] Jan Glete and Patrik Höglund added new insights into the ship's construction and life at sea.[32] In 2003 Fred Hocker became the Vasa Museum's director of research and launched a new research programme. A book describing the archaeological excavation appeared a few years later (the first volume in a planned series about the ship), and in 2011 Hocker summarized our knowledge of *Vasa* in a book of the same name.[33]

What do the written sources tell us?

What can we learn about the people of *Vasa* from the available sources and previous research? The correspondence and minutes of the inquest give us the names of seven people on board: captain Söfring Hansson, captain Hans Jonsson (deceased), vice-admiral Erik Jönsson (and his boy, but he is not named), lieutenant Petter Gierdsson, boatswain Peer Bertilsson, master Jöran Matsson, and master gunner Joen Larsson. The minutes also reveal many other names of people who sat on the bench or were heard as witnesses: Lasse Bubz, 'Hughu', Hughu's colleague, 'Mäster' Wellam, Hans Förrådh, Erich Larsson, Mayor Hans Nielson, Johan Hans Klerck, and Frans and Johan Isbrandsson. There is no indication, however, of which if any of them had been aboard the ship when it sank. Three more seamen 'of *Vasa*' – Mats Mickelson, Mårten Eriksson and Peder Eriksson – were accused of helping two seamen from the ship old *Svärdet* (Sword) to steal a chest from German seamen. Interestingly, they were tried in Stockholm on 11 August 1628, the day after the *Vasa* sank. Yet it remains unclear when and where the theft had taken place. The court ruled that the thieves should be detained and forced to run the gauntlet. We do not know if they had actually boarded *Vasa*, but it seems unlikely.[34]

There is no available source to tell us the actual number of people on *Vasa* on 10 August. According to various lists, the ship's complement was 133 seamen and 300 soldiers. Given the king's instructions to the Council in April 1628 and the low number of muskets found, it has been assumed the soldiers had not yet embarked, but were to join the others at Älvsnabben.[35] And if the ship had continued to Älvsnabben, who were the soldiers who would have joined it there? We do not know that either. In a draft list of navy personnel, two companies and their commanders' names are listed under *Vasa*, but it is hard to decipher – and since it was probably written in early 1628, it is likely it had changed by the summer.[36] What we do know, however, is that some seamen had their wives and children with them for *Vasa*'s maiden voyage. One estimate puts their number at 150, but there could have been more. The plan was for the passengers to get off at Vaxholm.

Why do we know so little about the people?

Evidently we know surprisingly little about the people on *Vasa*. A ship with perhaps 150 people on board sinks in Stockholm in plain sight of hundreds of eye witnesses, and yet we have little more than a handful of names and only one name from the 30 or so dead. Why?

Perhaps it is because many of the central sources are lost? The original manuscript of the inquest has been missing since the nineteenth century, and there was most likely a muster roll for the survivors, but it is nowhere to be found. Probably there were also other relevant letters and minutes which were not preserved. Or perhaps the foundering of *Vasa* was not seen as such a big deal back then? Plenty of ships sank in this period; people died all the time. The fact *Vasa* is now a world-famous museum exhibit does not necessarily mean the ship was considered important in the seventeenth century. Did the silence of the sources reflect a lack of interest? It seems unlikely, given the apparent effort put into finding a guilty party and trying to salvage the ship. Furthermore, we know that death mattered just as much then as now, and the ceremonial and care shown for the rich extended to ordinary people. *Vasa*'s first ever duty had been to salute the dead admiral Nils Stiernsköld, as the ship that carried his corpse entered the port of Stockholm in the summer of 1628. True, Stiernsköld far outranked everyone on *Vasa*, but surely it is fair to assume their deaths too would have left some trace? It has been said the church bells of Stockholm rang for the *Vasa* dead on the night of 10 August, but so far I have not been able to track the source down. It would be interesting to know more about seamen who died at sea. It seems their corpses were often thrown overboard – but was there any form of ceremony?[37] How were their families given news of their deaths?

Another alternative is that there are more sources, but they have been overlooked. Even though many skilled scholars have searched the archives, it is likely that some material has been neglected. In a study about the seamen, Urban Skenbäck confirms he has not had time to look for any other sources than the ones Hafström brought to light. In a memo, Jan Glete claimed there is plenty of source material of relevance to *Vasa* not yet analysed by researchers.[38] It should be noted that Glete was primarily looking for information on shipbuilding and naval organization, not individual seamen and their families, but his assertion could well be valid for that kind of material too. Perhaps it is time to return to the archives?

Back to the archives

There is every reason to return to the archives to look for traces of the people of *Vasa*. A good starting point would be the individuals we know by name – to map their personal history, family life, and careers and search the archives for broader background information. The local source material from Stockholm could be of interest in this context: the various taxation registers, law court records, and church registers for births, christenings, and deaths. We already know that some key figures in *Vasa*'s story such as Margareta Nilsdotter and Henrik Hybertsson appeared before the courts. Finding more information about the people associated with *Vasa* may well provide clues about the people aboard when it sank. Muster roles and administrative records from other parts

Figure 3.3. Women carrying water, Lorenzo Magalotti. Photo: Uppsala University Library.

of Sweden may also be relevant. And it would be interesting to search for more diplomatic material. Were there more foreign envoys present in Stockholm, and what did they report home? The dream would be to identify by name the people we know were on board the ship, and hence gather new information about their lives. In the absence of that, there are other means of finding out more about the people of *Vasa*.

One way to proceed would be a more general study of the seamen and soldiers in the seventeenth-century Swedish navy. How were they recruited, how long did they serve, and how many died at sea? In a newly formulated project I intend to study the seamen as a part of a household.[39] We know from previous research both that the navy experienced difficulties recruiting crews in the 1620s and that Swedish society relied heavily on the household norm. It is reasonable to assume that becoming a seaman – whether by forced conscription or on a voluntary basis – had an impact on the man's family and that the household adopted certain strategies when it came to making a living and finding somewhere to live. To name one example, seamen's wives were allowed to produce certain items despite not belonging to a city guild.[40] With the establishment of a fixed system of recruitment, the job came to define not only the seamen, but also their wives and children. Nils Erik Villstrand's studies reveal how fruitful it can be to look at the manning of the navy from a local perspective.[41]

The women on board *Vasa* when it sank are of special interest. We know that they were not exceptions (Fig. 3.3). AnnaSara Hammar and Mirja Arnshav have found women on warships both in port and at sea.[42] According to a draft of the Sea Articles of 1628, 'whores' were not allowed, but bringing one's wife was permitted if the ship was in home waters and not about to engage the enemy.[43] The same clause was included in the Sea Articles of 1644. Hammar states that the rules were probably followed, and that one was more likely to find women and children on small ships going short distances. But there were exceptions. In 1677, for example, a wife and her baby unintentionally experienced a battle, as she was delivering a food package to her husband.[44]

Sources indicate there were children on *Vasa* who were only passengers, but there were also ship's boys who actually worked in the navy. According to a manning plan for the navy from 1628 it employed a hundred boys.[45] The fact that Erik Jönsson was reportedly in *Vasa*'s great cabin with his boy makes this a promising line of research. Might Admiralty sources perhaps reveal more about them? Of the human remains found at the wreck of *Kronan*, twelve people were under 18 (of whom seven were younger than 14).[46] Despite recent attempts to discover more about the ship's boys, we actually know little about them.[47]

There were also several professional categories worth examining, such as ship's chaplains. When Nils Stiernsköld was about to die after the Battle of the Gdańsk Roadstead in 1627, the ship's chaplain Berthil administered his last rites.[48] According to contemporaneous sources there were supposed to be five chaplains and one superintendent for the entire navy.[49] Who was the superintendent of the navy, and how were the chaplains organized?[50] Sources for the cathedral chapter of Uppsala can probably reveal more.[51] Was there a chaplain on *Vasa* on 10 August 1628? Stiernsköld's fate in 1627 also brings to mind another profession worth investigating. Before Berthil the chaplain was summoned, the ship's barber surgeon had amputated Stiernsköld's injured arm. There were supposed to be 24 barber surgeons in the navy, and it has been assumed there was one associated with *Vasa*.[52]

With some creativity, perseverance, and luck it should be possible to find new information. But it would also be useful to reread the standard *Vasa* sources with new research questions in mind. Most people who have searched the archives for *Vasa* material were after its construction, sinking, and salvage, and not the people on and around the ship. New questions should provide new answers. Take the Oxenstierna letter, and especially the formulation about the women and children who 'wanted to come along' to Vaxholm: it gives agency to women in an unexpected way, showing women and children had wills of their own and the capacity to act on their wishes. Similarly, it would be worth revisiting the inquest, not to find out why the ship sank or how many died, but rather to look at the people who were in the room. Who was summoned, what were their roles, and what does that tell us about the division of labour, the nature of the work, social hierarchies, and so forth? The court material and financial records can tell us more about the economic relations between individuals and social networks. By getting to know the key figures in the *Vasa* story, by studying not only them but also their families, business relations, and social networks, others may appear who were on board *Vasa* or had a role to play. Stockholm and the navy were both small circles in the 1620s, and a thorough study of correspondence would likely reveal new names and connections. Yet we have not only written sources at our disposal to tell the story of the people of *Vasa* – some of them can speak for themselves.

Human remains

Over 1,000 human bones were recovered during the salvage and excavation from inside and around the ship (Fig. 3.4).[53] The interpretation has varied over the years, but the latest research – uniting context analysis, osteological analysis, and DNA analysis – suggests there were eleven or twelve adult skeletons found inside the ship and four or five people

Figure 3.4. One of the *Vasa* skeletons. Photo: Anneli Karlsson, Vasa Museum/ SMTM.

outside.[54] Among the bones inside the ship was a single upper arm bone from a child under 10 years old, and outside a pair of feet was found in a pair of boots. Ongoing DNA analyses are expected to confirm or adjust earlier findings regarding the sex of the people and whether any of them were related.[55]

What can the skeletons tell us? They confirm that at least two women and a child were on board. They also say something about the age and general health of the people of *Vasa*. Most men were in their twenties and thirties, but the skeletons range in age from teenagers to people in their fifties or sixties. The average height was 165–166 cm (the shortest was 160 cm and the tallest 176 cm). Most had been injured at some point in their lives – they had healed broken bones.

The skeletons have not been identified. For one of them, however, there is evidence he might have been captain Hans Jonsson – the only deceased person mentioned by name in the written sources. If we assume that around 30 people died that means we have remains for at least half of them, so there is a 50 per cent chance that Hans Jonsson's remains are among them. According to the sources he was trapped inside the ship, which increases the chances of him being among the recovered remains. Since he was referred to as 'old' and was a man of a certain

Figure 3.5. Reconstruction of skeleton B, 'Beata'. Photo: Anneli Karlsson, Vasa Museum/SMTM.

Figure 3.6. Spoons. Photo: Anneli Karlsson, Vasa Museum/SMTM.

social standing, the only skeleton to match would be 'Johan', who was the oldest and reasonably well dressed. Hans Jonsson had a long career and there should be more information to be found about him in archival sources. Several of the skeletons were found with clothing and personal possessions – valuable information about who they were (Fig. 3.5).

Amazing artefacts

Objects possess emotional power. Holding a spoon that someone once took aboard the ship can evoke the feeling that it transcends time. Objects are easy to relate to. We all use spoons every day, we all wear clothes and shoes, and those are things we have in common with the people of *Vasa* despite everything that separates us – time, worldviews, ways of life. The meat and drink on board the ship remind us that the people of *Vasa* had the same need for food and drink as we have; the chamber pots remind us they had other human needs too. Their combs, pipes, and board games serve as reminders of everything that unites us people across the centuries: objects with a unique ability to spark our emotions and establish reassuringly common ground. But they can also appear banal. Saying that humans need nourishment, that they need to relieve themselves, that since the beginning of time they have dressed and tried to embellish themselves, is stating the obvious. A unique sensation in a museum is not necessarily an interesting scholarly problem. So how best to ask research questions about *Vasa* objects?

The fact of the matter is that there are over 40,000 objects in the Vasa Museum collections, and all can contribute valuable and unexpected knowledge aplenty. Putting to one side the ship parts, artillery and weaponry, shot (9,000 items), and human remains and there are 20,000 objects related to the people of *Vasa*, either as personal belongings or as commodities and items used in everyday life. The collections are unique in several ways. Since we know the time of the sinking we can date the objects – we know they were made before 10 August 1628 (with the exception of some artefacts added during the salvage attempts in the seventeenth century or dropped on the wreck later). We also know that the objects were connected to the people on board or to the operation of the ship. With the exception of a gold ring, a silver spoon, an exclusive table clock, and a brazier, only few exclusive objects were found.[56] There were silver coins, a little velvet pouch, a Westerwald tankard, and some items of clothing made from high-quality fabric, but the vast majority of the objects reflect the broader strata of society rather than the elite: in contrast to many other museum collections with objects from the seventeenth century, they did not belong to royalty or nobility. It also means the kind of everyday objects which were used until they fell to pieces and never made it into museums abound in the Vasa Museum collections. There are clothes, sewing equipment, spoons, plates, bowls, tankards, chests, casks, boxes, coins, knives, games, books (severely fragmented), combs, tobacco pipes, cooking pots, chamber pots, lanterns, fishing gear, various tools, and much more (Fig. 3.6).

The objects were not recorded in detail during the excavation, but they were given a number and noted in a find ledger. As of 2003 an ongoing documentation project led by Fred Hocker has seen museum staff and visiting students and experts work to resolve this by dividing the finds according to five major themes, published as (*i*) the salvage and excavation process, and to come (*ii*) the rigging and sailing the ship, (*iii*) building the ship (*iv*) the crew as individuals, (*v*) the crew as a community, and (*vi*) naval warfare.[57] Each theme is divided into smaller find groups, and in each find group every object is examined, sketched, measured, and photographed and all data is entered into the museum's finds database, Primus.[58] In this fashion a substantial part of the collection is now documented, and several find groups have been described and analysed in Master's dissertations at various universities. All this work provides a great starting point for the research about the people of *Vasa*.

What happens if we let the objects lead the way and, as some scholars suggest, take a 'Grand Tour' among them or 'bathe' in them?[59] By spending a great deal of time with the objects, getting to know them, and becoming an expert the researcher should see new things and ask unexpected questions. Not just seeing them as material culture, but actually touching them, smelling them, and observing them closely will give new insights. Was it heavy, light, fragile? Could one person carry it or was it a job for several people? The objects can tell us about practices not recorded in the written source material. The fishing equipment in the *Vasa* collection points to the practice of fishing at sea – hardly surprising, but not part of how provisioning for the navy is normally described. The great variety of animal and fish bones found on *Vasa* – cow, pig, sheep or goat, roe deer, domestic fowl, goose, mallard, black and willow grouse, cod, pike, burbot (freshwater cod), ling, herring, and perch – offers a far more colourful image of the food at sea compared to the list of provisions that specify bread, beer, meat and dried fish, herring, salt, and peas.[60] To be fair, the seamen were supposed to feed themselves when the ship was in Stockholm waters, yet the provisions can give interesting information about food habits, hunting, and trade.

One way of approaching the objects is to study them one by one. The idea of making object biographies is to include the entire lifespan from production, via trade and consumption all the way to becoming a museum object. This approach has been tested in the project 'Gendered

Figure 3.7. One of the board games from *Vasa*. Photo: Anneli Karlsson, Vasa Museum/SMTM.

interpretations' in collaboration with the Victoria & Albert Museum in London and the universities of Lund and Plymouth. The aim has been to retrieve unknown histories of gender and sexuality by writing object biographies. Among the *Vasa* objects studied in the forthcoming publication is a *svepask* or bentwood box with the initials MOD – indicating that it belonged to a woman – and a thimble, a hat, a board game (nine men's morris) and more (Fig. 3.7). Together they exemplify how object biographies can help write the history of the people of *Vasa*.[61]

Another way is to look at the closed finds. Although many objects had moved around on the wreck and lost their original placing, there were many closed finds such as chests, barrels, and boxes that still had the same contents as when the ship set sail: food, various forms of equipment, clothing, shoes, tools for repairing clothes and shoes, and much more. They offer a possibility of reconstructing what people took with

Figure 3.8. On board *Vasa*. Photo: Anneli Karlsson, Vasa Museum/SMTM.

them and by extension people's lives. A more thorough analysis of the closed finds would be the best way to start researching the people of *Vasa*. As has been pointed out, the archaeological site was less disturbed than was originally thought. That means it is also vital to consider the find context of the *Vasa* material.[62] Placing the objects in their correct physical context will help us understand the division of space on the ship – how were objects and people placed? This in turn will tell us more about social hierarchies and how work was organized.[63]

There are also opportunities to create new contexts. Objects can be divided into different themes by production or use. How did people eat, sleep, dress, amuse themselves, fight, and die? An ongoing project about *Vasa* garments and shoes is one example. Since there was no military uniform in the navy at the time and the seamen were conscripts, their clothing is likely to represent a cross-section of Swedish society. The project can tell not only how people were dressed but if their clothes were old or new, in good or bad condition, home-made or bought. This will give valuable insights into the differences in social and economic status.[64] Finds of different kinds also say something about eating habits. Why were there so many spoons but so few bowls? Surely plates were a bit unpractical if the commonest food was yellow pea soup? What about drink? We know the crew was supposed to be served 3 litres of (weak) beer a day each, but there were also flasks with stronger alcohol on *Vasa*. Who drank it, and in what context? After all, the question of sobriety came up several times at the inquest and we can assume that the use and misuse of alcohol was widespread.

There is also a lot to gain from seeing the collection as a whole. What can the objects tell us about the people on board and their status, health, pains, and pleasures? What can they say that goes beyond the objects themselves? A highly interesting aspect is that so many were marked, either with owner's marks or initials, as a study by the curator Irene Lindblom has shown.[65] Do the initials on different objects indicate their owners could read and write?

Finally, as for all source material, gaps and silences can speak volumes. Even though we know that some materials are missing because they do not withstand water well and have diluted or corroded away (which is the reason there are no iron objects), that does not account for all the gaps. Some things may have been rescued with the survivors or salvaged shortly after the sinking. Yet is likely that some objects are missing because they were never brought on board. This is the case with muskets – the few examples in the collection came nowhere near arming 300 soldiers, which has been taken to mean the soldiers were not yet on the ship. A bit surprisingly there are no musical instruments (in contrast to *Kronan*, which foundered in 1676 with several instruments).[66]

Does it make sense that the found artefacts corresponded to the belongings of 150 people? Was everything on the ship intended to be there for the remainder of the journey or is it possible some things were sent on the ship for just part of the trip? This could indicate who was on board to stay and who was a guest (Fig. 3.8).

Multidisciplinary ways forward

As should be apparent from this account, written sources, human remains, and objects all have interesting things to say about the people of *Vasa*. Yet there is something better still, and that is the possibility of using them all jointly. Taken together, they offer a unique opportunity to approach the lived reality and ways of life of the broader strata of society in the 1620s. The objects can bring new phenomena to our attention and help us to ask new questions. By combining the different materials we can write a fuller and more encompassing story.

Studying *Vasa* can add not only to the knowledge of the ship itself and life at sea, but also to our understanding of Swedish society in the 1620s. Since seamen were either allotted to the navy or conscripted from peasant families on the coasts or ordinary town dwellers, and since some had their families with them, they can be seen as representatives of majority society. Most people on board *Vasa* did not belong to the upper classes, and none belonged to the nobility. *Vasa* can thus tell us a great deal about who was recruited, everyday life at sea, human relations and family life, what people ate and drank, how they entertained themselves, and much more. If we study written sources alongside objects in the Vasa Museum collections and the human remains, we can learn more not only about the crew, but also about the people who commissioned the ship, and the ones that built, transported, wove, painted, polished, and so forth. *Vasa* can thus serve as a key to understanding the maritime, economic, and political history of Sweden.

One way would be to focus on the individuals and try to find out as much as possible about each one – micro history, in other words. It would also mean making the most of the information we have about the skeletons, whether their age, physical appearance, medical conditions, or personal belongings. If both written sources and human remains are scrutinized carefully it might also be possible to put names to the skeletons or to strengthen earlier assumptions. It is also possible to use scholarly tools from the other end of the scale, and, inspired by global history, view both individuals and objects as integral to international trade and knowledge exchange. Even though the majority of the ordinary seamen were conscripted from farms and towns across Sweden–Finland, many officers and shipbuilders were hired in Germany, the Netherlands, and Scotland.

Combining written sources, human remains, and objects also offers the chance to compare theory and practice. The objects can reveal a much more complex reality than the bureaucratic lists in the archives – the presence of women and children, for example, or all the activities outside fighting sea battles. They can also help us make comparisons over time and observe changed practices. (The professionally butchered cattle in the *Kronan* material may perhaps confirm the professionalization of the navy since *Vasa*'s day.) The artefacts could take us past basic assumptions and preconceptions.

There are countless possibilities to ask interesting questions of the people on board *Vasa* on its disastrous maiden voyage. Having built, rigged, packed, visited, and sailed the ship and been there for its dramatic sinking, they are well worth examining. Even more important, however, is that they can serve as a medium to discover more about life in Stockholm in the 1620s. By observing them in the looking glass, we can glimpse behind them the rest of Swedish society.

Notes

1 Letter from Gabriel Oxenstierna 23 Aug. 1628, printed in *Rikskansleren Axel Oxenstiernas skrifter och brefvexling, Afd. 2, iii/1: Gabriel Gustafsson Oxenstiernas bref 1611–1640, 2: Per Brahes bref 1633–1651*, ed. Per Sondén (Stockholm 1890) (hereafter *AOSB*), 163. He was mistaken about the number of cannon – according to an inventory from the summer of 1628 there were 64 – but it is possible he did not count the two smallest ones, two falconets, or he was just ill-informed.

2 For the manning of *Vasa*, see Georg Hafström, 'Skeppet Wasas bemanningsfråga', *Tidskrift i Sjöväsendet* 10 (1970).

3 Emma Hocker, *Preserving Vasa* (London 2018), 105–118.

4 Riksarkivet (Swedish National Archives), Stockholm (RA), Rådets registratur 1628, fol. 659–63.

5 I would like to thank my colleague Inger Elgestedt for bringing the difference in spelling to my attention.

6 See *Svenska Akademiens Ordbok* (*SAOB*) www.saob.se/, s.v. 'omkomma' and 'undkomma'.

7 Abraham Brahe, *Tidebok* (Stockholm 1920), 170; Gustav Edvard Klemming (ed.), 'Anteckningar af Johannes Thomæ Agrivillensis Bureus', *Samlaren* 4 (1883), 113.

8 Rigsarkivet (Danish National Archives), Copenhagen, Tyske Kancelli, Udenrigske afdeling, Sverige: Indberetninger fra forskellige agenter og residenter (1622–1639), letter from Erik Krabbe, 17 Aug. 1628.

9 The National Archives of the UK (TNA), London, James Spens to Secretary Coke, 25 Aug. 1628, copy at the Vasa Museum.

10 *AOSB* 1890, 163.

11 *Svenska riksrådets protokoll* (hereafter *SRP*), i: *1621–1629* (Stockholm 1878), 102–103 'Han svor att altt folk var nycktertt'; 'satte han hvar och en vedh sitt embethe och platz'.

12 *SRP* 1878, i. 103–104.

13 *SRP* 1878, i. 104, 14 Aug. 1628.

14 Most likely Johan Hans Klerk, who was a witness at the inquest, and Arvid Forbus. Both were of Scottish descent and figured prominently in the Swedish navy.

15 *SRP* 1878, i. 107.

16 *SRP* 1878, i. 111.

17 *SRP* 1878, i. 111; RA, RA:s ämnessamlingar, M-serien, M 1754 has an incomplete transcription of the minutes, published in Georg Hafström, 'Äldre tiders bärgningsarbeten vid vraket av skeppet Wasa', *Tidskrift i Sjöväsendet* (1958), 751–8. The original minutes were in the former collection RA, Oxenstiernska samlingen, Handlingar om Svenska Flottan but are now lost (see *SRP* 1878, i.).

18 Hafström 1958, 771; *SRP* 1878, i. 111.

19 Quoted in Hafström 1958, 777.

20 Hafström 1958, 802.

21 Lars Ericson Wolke, *Stridens verklighet: Döden på slagfältet i svensk historia 1563–1814* (Lund 2020), 222: 'låt oss nu se att det icke går oss i hand som det gick med Wasen i salig konung Gustaf Adolfs tid vid Stockholm'.

22 I would like to thank Peter Sjökvist who kindly translated the text from Latin to Swedish.

23 Johannes Schefferus, *En bok om det svenska folkets minnesvärda historia*, ed. Allan Ellenius & Kurt Johannesson, tr. Birger Bergh (Stockholm 2005), 56.

24 Carl N. Bechstadius, *Then adelige och lärde swenske siö-man* (Stockholm 1734). For *Vasa* in the literature, see also Georg Hafström, 'Några problem kring regalskeppet Wasa', *Forum Navale* (1963) and Carl Olof Cederlund, 'From Liberton to Franzén', in Carl Olof Cederlund, *Vasa I: The Archaeology of a Warship* (Stockholm 2006).

25 In addition to Baazius and Bechstadius, Rüdling also referred to Laurentius Paulinus Gothus' *Historiæ arctoæ* of 1636, but that concerns Queen Maria Eleonora's travels and not Vasa.

26 Carl Gustaf Törnquist, *Utkast till swenska flottans sjötåg* (Stockholm 1788).

27 Abraham Peter Cronholm, *Sveriges historia under Gustaf II Adolphs regering* (Stockholm 1857).

28 The sources for Ahnlund's more questionable claims are not known. For example, at least one shipmaster, Jöran Mattson, survived – he was interrogated at the inquest.

29 Both Hafström and Fälting have described Ahnlund's joy as the mast was salvaged. Ahnlund died in January 1958.

30 About the early years of research: Hans Soop, 'Vasa och den vetenskapliga forskningen', in *Mitt i strömmen. En vänbok tillägnad Lars-Åke Kvarning* (Stockholm 1996).

31 Ingrid Kaijser, Ernst Nathorst-Böös & Inga-Lill Persson, 'Ur sjömannens kista och tunna: personliga tillhörigheter på Vasa', *Wasastudier* 10 (Stockholm 1982); Urban Skenbäck, 'Sjöfolk och knektar på Wasa', *Wasastudier* 11 (Stockholm 1983); Katarina Villner, 'Blod, kryddor och sot: Läkekonst för 300 år sedan', *Wasastudier* 14 (Stockholm 1986).

32 Jan Glete, 'Kontrakt, bestick och dimensioner: Vasa och de stora skeppsbyggnadskontrakten under Gustav II Adolfs tid: En sammanställning av data ur kontrakt, räkenskaper och administrativt källmaterial rörande flottan', draft (2002); Jan Glete, *Swedish naval administration, 1521–1721: resource flows and organisational capabilities* (Leiden 2010); Patrik Höglund, 'Vasa: Arkeologiska fynd och ett fartygssamhälle', *Forum Navale* 52 (1997); Patrik Höglund, 'Örlogsskeppet Vasa och ståndssamhällets rum', in Staffan von Arbin (ed.), *Tjop tjop! Vänbok till Christer Westerdahl* (Skärhamn 2015).

33 Cederlund 2006; Fred Hocker, *Vasa* (Stockholm 2011).

34 *Stockholms tänkeböcker*, xvii: *1628*, ed. Jan Gejrot (Stockholm 1998), 93.

35 Skenbäck 1983, 49.

36 Skenbäck 1983, 21.

37 For deaths at sea, see Villner 1986, 72; Katarina Villner, *Under däck: Mary Rose–Vasa–Kronan* (Stockholm 2012), 75–7; Ericson Wolke 2020, 279–80.

38 Glete 2002, 3.

39 'Seamen, soldiers, wives and everyday life: A material history', part of the research programme *Den glömda flottan: Sveriges 'blåa' kulturarv ca 1450–1850* ('The forgotten navy: Sweden's maritime heritage, c.1450–1850'), financed by Riksbankens Jubileumsfond.

40 Olle Törnbom, 'Båtsmanshushållets uppkomst', *Forum Navale* 9 (1948), 57–8.

41 Nils Erik Villstrand, *Båtsmanshållet på Åland och i Finland under 1620-talet* (Åbo 1979); id., 'Manskap och sjöfolk inom den svenska örlogsflottan 1617–1644', *Historisk Tidskrift för Finland* (1986); id., ''Bondpojkar doppade i vatten': Svensk sjömilitär rekrytering ur ett jämförande perspektiv (1500–1800)', in *Människan i flottans tjänst* (Åbo 2001).

42 Mirja Arnshav, ''I Kaijutan war een hop qwinfolk och barn': kvinnor ombord på 1600-talets örlogsfartyg', *Forum Navale* 73 (2017); AnnaSara Hammar, 'Kvinnor till sjöss på Vasas tid' (unpub. 2015), preparatory work for the Vasa Museum exhibition *Kvinnorna*.

43 Article 58, quoted in Sven-Gunnar Ingemar Haverling, 'Ett projekt till sjöartiklar från år 1628', *Forum Navale* 9 (1948), 110.

44 Hammar 2015.

45 'Siööfolcks staten som nu reformeras på efterfölliande Sätt Anno 1628', see Skenbäck 1983, 37.

46 Anna Kjellström et al., 'Människorna ombord: Nya osteologiska perspektiv', in Lars Einarsson (ed.), *Skeppet, staden, stormakten: Människor och samhälle under regalskeppet Kronans tid* (Kalmar 2015), 58.

47 Maria Sjöberg, 'Hur pojkar blev karlar: skeppsgossar och andra pojkar i den svenska krigsmakten 1600–1800', Christer Kujava & Ann-Catrin Östman (eds.), *Svärdet, ordet och pennan: kring människa, makt och rum i nordisk historia: Festskrift till Nils Erik Villstrand* (Åbo 2012); Höglund 1997, 40–3.

48 This was described in the funeral sermon. David Gudmundsson, 'Konsten att dö som en kristen krigare: Amiral Nils Stiernsköld och skeppsprästen Berthil vid Danzig år 1627', *Religionsvetenskaplig Internettidskrift* 2/10 (2011).

49 Skenbäck 1983, 37.
50 Patrik Höglund, 'Skeppssamhället: Rang, roller och status på örlogsskepp under 1600-talet' (PhD thesis, forthcoming).
51 It is also worth noting that the ship's priest Lars Arvidi appeared several times before the city court in Stockholm in 1628, see Stockholms stad, Stadsarkivet, Personer i tänkeböckerna [catalogue], sok.stadsarkivet.stockholm.se/Databas/personer-i-tanke-bockerna/Sok?sidindex=469.
52 Skenbäck 1983, 37; Höglund 1997, 39; Villner 1986.
53 This passage is based on information from Fred Hocker.
54 See Allison N. Miller Simonds, 'Who Are You? An Archaeological Examination of the Human Remains Associated with Vasa' (MA diss., East Carolina University 2017); Isolde Green Jungstedt, 'The people behind the bones: MLMNI and water taphonomy on the Swedish warship Vasa' (MA diss., Stockholm University 2018); and a summary by Fred Hocker in an internal Vasa Museum memo, 'Vasa Research: Artefact Group Research Methodology', 2018.
55 This research is led by Marie Allen of Uppsala University's Department of Immunology, Genetics and Pathology.
56 Hans Soop, *Silver, brons, mässing, tenn: Bruksföremål från örlogsskeppet Vasa* (Stockholm 2001).
57 Hocker, 'Vasa Research' 2018.
58 Hocker, 'Vasa Research' 2018, 4.
59 Ulrika Torell, 'Grand tour bland tingen', and Marie Ulväng, 'Textilbadet: Kläder och konsumtion', in Anna Maria Forssberg & Karin Sennefelt (eds.), *Fråga föremålen: handbok till historiska studier av materiell kultur* (Lund 2014).
60 Ulrica Söderlind, *Skrovmål: Kosthållning och matlagning i den svenska flottan från 1500-tal till 1700-tal* (Stockholm 2006).
61 Anna Maria Forssberg & Svante Norrhem, *Föremålens hemliga liv: Kön och genus i Vasamuseets samlingar* (forthcoming 2021).
62 The excavation and the placement of closed finds is described in Cederlund 2006, pt. iii; see also Kaijser et al. 1982.
63 This is the topic of Höglund forthcoming.
64 See, for example, Anna Silwerulv's chapter in Forssberg & Norrhem 2021.
65 Irene Lindblom, 'Märkta föremål från Vasa' (unpub. Vasa Museum report 2013), 2 (not paginated).
66 Lars Einarsson, *Regalskeppet Kronan: historia och arkeologi ur djupet* (Lund 2016).

CHAPTER 4

Swedish vessels in the Prize Papers

Cases from the American Revolutionary War, 1776–1783

Leos Müller

Trade under neutral flags is not a modern phenomenon. Even in the eighteenth century, Swedish ships under a neutral flag traded with and between belligerents, and the American Revolutionary War saw a boom in Swedish shipping. But Britain, which dominated the seas, tried to curb and even stop the trade under neutral flags. This essay considers Swedish ships seized by the British navy and privateers and the patterns of Swedish shipping in wartime in 1776–1783, using the ship seizures recorded in the Prize Papers – an extraordinarily rich and underused archive.

In the eighteenth century, the Swedish merchant fleet expanded considerably. This has been explained by pointing to Sweden's mercantilist policy, the transport needs of foreign trade, and institutional improvements (legislation, peace treaties with the Barbary States, etc.).[1] An underrated and often misunderstood factor behind the expansion, though, was foreign demand for Swedish shipping capacity – tramp shipping under the Swedish flag. In the tramp trade, cargo vessels did not trade between fixed ports, but took cargo wherever they could for any port.

Swedish tramp vessels were often employed by foreigners to carry cargo between foreign ports, without touching Sweden. They might stay away from Sweden for years. There are many reasons why the literature has overlooked Swedish tramp shipping. One of the most obvious reasons is the sources. Sweden has well-preserved, detailed trade statistics produced by the Kommerskollegium (Board of Trade), but the sources for shipping businesses, and especially tramp shipping, are far scarcer and more difficult to evaluate.[2] The key problem was the nature of tramp shipping as, in principle, overseas trade.

In the records of the Board of Trade there are two series concerning Swedish ships engaged in foreign trade: the registers of *sjöpass* or sea-passes (which identified ships as being protected under Sweden's treaties with North African countries) and the registers of *fribrev* or sea-briefs (which identified Swedish ships employed in foreign trade).[3] They include information on ships' names, tonnages, homeports, shipmasters, shipowners, cargo, and even their first destinations. But we lack information about what all the ships were doing away from Sweden. We do not know their other destinations, cargo, and patterns of shipping. Swedish-flagged vessels went from port to port looking for profitable cargo to carry, but none of it is visible in the Board of Trade records. There is additional evidence that Swedish vessels were sailing the North Sea, the Mediterranean, the Atlantic, even the Indian Ocean with goods belonging to foreigners. It is possible to trace their movements in private correspondence between shipowners, shipmasters, commission agents, and consuls – in fact, Swedish consuls had to report all Swedish vessels visiting their district and document their movements[4] – but unfortunately the majority of such shipping lists are gone, as is most of the private correspondence of shipowners and shipmasters.

This essay thus examines Swedish shipping patterns by using the Prize Papers. The Prize Papers of the British High Court of Admiralty (HCA), held in The National Archives of the UK, comprise a large number of documents relating to vessels of all nationalities taken as prizes by British privateers or the Royal Navy, and prosecuted in the prize division of the Admiralty Court.[5] Each case has documentation of the seizure of the prize, the stated reasons, the vessel's identity documents,

Figure 4.1. The snows *Resolution* and *L'Apparance* attacked by the British cutter, 5 December 1793. The image is from the French Revolutionary Wars, but similar encounters took place between British privateers and Swedish merchant vessels in 1778–1783. Photo: Cecilia Nordstrand, Swedish National Maritime Museum/SMTM.

bills of lading, correspondence, and so on. The quality and quantity of the documentation varies enormously: some cases are extensively documented and include the bulk of the correspondence in transit by ship, while others are more sparse. Here I am especially interested in the interrogatories, the standardized sets of written questions formally put to the captured vessel's crew that they had to answer. For each prize taken, the shipmaster and two or three mariners, or sometimes passengers, were asked specific questions relevant to the prize case, for example the nationality of the crew and vessel, ownership of the cargo, voyage details, home port, ports of call, and destinations. The interrogatories, in other words, provide information about the vessel's movements from its departure to the moment of seizure. As the quality of interrogatories varies from case to case, however, the information is best completed with other sources.

The essay focuses on Swedish vessels taken in the American Revolutionary War (1776–1783), a war in which Sweden stayed neutral. The war began as a rebellion of North American colonists against Britain, but from 1778 it turned into a European great power conflict, engaging on the pro-American side first France (1778), then Spain (1779), and finally the Dutch Republic (1780). The northern powers – Sweden, Denmark, and Russia – stayed outside the conflict. The American Revolutionary War was in many ways a maritime conflict. From as early as 1776 American privateers were cruising the Atlantic and North Sea, searching for British prizes. A couple of years later they had been joined by French and Spanish vessels. The British replied in kind, with Royal Navy and a large number of private ships of war (privateers) engaged in chasing the enemy. And of course, naval operations in the West Indies and North America did play a vital role in the outcome of the conflict.[6] Maritime warfare opened a niche of highly profitable but risky tramp shipping under the neutral flags of Denmark and Sweden.

I will consider how the Swedes balanced the risks and rewards of tramp shipping under wartime conditions by looking at how many Swedish vessels were taken as British prizes, on which routes and for what reasons, and the HCA's decisions in each case.

Neutrality in the American Revolutionary War

In 1775 there were reports of renewed tension between North American colonists and London, and war seemed increasingly likely. In Sweden, as in Denmark and the Dutch Republic, this was viewed as high politics, but also as news of a profitable opportunity. The three middle-range states had successfully traded under neutral flags in the Seven Years War (1756–1763). They each had large merchant marines and extensive foreign trade, and had succeeded in balancing their foreign policies between Britain and France. But the fact that they were neutral states did not mean they adopted the same policies towards the belligerents.[7]

The Dutch Republic and Denmark had colonies in the West Indies and their transatlantic trade was very important. They traded with the Americans as well as with the other belligerents. The Dutch were, too, the most important suppliers of weapons to the American rebels. Not surprisingly, the first nation to recognize the US independence was the Dutch Republic, with its 'First Salute' to the US flag in the Dutch West Indian island of St. Eustatius, in November 1776.[8] The Danes, on the other hand, prohibited trade in weapons with American rebels and kept their relations with Britain friendly.[9] Much of the Dutch and Danish foreign policy in 1776–1783 might be explained by their commercial interests in the Atlantic trade and West Indies.

Sweden was interested in the Atlantic trade, but did not participate directly, since until 1784 it lacked a colony in the West Indies. Swedish vessels were chartered for voyages to the West Indies by other parties, the French and Spanish especially, but only on a limited scale.[10] Sweden's major commercial interest was trade with southern Europe and tramp shipping there. Sweden was a big exporter of iron and naval stores (tar, pitch, boards), the latter being strategically sensitive goods – contraband of war, forbidden to be supplied by neutrals to belligerents in time of war under British law.[11] It was the British understanding of the legality of the Swedish export trade which would frame the limits of Sweden's maritime neutrality. Much of Swedish foreign trade was with southern Europe and the Mediterranean, and there was also the large market for tramp shipping.[12]

In February 1778, France recognized the independence of the United States, and soon war between France and Britain broke out. Sweden, Denmark, and Russia discussed the possibility of a joint defence of neutral trade and shipping, primarily against British supremacy at sea, but they had different interests in the conflict and perceived one another as competitors. In 1778, Denmark suggested to Russia that they join forces to protect shipping in the northern Atlantic. The American privateers were cruising coastal Danish–Norwegian waters, seizing British vessels with goods from northern Russia. Britain protested at the American seizures and asked the Danes to guarantee safety of the Danish–Norwegian maritime routes. Denmark thought protecting the route from Russian Archangel to Britain along Norway's long coast was in both Russian and Danish interests, and so approached Empress Catherine II. The Empress was not interested.[13]

Late 1778 and 1779 were chaotic, with British and French privateers seizing many neutrals. In February 1780, Catherine II stole a march by issuing a declaration of the protection of neutral trade and shipping. She required belligerents to recognize the neutrals' rights to trade and sail freely, and she invited the other neutral powers to join her in the defence of neutral rights.

The immediate cause of Catherine II's declaration was the seizure of Russian vessels in the Mediterranean by the Spanish, and for that reason the British initially perceived the declaration as targeted against Spain and France. In the long term the declaration had an anti-British stance which baffled London: Russia had few merchant vessels and most of its foreign trade was carried on British and Dutch bottoms, and more broadly there were no obvious strategic conflicts between Russian and British foreign policy interests.[14] The coordinated protection of neutral rights at sea was important to Sweden and Denmark, though, and after some hesitation they welcomed the Russian initiative. After a couple of months of negotiations, St Petersburg, Copenhagen, and Stockholm formed the First League of Armed Neutrality. Between 1780 and 1783 Danish and Swedish shipping and trade flourished, and the British harassment of neutral shipping declined substantially.

The Dutch Republic, too, welcomed Russia's initiative, proclaiming Catherine II the protector of the liberty of the seas. Yet before it could join the League, Britain declared the war on the Dutch Republic. The League of Armed Neutrality did not protest. The fact that in early 1781 the Dutch carrying capacity disappeared from the international freight market was the major reason for the Danish and Swedish boom over the next couple of years.

Swedish vessels in the Prize Papers, 1778–1783

To chart how Swedish-flagged shipping and British prize-taking were interrelated, I have used a combination of three sources: the Swedish sea-pass registers, the Swedish diplomatic records of prize cases (Diplomatica Anglica), and Swedish prize cases in the Prize Papers. Sweden's sea-pass registers – which included the Mediterranean passes that iden-

Table 4.1. Swedish prizes taken and Swedish trade, 1778–1783.

Year	Prizes taken *	Ships ASP †	Ships FB ‡	Arrivals Marseilles §
1778	35	287	690	42
1779	17	282	724	30
1780	8	320	726	22
1781	8	373	832	42
1782	5	441	933	52
1783	1	339	978	51
1778–1783	74	2042	4883	239

Sources:

* Prizes taken by the British between August 1778 and January 1783, from Riksarkivet (Swedish National Archives), Stockholm (RA), Diplomatica Anglica, Handlingar ang. uppbringningar 1764–1793, vol. 443.
† Number of Mediterranean passes issued in 1778–1783, from RA, Kommerskollegium, Huvudarkivet, CIIb, Sjöpassdiarier, Algeriska sjöpass (ASP).
‡ Number of sea-briefs issued in 1778–1783, from RA, Kommerskollegium, Huvudarkivet, CIIc, Fribrevsdiarier (FB).
§ Number of Swedish vessels arriving at Marseilles, from Charles Carrière, *Négociants marseillais au XVIIIe siècle* (Marseilles 1973), 1061.

tified Swedish ships bound for destinations beyond Cape Finisterre in north-western Spain as being protected under Sweden's treaties with Barbary States – are a reliable source for Swedish vessels involved in long-distance trade (the Mediterranean, the Atlantic, Spain and Portugal, and the Indian Ocean) and recorded the ships' dates of departure and arrival and first presumed destination.[15] The information in the Swedish sea-brief registers is thinner than in the sea-pass registers – there is no information about destination, cargo, or date of return in the document – but sea-brief registers do include *all* vessels, including those in the Baltic and the North Sea.

A comparison of the sea-brief and sea-pass registers shows that about 40 per cent of all Swedish vessels in the period 1778–1783 applied for Mediterranean passes, and accordingly were employed in long-distance shipping (Table 4.1). (In tonnage the proportion was even greater, because the average tonnage of vessels employed beyond Cape Finisterre was higher than that of vessels sailing in Baltic and North Sea waters.[16]) There are two apparent conclusions to be drawn. First, in comparison with the total shipping activity, the number of prizes was low – less than 2 per cent of all Swedish vessels employed in foreign trade in the five-year period. Second, half of the prizes were taken in the space of four months at the start of the war, in late 1778. The British took few prizes in 1780–1783. One explanation is Catherine II's League of Armed Neutrality, yet the decrease was also related to the fact that the HCA Prize Court ruled that most Swedish vessels taken in 1778 should be freed, and that only cargoes of naval stores were prize and paid for. If in a prize case it was found there was no obvious abuse of a neutral flag, the shipmaster was free to go. Why would privateers make the effort if the outcome were so uncertain?

The study of the prizes taken falls into two. In the first part I look at the Swedish vessels taken between August and December 1778, the four months when British privateers took thirty-five Swedish prizes. In the second part I analyse the period between 1780 and 1782 when there were a few but nonetheless remarkable cases of apparent abuses of the neutral flag.

Prizes taken in late 1778

Of the thirty-five Swedish ships taken as British prizes between August and December 1778, the majority had sailed from Sweden and the Baltic. Twelve gave Swedish ports as their last port of call. Stockholm dominated, and with one exception (*Brita Cecilia*) gave Stockholm as their home port. Two came from Finnish ports – Nykarleby (Uusikaarlepyy) and Uleåborg (Oulu) – and others from Gothenburg and Strömstad on the Swedish west coast and Västervik on the east coast. Six ships gave non-Swedish Baltic ports as their last port of call: five came from St Petersburg and one from Königsberg (Kaliningrad). *Concordia Affinitas* (home port Ystad in southern Sweden) gave Hamburg as her last port of call. Surprisingly, five vessels mentioned English towns as their last port of call, yet they too were seized as British prizes. All told, twenty-four of the ships were taken prize as they headed south from northern Europe. The majority gave as their destination a French port, an obvious reason for seizure, but it did not mean that was their final destination. Cadiz, Barcelona, Genoa, and Livorno also featured as destinations.

The dates of seizure, the privateer, and the English port to which these vessels were taken say nothing about the legal character of trade. They were captured in the North Sea or English Channel by a small group of privateers, often even on the same day, which might indicate that they were sailing together. For example, on 2 September *Joseph* seized *Sex Bröder* (home port Strömstad) and on 4 September *Gustaff* (home port Stockholm); both ships were taken to Dover to await the HCA Prize Court's decision and soon were set free. On 10 September, the privateer *Phoenix* seized *Prudentia* (home port Västervik) and *Anna Maria* (home port Wolgast in Swedish Pomerania), and both were taken to Rye in East Sussex. These too were released in early 1779, with freight paid, and goods, such as naval stores, purchased by the Navy Board.

The remaining eleven ships were engaged in the tramp trade between French, Spanish, and Italian ports. The first one taken as a British prize in 1778 was *Johanna Elisabeth* (*La Jeanne Isabelle* in the Prize Papers) under Captain Mattias Backström (home port Stockholm), sailing from Alicante to Dunkirk and Ostend with a Spanish-owned cargo of brandy, wine, almonds, and fruits. It was seized by HMS *Kite* on 6 August and brought to Dover, where the vessel was later released as Swedish property, but part of the cargo was condemned.[17] *Johanna Elisabeth* had obtained a Mediterranean pass on 17 September 1777 and seems to have remained overseas almost two years until 8 September 1779, when the sea-pass was returned to the Swedish authorities.[18] Being taken prize in August 1778 did not appear to affect the captain's or shipowners' willingness to continue in the tramp trade.

Only three vessels in the autumn 1778 sample – *Wandringsman* (Wanderer), *Winberget* (Vineyard), and *Krönta Ankaret* (Crowned Anchor) – gave Swedish ports as their final destination, and all were carrying wine, sugar, coffee, and other goods from Bordeaux. They were loaded in France, and thus the nationality of their cargo was unquestionably more problematic in comparison with vessels departing from Swedish or Baltic ports.

Wandringsman, under captain Erland Lundström, was seized on 2 September as it sailed from Bordeaux to Uddevalla, and was taken to Rye by a privateer, *Resolution*. A small vessel, only 50 tons (25 heavy lasts), its home port was Uddevalla on Sweden's west coast. It was released on 27 September as being Swedish property, but its cargo, consisting of wine, sugar, and coffee, was partly condemned as French property.[19] No Mediterranean pass had been issued for it before its capture, possibly because what was planned was a round voyage, Uddevalla–Bordeaux–Uddevalla. But the following year, in November 1779, the captain applied for a sea-pass for a voyage to France and now beyond 'according to orders'.[20]

On 9 September, a week after *Wandringsman* was seized, HMS *Kite* took *Winberget*, under captain Anders Bjur (Biur), as it made its way from Bordeaux home to Stockholm. The cargo consisted once again of wine, sugar, coffee, cocoa, etc. The ship was taken to Falmouth. In January 1779 it was released as neutral Swedish property, with part of the cargo confiscated as French property. Another presumably Swedish part of cargo was disputed by the captor until 1782, when the High Court of Appeals for Prizes returned it to the Swedish owners.[21]

The third ship taken on a voyage from Bordeaux was *Krönta Ankaret*, under Master Peter Renström. The vessel, a sloop, was bound for its home port of Karlskrona when it was seized off the Isle of Wight on 10 October by the well-known *Resolution* and brought into Poole, the privateer's home port. The ship had a rich cargo of luxury groceries and French wine, and the resultant case produced substantial documentation. The master's answers to the interrogatories reveal that *Krönta Ankaret* had left its home port, Karlskrona, a naval base in southern Sweden, in June 1778 with a crew of six, all Swedes. The cargo was loaded at Bordeaux in September and on 25 September it left France, being taken two weeks later. The timings indicate the sloop had gone straight from Karlskrona to Bordeaux and was on the home leg of its round voyage, similar to *Wandringsman* above.

Krönta Ankaret's tonnage was 52 tons, small in comparison with the average Swedish ship, but its cargo was highly valuable. In his answers to the interrogatories, Master Renström said it had loaded 'Tobacco, Sugar, Coffee Rice Prunes Wine Indico Vinegar Almonds Oil Silk Cordials

Perfumes Olives & Capers Cork & Cotton the particular Quantity of each this deponent cannot set forth'. He also said all goods on board had Swedish owners, as proved by 15 bills of lading 'all true and genuine'. To prove the cargo was indeed Swedish property, the Karlskrona merchants produced a list of all the goods, with hundreds of bottles and barrels ('oxhufwed') of wine detailed, but not until April 1779, six months after the seizure. While the sloop was released in January 1779, the ownership of the cargo had not been settled. It was not until February 1782 that the High Court of Appeals for Prizes decided in favour of the Swedish owners.[22]

The case of the 140-ton *Anna Maria* (home port Wolgast in Swedish Pomerania) was a complex story of the tramp trade between the eastern Baltic and Western Europe. It was seized in the Channel on 10 September 1778 and taken to Rye. In the responses to the interrogatories it was said *Anna Maria* traded between the Baltic and France. The mariner who was questioned, 33-year-old Marten Mietner from Wolgast, described three part-voyages *Anna Maria* made from the Baltic – part-voyages being understood as legs of one uninterrupted voyage from the home port. The first began at Wismar, also in Swedish Pomerania, with a cargo of grain for Bordeaux. After delivering the grain to Bordeaux the vessel loaded French goods (coffee and brandy) for Königsberg in Prussia. The second part-voyage went from Königsberg to Amsterdam, once again with a cargo of grain. After returning to the Baltic, *Anna Maria* loaded hemp and flax at Königsberg and Pillau (Baltiysk) on 3 August 1778. The final destination of this third part of the voyage was Nantes. The vessel was seized en route to Nantes.[23] There was no Mediterranean pass issued for *Anna Maria* from Wolgast. The captain was apparently sailing only between the eastern Baltic, France, and the Dutch Republic. The outdrawn voyage was a typical shipping pattern of vessels from Swedish Pomerania.

Aurora, a larger vessel at 220 tons, had its home port in Gamlakarleby (Kokkola) in northern Finland. It was taken by the privateer *Kent* off the Lizard in south-west England on 14 September 1778, and brought to Falmouth. In his answers to the interrogatories, the mariner Eric Åhman, aged 27 and like the ship from Gamlakarleby, said *Aurora*'s voyage began in August 1777 in its home port.[24] (This is confirmed by the ship's Mediterranean pass.[25]) It had a cargo of tar, pitch, and deals for London and Falmouth. On the next leg, it went from England to Venice, then from Venice to Marseilles. In Marseilles it was contracted for a cargo of olive oil from Port-Maurice in Liguria to Havre de Grace (Le Havre) in France. This final leg started in July 1778 in and around Port-Maurice, collecting the cargo of oil. It is not obvious if it stopped anywhere on its voyage from Italy to France before being seized off the Lizard. After a couple of months, *Aurora* was set free on 29 January 1779, but the cargo was declared French property and therefore condemned. Among the Prize Papers is a charter party, as such contracts are known, dated in Marseilles for the voyage from Port-Maurice.[26] *Aurora* did not return its Mediterranean pass until the next summer, in August 1780. It seems to have continued in the tramp trade for another eighteen months, and was away from home in Finland for three years.

Three peculiar cases were ships taken first by American privateers, then retaken or liberated by the British privateers. All three were on their way from British ports; the Americans were cruising in British waters. *Henrica Sophia* (home port Stockholm), was bound from London to Tenerife with an English cargo of piece goods. In the autumn of 1778 she was taken by an American privateer and then retaken by a British one. According to the entry in the Swedish sea-pass register it was a small vessel – only 50 tons – and the pass, issued on 23 May 1776, seems never to have been returned to the Swedish authorities.[27] In May 1776, its recorded destination was Portugal, but when seized in 1778 it was sailing from London to Tenerife. The second ship, *Maria*, under Master Johan Dahlman, was sailing from Yarmouth to Genoa and Livorno when it was captured by American rebels. It was retaken by the frigate *Glasgow*. The Swedish documentation indicates that the privateer and the shipmaster made a deal with the British and *Maria* continued its voyage.[28] The third vessel taken by an American privateer was *Anna Lovisa* (home port Stockholm), carrying pilchards (sardines) from Mount Bay (Cornwall) to Civitavecchia in Italy.[29] It was retaken by the British cutter *Alderney* on 9 February 1779, and brought to Falmouth. There was no case brought in the HCA Prize Court and the ship was set free. Of these three retaken Swedish vessels, only *Maria* under Master Dahlman can be traced in Prize Papers, obviously because the other vessels were immediately released, although all three are documented in the Anglo-Swedish diplomatic sources.

The British were undoubtedly harassing Swedish neutral shipping in the autumn of 1778. They stopped a large number of vessels loaded with naval stores for French destinations. Yet vessels were released and cargo was purchased or released as neutral property. After some delay, most vessels seemed to have continued on their way. These cases also indicate that shipping patterns from western Sweden and Pomerania differed from the Baltic, eastern Sweden, and Finland. Vessels from western Sweden and Pomerania had ports of call in France, the Dutch Republic, and the Baltic, and were not planning to go to southern Europe, having not applied for Mediterranean passes. Vessels from Stockholm and Finland, on the other hand, did apply for Mediterranean passes, because they were looking to join the tramp trade in more distant waters.

Prizes taken in 1780–1783

The situation between Britain and the Scandinavian powers changed at the beginning of 1780. It was sparked by Spain's entrance into the American Revolutionary War – in June 1779, it had joined the war on the American and French side. In the winter of 1779–80 the Spanish effectively blockaded Gibraltar, and Spanish privateers preyed on shipping, which affected the neutral flags. The Swedish consul in Cadiz reported that between September 1779 and April 1780 the Spanish privateers took 32 Swedish prizes to Algeciras, Cadiz, and Ceuta.[30] The ships were released while the cargo, if proved British property, was condemned. The procedure differed little from the British jurisdiction, but Spanish prize-taking in Gibraltar damaged charterers' trust in the Swedish flag: potential customers were worried by the risk of employing Swedish tonnage, as was noted by the consul in Cadiz. There was a discernible decline in the number of Swedish arrivals in Marseilles in 1780 (Table 4.1).

Figure 4.2. The English Channel (above) and the Baltic Sea (right). Maps: Lönegård & Co.

In January 1780, the Spanish in Gibraltar seized a Russian-flagged ship bound for Malaga and Livorno. In commercial terms it was insignificant – the Russians had few vessels in the Mediterranean – but Catherine II was furious. She threatened to send a Russian naval squadron to the Mediterranean. In February, she issued her proclamation of neutral rights, which was sent to all belligerents. The proclamation declared that shipping under neutral flags must be left free and unharmed by belligerents.[31] Catherine II went on to invite Sweden and Denmark to form an armed naval league to defend neutral trade and shipping. This caught the Danes and Swedes off guard, if only because Catherine II had declined a similar Danish proposal in 1778. Over the course of the spring and summer the three countries negotiated a naval collaboration, and in July and September 1780 they signed the mutual conventions, in which they promised that from the late spring of 1781 they would form a joint naval force to defend neutral shipping. Joint Danish–Swedish fleets did

Figure 4.3. The Empress of Russia, Catherine the Great as the protector of the free sea (*Mare liberum*). On the reverse are the coats of arms of Russia, Sweden, Denmark, and the Dutch Republic. A Dutch medal made in 1780 to commemorate Catherine's declaration of armed neutrality. Photo: Martin Tunefalk, Economy Museum – Royal Coin Cabinet/Statens Historiska Museer/SHM.

indeed patrol the North Sea in 1781, but the Russians were absent as the focus of foreign policy shifted south again.

What was more important from the Danish and Swedish point of view was the outbreak of the Fourth Anglo-Dutch War (1780–84). The Dutch, too, had intended to join the League of Armed Neutrality, but the outbreak of war in December 1780 made it unfeasible (Fig. 4.3).[32] The Danes and Swedes were left as the only two substantial merchant marines outside the war, and they exploited the situation.

As shown by the Swedish cases in the Prize Papers for the period 1781–83, the British left Swedish shipping unmolested. Of the fourteen Swedish prizes taken between 1781 and 1783 at least four were an apparent abuse of the neutral flag: *Anna Greta Helena*, *Amphion*, *Villa Nova*, and *Sverdsfisken* (Swordfish). The remaining cases repeated the history of the prizes seized in the autumn of 1778: nine vessels carrying iron and naval stores (tar, pitch, hemp, masts, and boards) from the Baltic Sea to French destinations, which were caught and released, their cargo purchased by the Navy Board.

What, then, of the cases of the apparent abuse of the neutral flag? *Anna Greta Helena* was one of the most illuminating cases of how even a small Swedish vessel could be employed illegally in wartime, but also what the interrogatories and other documentation can tell us about such cases.[33] *Anna Greta Helena* was a small Stockholm brig of about 70 tons (34.5 heavy lasts). The shipowners were the Stockholm-based Gustav Lindblad & Co. The vessel left its home port on 2 October 1780 with a cargo of pitch for the well-known Swedish trading house of Jan & Carl Hasselgren in Amsterdam.[34] It arrived in Amsterdam on 30 November, just before the outbreak of the war between the Dutch and British. On 28 February the brig left Amsterdam in ballast with only provisions for the crew, planning to cruise off the Western Islands (the Azores) until August 1781. It was taken on 30 March by the privateer *Harlequin* off the island of Flores in the Azores. The crew and an odd Dutch passenger were moved over to the privateer while *Anna Greta Helena* was 'destroyed' at sea.

The crew was taken to Liverpool where the captain, crew, and the Dutch passenger answered questions in June 1781. Captain Petter Ferenstrom's story was that the brig went to the Azores to warn Swedish vessels about the outbreak of the war between the Dutch Republic and Britain. This was apparently untrue as there were few Swedish vessels that far distant, and those that were were not threatened by the outbreak of the war. Ferenstrom had sailed to the Azores without the knowledge and approval of the Stockholm shipowners. The Dutch passenger on board was to be taken to Setubal in Portugal, their ultimate destination after cruising the Azores.

The Dutch passenger's answers, the privateer's report, and the seized documents reveal a different story. Philip Hendrik de Haart had been commissioned by the Dutch East India Company (VOC) to inform arriving Dutch vessels about the outbreak of the war. De Haart was supplied with a bundle of the VOC documents he was supposed to destroy – by throwing them overboard – if the British took the ship. As the privateer reported, De Haart failed to do so. The seized Dutch papers confirmed De Haart's real role as a VOC officer and his orders confirm the secret nature of the mission:

> You shall see to it that none of the Company's letters or papers are taken off board … In case (God forbid) you are happened upon by the enemy, you shall promptly throw all Company papers and also copies of this order overboard, the same in the meantime prepared in such a way that they sink.[35]

The Swedish captain protested at the seizure and destruction of the ship, and even claimed that he and his crew were robbed by the privateer. But in May 1782 the High Court of Appeals for Prizes confirmed the confiscation of the vessel and its property because it had been employed by the enemy.

In April 1782, the British stopped a French convoy destined for Isle de France (Mauritius) in the Indian Ocean that included two Swedish vessels: *Amphion*, under Master Sven Maybom, and *Villa Nova*, under Master Anders Höög.[36] *Amphion* was a large ship, about 700 tons (285 heavy lasts), while *Villa Nova* was a snow of 260 tons (128.5 heavy lasts). The home port of both was Gothenburg, which *Amphion* left in August 1781 and *Villa Nova* six months later in January 1782.[37] *Amphion* first went to Lorient on the Atlantic coast of France with a cargo of deals, iron, and tar. Afterwards, she was chartered for a voyage from Brest to Isle de France. *Villa Nova*, too, was contracted by the French for the same route. The two vessels were seized off the island of Ushant, Brittany, on 12 April 1782, and taken across the Channel to Plymouth. Apparently, the British naval vessels had been patrolling the waters outside Brest.

The documentation of *Amphion*'s case is detailed, with three interrogatories, including documents translated from French and Swedish. The reason is clear. This was a big ship with a valuable illegal cargo bound for Isle de France. *Amphion*'s was a mixed cargo of iron and copper kettles, coals, nails, wine, brandy, vinegar, pork, medicines, etc., all specified in bills of lading. In addition, the ship was carrying cash: 14,400 livres in two chests and a barrel containing 2,000 dollars (probably Spanish). In time of war the money/cash was defined as contraband of war, and so would be found a legitimate prize.

The documents show the ship had been built only the year before, in 1781 in Torneå (Tornio) in the Gulf of Bothnia, and under the supervision of the same master, Sven Maybom. This indicates that the ship was built in the wartime boom and on the direct orders of its Gothenburg owners, the trading house Arfwidson & Söner. *Amphion* had a crew of 44 men, all Swedes and all hired in Gothenburg in October 1781. The freight contract for Isle de France (Mauritius) had been negotiated between Mr Berard, the Swedish consul in Lorient, and the Commissary of the French Marine.

Amphion and *Villa Nova* were snatched by the British navy just outside Brest, but these two vessels were not exceptions. For example, in March 1783 a similar contract was signed in Lorient chartering six Swedish ships for a voyage to the Dutch East Indies via the Isle de France. The charterer in that case was the VOC, and the vessels were chartered for the return voyage from Batavia (Jakarta) to Amsterdam with Dutch colonial goods. Three of the vessels, *Orion*, *Fru Johanna*, and *Conjuncturen*, had the same owners as *Amphion* – Arfwidson & Söner in Gothenburg. The charter party with *Conjuncturen* is the most interesting: it was chartered for a voyage between Martinique in the West Indies and Batavia in the Dutch East Indies. The owners, Arfwidson & Söner was a big exporter of salted fish (probably to be food for slaves) and that was what *Conjuncturen* carried to the West Indies, before she was chartered for the trip to the Indian Ocean.[38] The charter party with the VOC was signed in 1783 and voyages continued over the next two years. None of these six chartered vessels seems to have been seized by the British, most probably because the dangerous part of the voyage, from Batavia to Amsterdam, began in 1784 when the war already was over.[39]

There were two prizes with direct connections to the West Indies in the Swedish diplomatic records (Diplomatica Anglica), but they have not so far been traced in the Prize Papers. The first was *Hertiginnan af Södermanland* (Duchess of Sörmland) (home port Stockholm) under Master Peter Alfving. The shipowner was the well-known Stockholm trading house, Chr. Hebbe & Söner. The vessel and its cargo of sugar were seized en route from Havana, Cuba, to Spain on 14 August 1779. Both vessel and cargo were condemned as Spanish property on 1 February 1780.[40]

Sverdsfisken (home port Karlskrona) was a ship of about 350 tons under Master Jacob Hackert. According to its Mediterranean pass, the ship left Karlskrona on 29 August 1780.[41] A year later, on 23 August 1781, it was seized en route from Bordeaux to Saint-Domingue (Haiti), a French colony in the West Indies, with a cargo of wine, brandy, and linen, and taken to Liverpool. The owners of the cargo were the merchants Erdman, Schröder & Co. in Westphalia and Prussia. The ship was set free by the HCA Prize Court's decision of 15 March 1782, while the question of the cargo remained unresolved.[42] In November the same year, *Sverdsfisken* applied for a new Mediterranean pass, once again with the vague destination 'the Mediterranean and so on' – so six months after being captured it was working in tramp shipping again.[43]

Conclusions

I have identified 60 Swedish prize cases in the Prize Papers in the decade 1775–85, which was dominated by the American Revolutionary War. The Diplomatica Anglica collection in Stockholm lists 74 prizes taken between August 1778 and January 1783, most of which could be found in the Prize Papers in London. In the remaining cases, there were good reasons why the vessels were not documented in the Prize Papers, the example here being when Swedish vessels were seized by Americans and retaken and released by British privateers.

The Prize Papers provide information about the vessels and their voyages that cannot be traced in Swedish sources. The documentation, in particular the interrogatories, display the scope of Swedish shipping in the period. There were two typical patterns of how the shipping business was organized. The first saw vessels on round voyages between Sweden or the Baltic and destinations in Western Europe, in particular Britain and France. Their homeports in Sweden were not necessarily ports of call. Many had home ports of limited trade significance, such as Uddevalla, Karlskrona, or Wolgast. The second pattern of shipping included tramp shipping in southern Europe and the Atlantic.

There were a few examples of the obvious abuse of Swedish neutrality. The majority of seized vessels were released after a couple of months at most and continued to trade thereafter. A comparison of shipping activities (the number of registered voyages) and prizes seized in 1778–1783 shows that the risk of being taken prize did not affect business much. But, even when released, the vessels lost time, and sometimes freight and cargo. Prize-taking damaged the reputation of the Swedish flag, and that meant lost customers.

An interesting detail in the Prize Papers is the national character of the crews. The interrogatories for the period 1778–1783 show that the Swedish vessels had entirely Swedish crews, as is borne out by surviving crew lists. For the answers to the interrogatories, the court officials often employed translators from Swedish and Dutch, the two dominant languages used by Swedish seamen. The predominance of Swedish-born crews on Swedish ships contrasted with other merchant marines, not least the Dutch and Danish, which had far more multinational crews. In fact, Swedish seamen contributed heavily to the manning of the Dutch and Danish fleets.[44] Undoubtedly, this was an outcome of Sweden's mercantilist policy and the fact that the Swedish homeports were in the northern European periphery, far from shipping hubs such as

Amsterdam or Copenhagen. In addition, Swedish seamen wages were low in comparison with all other maritime nations.

A study of Swedish prizes seized in the American Revolutionary War confirms, too, the different geographies of Danish and Swedish shipping. In comparison with Danish shipping there were relatively few Swedish vessels employed in the Atlantic trade or in shipping to the West Indies. This would change during the next wartime boom of neutral flags, the French Revolutionary and Napoleonic Wars.

Notes

1 Eli F. Heckscher, *Den svenska handelssjöfartens ekonomiska historia sedan Gustaf Vasa* (Uppsala 1940); Staffan Högberg, *Utrikeshandel och sjöfart på 1700-talet: Stapelvaror i svensk export och import 1738–1808* (Stockholm 1969); Leos Müller, *Consuls, Corsairs, and Commerce: The Swedish Consular Service and Long-Distance Shipping, 1720–1815* (Uppsala 2004); Leos Müller, 'The Forgotten Age of Swedish Shipping: The Eighteenth Century', *International Journal of Maritime History* 24/2 (2012), 1–18.

2 For a review of trade statistics and the literature on the Board of Trade, see Rolf Vallerö, *Svensk handels- och sjöfartsstatistik 1637–1813: En tillkomsthistorisk undersökning* (Stockholm 1969); Högberg 1969; and more recently Henric Häggqvist, *On the Ocean of Protectionism: The Structure of Swedish Tariffs and Trade 1780–1830* (PhD thesis, Uppsala 2015); Rodney Edvinsson & Christoffer Tarek Gad, 'Assessing trade in the mercantilist era: Evidence from a new database on foreign trade of Sweden–Finland, 1738–1805', *Scandinavian Economic History Review* 66/3 (2018), 226–45.

3 For sea-passes, see Leos Müller, 'Under svensk flagg i Medelhavet: Algeriska sjöpass 1770–1800', in Marie Lennersand & Leos Müller (eds.), *Från Afrikakompaniet till Tokyo: En vänbok till György Nováky* (Stockholm 2017); for sea-briefs, see Jan Kilborn, *Fartyg i Europas periferi under den industriella revolutionen: Den svenska utrikes handelsflottan 1795–1845* (licentiate diss., Gothenburg University 2009).

4 For Henrik Gahn's ship lists from Cadiz in the 1770s, see Müller 2004, 112–113.

5 The collection of Prize Papers has been used by researchers to address a wide range of historical questions. See Margaret R. Hunt, 'All At Sea: The Prize Papers as a Source for a Global Microhistory: Conference Report', *German Historical Institute London Bulletin* 37/1 (2015), 124–35. The research for the present essay is part of 'På spaning efter kunskap om världen: Skandinaviska resenärer till sjöss 1650–1810', a project funded by the Swedish Research Council, detailed at 'The Scandinavian Prize Papers' http://prizepapers.se/home/. The Prize Papers include some 3,000 Scandinavian vessels seized in the period 1650–1820, of which 500 were Swedish (and Finnish) and 2,500 were Danish (and Norwegian), the majority taken in the wars of 1756–1763, 1778–1783 and 1793–1815. The numbers of Danish and Swedish prizes were broadly similar until the outbreak of the Anglo-Danish War of 1807–1814.

6 Donald J. Stoker, Kenneth J. Hagan & Michael T. McMaster (eds.), *Strategy in the American War of Independence: A Global Approach* (London 2010).

7 Ole Feldbæk, 'Eighteenth-Century Danish Neutrality: Its Diplomacy, Economics and Law', *Scandinavian Journal of History* (1983), 3–21; id., *Dansk neutralitetspolitik under krigen 1778–1783: Studier i regeringens prioritering af politiske og økonomiske interesser* (Copenhagen 1971); Dan H. Andersen & Hans-Joachim Voth, 'The Grapes of War: Neutrality and Mediterranean Shipping under Danish Flag, 1747–1807', *Scandinavian Economic History Review* 1 (2000), 5–27; *Wim Klooster, Illicit Riches: Dutch Trade in the Caribbean* (Leiden 1998).

8 Barbara W. Tuchman, *The first salute* (New York 1988); Victor Enthoven, 'Dutch maritime strategy', in Stoker, Hagan & McMaster 2010, 178–85.

9 The Danes prohibited weapon exports to the West Indies (Feldbæk 1971, 80–2).

10 See, for example, transports of Spanish troops to Cuba in the 1760s. Müller 2004, 110.

11 On the differences in Danish, Dutch, and Swedish trade and shipping interests in 1776–1780, see Leos Müller, 'The League of Armed Neutrality and Sweden's Policy in the Late Eighteenth Century', *Revue d'Histoire Nordique* 14 (2012), 135–37.

12 Müller 2012, 137.

13 Isabel De Madariaga, *Britain, Russia, and the Armed Neutrality of 1780: Sir James Harris's Mission to St Petersburg during the American Revolution* (New Haven 1962), 73–5; Nils Jahnlund & Olof Jägerskiöld, *Den svenska utrikespolitikens historia, ii: 1721–1792* (Stockholm 1957), 280–2; Knud J. V. Jespersen, Ole Feldbæk & Carsten Due-Nielsen (eds.), *Dansk udenrigspolitiks historie, 1648–1814, ii: Revanche og neutralitet* (Copenhagen 2002), 381–2.

14 The best review of British–Russian foreign relations in 1778–1781 is De Madariaga 1962.

15 The reliability of the sea-pass registers for Mediterranean passes does not mean they covered all vessels bound there. Some vessels had a sea-pass but did not complete the voyage or sailed to another destination, while often the first destination stated in the registers is vague. See Leos Müller, 'Swedish merchant shipping in troubled times: The French Revolutionary Wars and Sweden's neutrality 1793–1801', *International Journal of Maritime History* 1 (2016), 151; Müller 2017, 43, 41–5; also Müller 2004, 144–54.

16 Müller 2004, 143–4.

17 The National Archives (TNA), London, High Court of Admiralty (HCA), Prize Papers 32/365/24, *La Jeanne Isabelle*, 1778, master Mathias Backstrom; Riksarkivet (Swedish National Archives), Stockholm (RA), Diplomatica Anglica, vol. 443, Handlingar ang. uppbringningar 1764–1793, *Johanna Elisabeth*.

18 RA, Kommerskollegium, Huvudarkivet, CIIb, Sjöpassdiarier (Registers of sea-passes), 'Algeriska sjöpass' (APR), *Johanna Elisabeth*, pass nr 184 issued 17 Sept. 1777. The registered tonnage was 131 heavy lasts (260 tons).

19 RA, Diplomatica Anglica, vol. 443, *Wandringsman*; TNA, HCA 32/488/6, *Wandringsman*, master Erland Lundstrom.

20 RA, APR, *Wandringsman*, pass nr 268 issued 11 Nov. 1779.

21 According to notes in RA, Diplomatica Anglica, vol. 443, *Wandringsman* but there is no trace of the vessel in TNA, HCA; RA, APR, pass nr 94 issued 16 July 1777, returned 7 Jan. 1778.

22 RA, Diplomatica Anglica, vol. 443, *Krönta Ankaret*; TNA, HCA 32/385/4 Captured ship *Kronta Ankaret*, master Petter Renstrom.

23 RA, Diplomatica Anglica, vol. 443, *Anna Maria*; TNA, HCA 32/270/10 Captured ship *Anna Maria*, master Carl Valentien Bentzien.

24 RA, Diplomatica Anglica, vol. 443, *Aurora*; TNA, HCA 32/274/4 Captured ship *Aurora*, master Johan Gustav Lalin.

25 RA, APR, *Aurora*, pass nr 106 issued 21 July 1777, returned 21 Aug. 1780.

26 TNA, HCA 32/274/4 Captured ship *Aurora*, master Johan Gustav Lalin.

27 RA, APR, *Henrica Sophia*, pass nr 47 issued 23 May 1776.

28 RA, Diplomatica Anglica, vol. 443, *Maria*; TNA, HCA 32/395/13 Captured ship *Maria*, master Johannes Dahlman; RA, APR, *Maria*, pass nr 204 issued 1 Oct. 1777.

29 RA, Diplomatica Anglica, vol. 443, *Anna Lovisa*; RA, APR, *Anna Lovisa*, pass nr 89 issued 15 July 1777.

30 Müller 2004, 113–114.

31 De Madariaga 1962, 172; Müller 2012.

32 Enthoven 2010.

33 TNA, HCA 32/270/3 Captured ship *Anna Greta Helena*, master Petter Ferenstrom; RA, APR, *Anna Greta Helena*, pass nr 259 issued 25 Sept. 1780.

34 The Hasselgrens served as Swedish consuls in the city (Müller 2004, 92).

35 TNA, HCA 32/270/3 Captured ship *Anna Greta Helena*, seized Dutch document: 'U zulle zorgen dat geen van d Compagnies brieven of papieren van boord werden gebragt, als … Ingeval (dat Godt vertroede) Ue door den vijand mogt gecomen worden, zulle Ue bij tyds alle Compagnies Papieren en ookt afschrift van deeze order overboord werpen, dezelve inmidels zodanig gepropageerd hebbende, dat die moeten zinken'.

36 TNA, HCA 32/267/20 *Amphion*, master Sven Mayborn; TNA, HCA 32/474/4 *Villa Nova*, master Anders Hoog.

37 RA, APR, *Villa Nova*, pass nr 4 issued 15 Jan. 1782, master Anders Höög, home port Gothenburg, destination 'Westersjön' ('the Western Sea'); RA, APR, *Amphion*, pass nr 188 issued 20 Aug. 1781, home port Gothenburg, destination 'Frankrike och vidare efter ordres' ('France and onwards by order').

38 The charter party is described in detail in Jan Kronholm, *En sjöresa till Ostindien. Fregattskeppet Concordias färd till Batavia 1782–1785*, Jakobstads museums publikationer nr 28 (Jakobstad 2016), 73–76. On Concordia's destiny see also Clas Fredrik Hornstedt, *Brev från Batavia. En resa till Ostindien 1782–1786* (Stockholm 2008).

39 In 1795, there is a prize case relating to the Swedish vessel *Conjuncturen*, but it is too early to establish that it was the same vessel *Conjuncturen*, master Hallberg, seized in 1795, TNA, HCA 32/547/95, TNA.

40 *Hertiginnan af Södermanland*, RA, Diplomatica Anglica, vol. 443, the list of seized vessels, ship nr 42. The decision was confirmed by the Appeal Court.

41 RA, APR, *Sverdsfisken/Svärdsfisken*, pass nr 246 issued 18 Sept. 1780 but with no return date given.

42 RA, Diplomatica Anglica, vol. 443, *Sverdsfisken*, nr 68 on the list of seized ships.

43 RA, APR, *Svärdsfisken*, pass nr 419 issued 25 Nov. 1782.

44 Aske Brock & Jelle Van Lottum, 'Rural maritime labour migration to Copenhagen and Stockholm (1700–1800)', *Continuity & Change* 34/2 (2019), 231–52; Alexander Klein & Jelle Van Lottum, 'The Determinants of International Migration in Early Modern Europe: Evidence from the Maritime Sector, c.1700–1800', *Social Science History* 44/1 (2020), 143–67.

CHAPTER 5

On the honour of the naval ensign

The Swedish navy and the symbolism of naval and merchant flags, *c.*1700–1950

Fredrik Kämpe

National flags developed at sea. They were symbols of the states and monarchs the ships belonged to, and ceremonies for how naval ships in particular were to behave towards foreigners. An officer was expected to fight to the death to protect the honour of the flag. Such behaviour often clashed with other shifting goals, however, forcing naval commanders to choose between defending the flag's honour and succeeding in their mission. This essay examines the language of honour and how the Swedish navy between c.1700 and 1950 treated its flag. The honour of the flag served a military purpose that remained remarkably stable despite massive changes to society. At the same time, commanders and decision-makers have shown a surprising degree of pragmatism in order to achieve success.

Even though they are everywhere, most of us give little thought to the meaning of flags in our daily lives. In some countries, such as Sweden, Denmark, and the US, it is common to fly a national or regional flag when celebrating a birthday, the national day, or important national events such as royal weddings. In other countries, where it is less common for private individuals to fly flags, national flags still serve a purpose at major sporting events and international festivities, and can be found on everything from clothing to coffee mugs. National flags are not the only type of flag, of course; we are used to seeing company flags flying above supermarket car parks, for example, where they serve a very practical purpose by signalling the shop's location. Although perhaps of secondary importance, this function is also true of national flags: they are colourful pieces of cloth that are eminently practical marks of identity. Yet usually we ascribe so much more meaning to national flags that describing them as simple pieces of cloth is to negate what they can mean, and what they have meant historically. If they did not mean something why wave them in celebration, and, at the other extreme, why burn them?

The widespread private use of national flags is a relatively recent phenomenon, however, fuelled by the revolutionary and nationalist movements of the late eighteenth and nineteenth centuries. Even then it was a slow process. At the end of the nineteenth century, many Swedes did not even know what the Swedish flag looked like.[1] In 1916, a society for the celebration of the 'Swedish flag's day' was founded and began handing out flags to encourage its use.[2] In light of its many uses today, we can conclude that – in the long run – their efforts paid off. Its limited use by the public before the twentieth century was because the Swedish national flag was a symbol of monarchy, government, militarism, and, although often forgotten today, the maritime sector.

Flags and similar symbols have been used by military organizations for thousands of years, and in the medieval period their use spread to ecclesiastical contexts and to European noble families, towns, and military orders. Such flags were the symbols of specific military units, families, or towns, however. Leading dynasties often incorporated national symbols in their coats of arms, and these symbols were often incorporated into the national flag and national coats of arms. The exact origins and order of such developments is often difficult to establish and differed between countries. For my purposes, however, the key point is that it was in the maritime sector that national flags were first widely used. The Swedish navy and merchant marine had been using the national

Figure 5.1. The naval officer and painter Jacob Hägg (1839–1931) produced this beautiful and informative chart of the world's naval and merchant flags, probably in the 1890s. It is difficult to imagine a clearer example of the close relationship between national flags and the sea. Photo: Cecilia Nordstrand, Swedish National Maritime Museum/SMTM.

flag for centuries when in the late nineteenth century it became usual for the Swedish Army to use it, or indeed for private individuals to have flagpoles.[3]

This essay deals with the Swedish national flag in a maritime context, and how it was connected to ideas of honour and national glory. Specifically, it is about various episodes from Swedish naval history, in order to trace the impact which the flag and its meanings had on Swedish history and historical memory. Although deeply associated with national honour, the Swedes found ways to be pragmatic about using the flag without questioning the notion of its honour.

It was not only in Sweden that the widespread use of the national flag began in the maritime sector. It was true for Europe as a whole. On the high seas, it was important to identify ships at a distance.[4] The sea was open to all states with a coastline, and, although they tried, no state could exercise complete control of the oceans. In fact, early modern states' control of their populations at home and in their overseas territories was often far more limited than we might imagine. The sea is vast and early modern states were too weak to control the oceans effectively.[5] Thus when ships from different nations – or city-states – met at sea, there were many competing ideas about how they should behave towards one another. The sea connected places and made it possible to travel, trade, and fight over vast distances. And precisely because the sea was contested and uncontrolled, the flag became an important mark of identity, of who the ship belonged to, of whom it served, and which laws it sailed under. By using different flags they could also hide or redefine the identity of a ship – everything that some notions of honour, security, or neutrality held to be impossible. The flag could both protect its bearers and put them in situations where the only option was to fight for its honour.

The essay has three parts. The first deals with the general questions of the evolution of national flags with special attention to Sweden and the maritime sector, with examples of how flags have been used and their memory culture. Building on this background, the second part gives specific examples of how the Swedish navy has treated the flag and how it has perceived the flag's honour over the course of 250 years. The third part draws a number of conclusions from these examples.

The evolution of national flags

To understand the reasoning of the Swedish state and navy in the question of the national flag, context is important. The history of the Swedish flag is central. So is vexillology in general, and the key fact that it has been an acceptable *ruse de guerre* to fly the 'wrong' flag to avoid suspicion. And so is the flag as a memory object, and what it tells us about flags as concepts. These contextual discussions will show that the examples from the history of the Swedish navy are part of a long and often complicated history of flag use.

The origins of the Swedish national flag are uncertain. It developed from flags that represented individual kings or the ruling dynasty, and its close connection to the state and the military – the navy and fortifications in particular – is clear. The evidence of its existence is scattered throughout the sixteenth and seventeenth centuries, but the exact look of the flags is never entirely certain. Early Swedish naval flags in the sixteenth century were probably blue with yellow and white horizontal stripes, but it is not known how widespread they were, nor whether they were formally adopted. In the seventeenth century there was an early version of today's double swallow-tailed naval ensign which was widely used. The proportions have changed since, as have the shades of blue and yellow, but the basic form and colours – a blue flag with a yellow Scandinavian cross, the horizontal bar of the cross forming the second of three tails – have remained the same.

The earliest picture of the double swallow-tailed naval ensign dates from 1626, while the earliest surviving ensigns were captured by the Dutch at the Battle of the Sound in 1658 and are today in the Rijksmuseum in Amsterdam. As far as we know, Sweden's flags were first regulated in a royal decree of 1663, which stated that civilians should not use the king's double swallow-tailed flag, but could use the yellow cross if they wished. It is not known, however, what other colours were used besides the yellow or gold of the cross; blue seems likely, but since nothing was

Figure 5.2. Reproductions of Swedish flags, hoisted outside the Swedish National Maritime Museum, show the range of national flags used by the Swedish navy and merchant marine in the past. The first two from the left are educated guesses of early flags while the last two are the modern naval and civilian flags. Photo: Anneli Karlsson, Swedish National Maritime Museum/SMTM.

said in the decree it cannot be assumed the merchant flag had by then taken on its form of a rectangular blue-and-yellow ensign. It does show, however, that the yellow cross was at times seen as the primary symbol of nationality, and not always the combination of blue and yellow.[6]

The evolution of the Swedish national flag was thus a long process about which little is certain. By around 1700, however, it was established custom for naval ships to fly the double swallow-tailed flag and merchantmen to fly the rectangular blue-and-yellow flag. It should be noted that both the double swallow-tailed and the rectangular flag were originally seen as the king's flags. But since a king's flag signalled that the ship was the property of the Crown, requiring certain ceremonies, and swallow-tailed banners had in earlier periods signalled royal command, it was logical that it was the rectangular variant which became the flag of choice for private use. In this way, the ceremonies could remain exclusive to the monarchy and its navy. Conflicts over the wrongful use of swallow-tailed flags continued into the eighteenth century, however.[7]

Since the naval ensign showed that the ship belonged to the king, it was treated as a symbol of the sovereign. If a ship surrendered or its crew and officers showed cowardice it reflected badly on the king. The flag's honour was therefore the same as the king's and the country's honour. It was to be defended to the death and no disrespect to the flag could be accepted.[8] This thinking, and imaginative ways to get around the problems created by such a rigid stance, can be found throughout Swedish naval history. It was also why it became so important to restrict the use of the double swallow-tailed flag. In the eighteenth century, there were several orders from the Swedish government that merchantmen should not fly the king's flag or a swallow-tailed variant – something they did in order to appear armed, because from a distance it was difficult to see how well armed and well crewed a ship was, and a naval ensign could scare off pirates and privateers. From the king's and navy's perspective, however, this practice risked the flag's honour and legitimacy and could not be tolerated. The repeated attempts by the Swedish government to ban the practice show it was difficult to control, as some merchants simply ignored the orders. The interest in appearing more naval has also been advanced as an explanation for why the Swedish East India Company for a period flew a swallow-tailed flag.[9]

In the nineteenth century, the flag became increasingly seen as a symbol of the state, and the Crown sanctioned some use of swallow-tailed flags by civilian public authorities and even private associations.[10] Only with the Flag Act of 1906 was the double swallow-tailed flag reserved for the armed forces and royalty, while civilians – private individuals and civilian public authorities – were allowed to fly flags of the rectangular sort, with specified colours and proportions.[11] The close connection between the honour of the royal sovereign and the development of the national flag is plain.

Adolf Erik Nordenskiöld, the leader of the *Vega* expedition to find the Northeast Passage (1878–80), hit upon an unusual solution to his flag problem.[12] According the art historian Torsten Lenk, Nordenskiöld asked the Swedish government to allow him to fly the naval ensign, but he was told no. Instead, he made the expedition ship, *Vega*, a member of the Royal Swedish Yacht Club, since at that time the club's vessels

Figure 5.3. Adolf Erik Nordenskiöld was refused permission to fly the naval ensign on his expedition to find the Northeast Passage (1878–1880), so *Vega* flew the flag of the Royal Swedish Yacht Club instead. A naval ensign with the club's insignia on a white field in the middle of the yellow cross, it contrived to make *Vega* appear more official than it really was. Here *Vega* seems to be flying the naval ensign, though. Photo: Cecilia Nordstrand, Swedish National Maritime Museum/SMTM.

had the right to fly a naval ensign as long as it had the club's insignia on it. Despite the government's rejection, Nordenskiöld was able to fly a flag which was very close to the naval ensign.[13] On the surface, his solution was similar to the one pursued by Swedish merchantmen in the eighteenth century, but Nordenskiöld's reason to appear naval was probably not as much about security as about identity. A naval ensign would make the ship look more 'official', adding to the expedition's glory.

As flags were used to identify ships from a distance, it should come as no surprise that it was common for merchant ships as well as privateers and naval ships to carry a range of flags. Simply changing the flag was the easiest way to hide the identity of a ship. This was often practised without formal permission from the country in question.[14] However, as the historian Cornel Zwierlein has pointed out, such practices could be beneficial and even promoted by states. By extending their protection to foreigners, states could increase the use of their flags. At those times when there was not much piracy and limited resources were spent on protection, the more ships that sailed under a French flag the more duty was paid to France, the more merchandise flowed through French ports, and, crucially, the more the French appeared dominant at sea. All this was in the interests of the French state. When there was more piracy, on the other hand, it was in the state's interests to limit the number of ships enjoying the expensive protection France offered to those flying its flag.[15] In the early modern Mediterranean, it was common to fly a French flag even if the ship and crew were not in the least French, encouraged by the limited French laws on the matter; however, at times when France was attacking rivals from other nations, a British flag might be more attractive.[16]

History is full of examples of the conscious use of false flags. For example, when Sweden in 1724 adopted a navigation law, Produkt-plakatet (Commodity Proclamation), it was intended to prevent transit shipments to and from Sweden on any but Swedish ships. This targeted Dutch ships in particular, and within the year Dutch shipping to Sweden had collapsed. Sweden could not conjure up ships from thin air, however, and much of the increase in Swedish shipping immediately after 1724 must therefore have been due to Dutch ships simply changing their flags.[17] Privateers sometimes used flags liberally. In 1759, in the Seven Years War, the privateer *Prince Ferdinand* under the command of Captain James Marifield captured the homeward-bound, salt-laden Swedish snow *Reparation* off Cartagena. The privateer had at first flown a British flag and pretended that she was only going to inspect the Swedes' papers, but had changed to the Prussian flag once the ships were side by side. The Swedish ship was taken into Cartagena and declared good prize by Prussian authorities.[18] Captain Marifield was obviously aware of the political situation and knew that the Prussian authorities were more likely to find in his favour.

A well-known example of a naval vessel using the 'wrong' flag comes from the Tripolitan War between the US and Tripoli (1801–1805). On 1 August 1801, in the first naval action of the war, the American schooner *Enterprise* tricked the Tripolitan cruiser *Tripoli* by flying the British flag. Lieutenant Sterrett, the commanding officer, asked the Tripolitans what had brought them to sea, and they, thinking the schooner was British, answered that they were looking for Americans but could not find any. The American schooner had then lowered the British flag, hoisted the American, and opened fire into the Tripolitan from short range, forcing it to surrender without a single American casualty. Back home, the Americans viewed this as a great victory.[19]

For the purposes of this essay, the liberal use of the British flag is interesting. The *Enterprise* tricked the Tripolitan cruiser, but fired only after raising its own flag, maintaining standards of honour which meant the engagement could be celebrated by the American public. There were examples in the twentieth century too. In the First World War, Sweden was neutral but Swedish merchant ships sailed in British convoys. On 17 October and 12 December 1917, German destroyers and light cruisers attacked and sunk four Swedish ships, killing 16 people on one of them. The Germans had attacked the convoys without warning. The Swedish Board of Trade, when they documented the losses, pointed out that the Swedish ships had flown the Swedish flag, seemingly thinking that the Germans, seeing the neutral flag, should have treated them with more care by letting the crews leave the ships before opening fire. Despite the fact that the Swedish ships were sailing in a convoy hostile to the Germans, the Board of Trade seems to have argued that the neutral Swedish flag should have protected Swedish crews.[20] As an example of ships flying their own flag while sailing under the protection of the 'wrong' flag, it was still a misuse of foreign flags, although not to hide their own identity; in fact, they were showing their real identity, hoping it would protect them. It shows how complicated the relationship between identity and flag could be. The Swedes wanted the protection offered by the convoy but also wanted to maintain their identity as neutrals. From a German perspective, however, neutral ships had no right to be in an enemy convoy and were fair game. Furthermore, since history is so full of examples of ships flying a false flag, the Germans might not even have believed they were actually Swedish. When a German submarine attacked the Swedish barque *Anton* without warning in June 1918, one of the German officers said they suspected that the ship was a disguised British ship and therefore armed.[21]

The practice of flying a false flag was an easy and even accepted way to disguise a ship's true identity. For a naval vessel, as long as it flew its own flag when it opened fire, there was no dishonour in tricking its enemies. The acceptance of this practice must be kept in mind when we consider the different examples below of how the Swedish navy has treated its flag throughout history. It points to the importance of the flag's symbolism, but also to the pragmatic solutions adopted when need arose. Merchant ships used a range of flags in order to improve their chances of arriving at their destinations unmolested: a change of flags was an easy way to increase security, and the dictates of commerce meant their view of honour had more to do with reliability than national glory. This often clashed with the king's and the state's views of honour, however. Adolf Erik Nordenskiöld's voyage to find the Northeast Passage (1878–80) shows yet another way the flag indicated a specific identity. The need to scare raiders was not as acute, although they did exist in the waters the expedition's ship *Vega* would navigate, but Nordenskiöld still chose the flag of the Royal Swedish Yacht Club, because it was a naval ensign with the club's insignia in the middle. The insignia would not have been visible from a distance and the ship would therefore appear more official than with a merchant flag. Although the reasons had changed, the impulse was the same as on merchantmen in the eighteenth century.

As flags were so important, the capture of an enemy's flag was something honourable for the capturer. Just as the flag should be defended to the death, risking your life to capture an enemy's flag was increasing your own and the nation's glory. Therefore, European states have treated captured flags with care, preserving them as trophies. They were important tools of communication, and as trophies they took on new meanings as mementoes of military victories. Early modern knowledge of how best to preserve textiles was limited, though, and many trophies have therefore been displayed in conditions unsuitable for their preservation. But their display was also an important part of their use as trophies. They had to be visible to the public. They were therefore often displayed in buildings accessible to the public, such as churches. Passing from mode of communication to trophy, they finally became cultural heritage, and the examples that have survived the passing of time and suboptimal conditions on display are today often found in museums. Despite the limited ability to preserve flags, trophies, because of the symbolism attached to them, have often survived better than they would have done in their countries of origin.[22] This is why the oldest Swedish national flags in the world are not in Sweden, but in Amsterdam, while Russia's Central Naval Museum in St Petersburg has a collection of Swedish naval flags.[23] Sweden has a large number of Russian and Danish flags and banners in Statens trofésamling (the National Collection of Trophies), which comprises over 4,000 trophies from a variety of countries and today is held by the Swedish Army Museum.[24]

Flags can also survive in museum collections as memories of loss. On 15 April 1943, the Swedish submarine *Ulven* was lost after hitting a German naval mine. For three weeks the entire country followed news and radio reports of the search, one of the biggest rescue operations in Swedish history. When the submarine was finally found on 5 May at 52 metres depth it was soon evident all 33 men on board had died instantly. The diver who went down to the *Ulven* brought back its flag to confirm the identity of the submarine that had been found. Sweden was neutral, but it became a reminder that war was close. The accident was one of the largest military incidents in Sweden in the war, and the loss of *Ulven* remains the Swedish submarine force's largest loss.[25] The *Ulven* was salvaged in August 1943, broken up in Gothenburg, and many of the objects handed to the Swedish National Maritime Museum, the flag among them, which is now on display in the Submarine Hall of the Naval Museum in Karlskrona. In the 1940s, submarines flew their flags even when diving; the flag in the museum is thus worn

Figure 5.4. The diver who went down to *Ulven* on 5 May 1943 brought up its flag to prove its identity. Photo: Mattias Billemyr, Swedish National Maritime Museum/SMTM.

from use, marking the loss of the *Ulven* even more clearly. This flag therefore took on yet another kind of symbolism. Rather than a symbol of victory, it was a symbol of death and grief. And as the submarine was lost in the line of duty, I would argue the preservation of its flag was also connected to honour.

In battle, banners or signal flags had a practical function. Troops rallied to their banners to maintain cohesion, and in the days of no radio when battles were fought in tight formation, banners and other signal flags were used for communication. Yet banners were also symbolically important and lavishly decorated, each associated with its particular unit and distinct from the rest.[26] National flags at sea worked a little differently. While varying from country to country and over time, flags on warships or merchantmen were always more important as concepts than as objects. They marked national identity, and were meant to be used continually, so were not as lavishly designed as infantry banners. When a flag wore out it was replaced with a new one, while the old one was patched up for further use or destroyed. Unlike a banner, a ship's national flag did not represent a specific ship; rather, it represented the fact that the ship was considered part of a state's territory and the laws of that state pertained on board. That is why at sea the concept of the flag was more important than the object. The notions of the flag's honour were bound up with the institution of the flag, with the state and the monarchy, rather than with the piece of cloth.

As trophies and museum pieces it is the other way around: flags as objects are more important than flags as concepts. In a museum or trophy room, it is important that the preserved flag is the actual flag of the episode it is supposed to represent. Yet it has not lost its symbolism connected to the institution of the flag, or to the victory or loss it calls to mind. Neither is the flag without importance when in use. Part of the reason for defending it to the death is to deny the enemy the chance to claim a trophy. And even if the flag's honour should be viewed more as a concept than as the honour of the actual piece of cloth, a flying flag signals the identity of a ship and lowering it signals surrender (and depending on the mast, it signals the rank of the commanding officer on board). Flag as object and flag as representing an institution are always present in the symbolism of the flag, although to different degrees depending on the situation. *Ulven*'s flag represents both the loss of the submarine and crew *and* the 'glorious' and dangerous work of the Swedish navy to keep the country safe from invasion.

The complicated evolution of national flags, their uses and misuses at sea, the tradition of taking trophies, and the preservation of *Ulven*'s flag all show the multiple meanings of their symbolism and notions. Throughout their long history, national flags have meant different things at different times to different people. As we will see, since 1700 the Swedish navy has been broadly consistent in its attitude towards its flag, but has nevertheless been pragmatic when that collided with other interests.

The naval ensign in action

When the massive three-volume work *Svenska flottans historia* about the history of the Swedish navy was published in 1942–1945, King Gustaf V prefaced the first volume in the following terms:

> May the history of the Swedish Navy and its memories encourage the Auxiliary Naval Corps, for whose benefit this work is published, as well as all the Navy's branches and its men, to carefully cherish and eagerly adhere to the Navy's beautiful traditions of loyalty to the flag, dedication to duty, and unfailing concern for the Navy's betterment.[27]

These words were written in the Second World War, but the grandiose tone was typical of this type of work in peacetime as well as wartime. The king lists loyalty to the flag first of the navy's traditions. The flag has been an important symbol for the navy, but that importance has had consequences for Swedish naval history in many, sometimes unexpected, ways. The honour of the flag was to be defended at all costs, yet it was recognised that such a stubborn view could cause problems for the Swedes, so they worked around the problem by inventing ways to handle the flag without calling its honour into question.

Perhaps the best-known example of a Swedish commander who refused to do anything that would risk the flag's honour was Gustaf Psilander at the Battle of Orford Ness on 28 July 1704. In fact, when the naval officer Arnold Munthe wrote his fourteen-volume work *Svenska sjöhjältar* ('Swedish Naval Heroes') in 1899–1923, the first volume was about Psilander and opened with Orford Ness. The 50-gun warship *Öland* under Psilander and a convoy of Swedish merchantmen were about to enter the English Channel when they met a squadron of nine English warships. Since the English considered these their home waters, they demanded that *Öland* lower its topsails to salute the English flag and Queen Anne. The Swedes refused, and after a battle lasting four and a half hours *Öland* was so badly damaged that Psilander gave the order to signal that he was in distress, whereupon the English ceased firing. The *Öland* was towed into an English port, Psilander and his officers were arrested and the convoy seized. They were released in late August.

The merchantmen were also returned to the Swedes, although some had to wait a long time for their sea-passes. After his release, Psilander had to repair his ship for the voyage home. Funds were difficult to come by, but after a couple of months *Öland* finally left England with nine merchantmen in early November. Because of the limited repairs and the many wounded among the crew, the ship foundered in a storm on its way home. Most of the crew survived, however.[28] After a few years' hiatus, Psilander went on to have a brilliant career in the navy and as a provincial governor in Visby and Kalmar.[29] As Munthe's work shows, Psilander is remembered as one of Sweden's foremost naval heroes.

To the modern reader, it might seem odd that Psilander did not just salute the English flag. This would have saved lives, his ship, and the convoy. In fact, as early as in 1831, when the Swedish Academy produced a commemorative coin of Psilander, the secretary of the Academy, Bishop Frans Michael Franzén, commented on Psilander's choice to fight. Franzén felt both reason and decency demanded that Psilander should not have risked human lives and such an expensive thing as a ship of the line over such a meaningless formality. Munthe, however, points to Psilander's all-important orders, of which Franzén was ignorant.[30] They spelt out that lowering the flag or any sails for a foreign man-o'-war was to be treated as if he had left the ship in their hands, and he would therefore be court-martialled and executed. If a foreign ship threatened violence if its demands were not met, Psilander should defend his ship as long as humanly possible. No one aboard was to lower the flag in surrender or to follow such an order. If an officer lowered the flag, he would be executed; if the crew did it, one in every ten men would hang and the rest would clean the privies.[31] Far more than a meaningless formality, in other words. Psilander as command-ing officer had little choice in the matter, since to give in and salute a foreign power's flag and sovereign, and thereby legitimize their claim of superiority, was considered as bad as handing the ship over to the enemy, while surrender was out of the question. This reveals a very stubborn, even touchy, concept of the flag's – and sovereign's – honour.

The *Öland* did fight for as long as it could. A quarter of the crew were killed or wounded and the ship was reduced to a (barely) floating

Figure 5.5. The Battle of Orford Ness (1704) has been depicted many times in Swedish marine art, here in 1914 by Jacob Hägg (1839–1931). As in reality, the flags show the nationality and status of the ships. *Öland* is flying the Swedish double swallow-tailed naval ensign, the merchantmen the rectangular merchant flag. Although Hägg was meticulous, the variant of the Blue Ensign that he has given the enemy ships was not adopted until 1801, almost a century later. Photo: Cecilia Nordstrand, Swedish National Maritime Museum/SMTM.

wreck.[32] Interestingly, Psilander never surrendered, but signalled by tying up his flag that the ship was in distress. This is something that both Munthe and another Swedish officer who wrote naval history, Gunnar Unger, mentioned in their descriptions of the engagement.[33] There was no dishonour in asking for help if your ship was in distress. Even after fighting for hours, Psilander refused to risk dishonour by surrendering or acknowledging the superiority of the English, and chose instead to simply acknowledge that his ship was no longer seaworthy. He maintained his own and his sovereign's honour, although at the cost of a quarter of his men. To the men of the Swedish navy writing naval history two centuries later, this fact still had meaning.

Psilander's fight came to symbolize how the honour of the flag and the king or queen came before anything else, but it was not an isolated example. In 1695, King Charles XI had ordered that since the English were demanding that all foreign ships passing the English Channel should lower their pennants to salute the English flag, Swedish convoy ships should simply not have their pennants hoisted after Skagen, the northernmost tip of continental Denmark.[34] This way, when they reached the Channel there was no pennant to lower and the Swedes' honour was not at risk. As Psilander's example shows, however, the English found other ways to demand salutes.

The risks involved in not complying with orders to defend the ship and its flag were very real. In the seventeenth and eighteenth centuries, several Swedish naval officers were condemned to death because they had lowered the flag in surrender or were found not to have defended its honour with enough determination. However, most of the condemned officers were pardoned at the last minute, their sentences commuted to imprisonment, demotion, or discharge.[35] Having to wait for such a pardon, even if one knew it would likely come, must have been stressful.

The notion of the honour of the flag was not only represented by the state. Naval officers were themselves also concerned with such notions. In 1710, Swedish naval officers expressed concern that privateers could fly the naval ensign rather than the merchant flag since they were at greater risk of being captured, something that would bring dishonour to the flag. King Charles XII, however, was not swayed by their concerns, and privateers continued to fly the naval flag since when privateering they were considered to be the Crown's ships.[36]

At the end of the Great Northern War in 1721, Sweden was severely weakened. The days of the Swedish Empire were over and the Age of Liberty had begun, royal power was weak and the Diet strong. Sweden also began to build up its merchant marine, but even if Sweden decided on a new, less bellicose course, it did not mean the rest of Europe had. If Swedish ships were to be safe outside the Baltic, they needed protection, just as when Psilander sailed with convoys two decades earlier. In

1724, Sweden founded the Konvojkommissariatet (Convoy Office) to organize and fund the protection of Sweden's shipping. For the rest of the eighteenth century, and especially from 1750 on, Sweden's trade policy centred on upholding its neutrality in European wars and negotiating and maintaining peace treaties with the North African Barbary States so they would not capture Swedish ships. Sweden negotiated peace with Algiers in 1729, with Tunis in 1736, Tripoli in 1741, and Morocco in 1763. By maintaining its neutrality, Swedish ships could join in the lucrative tramp trade, making money out of other people's wars.[37]

Swedish naval vessels had a part to play. They continued to convoy merchantmen through dangerous waters, but they also managed negotiations with the Barbary States and transported gifts to North African leaders. The questions of the flag and of how to behave when meeting foreign naval ships therefore remained important. Johan Henrik Kreüger, a Swedish naval officer and chair of the Convoy Office, wrote a book about Sweden's relations with the North African States published in 1856, in which he listed the Convoy Office's expeditions. From his descriptions, we can glimpse the meaning of the flag. The first convoy under the new disposition left Sweden in 1725, escorted by the 54-gun ships *Verden* and *Öland* (a different one from Psilander's). In 1728, when *Verden* was again going to convoy merchantmen to Portugal, the commander, Captain Nilsson, was instructed to fly a merchant flag to 'Cap Rocsent' (Cape Roca) on the Portuguese coast. After passing this point, the ship would hoist the naval ensign and pennant, but only until passing the same point on the return journey, after which the ship would again fly the merchant flag. If foreign naval ships demanded it, the convoy ship could therefore salute them in waters where she was flying the merchant flag. This was clearly to avoid confrontation with the British. However, Kreüger mentions no such regulations when *Verden* escorted ships carrying gifts for the Algerian dey in 1730, after the first peace treaty had been negotiated the year before.[38] Unger claims that the escort ships of this period flew merchant flags because Sweden's weakened state extended to its navy, and it was not until 1759 that the escort ships again flew the naval ensign in all waters.[39] This was not necessarily the case, however. For such a special convoy as in 1730 it was presumably important to fly the naval flag the whole way: the expedition's purpose was diplomatic and demanded an official presence. Neither Kreüger nor Unger provide detailed references, however, so to be certain one would have to find the orders for this specific expedition.

After 1730, there was only one expedition in the space of 25 years. In 1745, the frigate *Fama* carried a Tripolitan envoy back home who had visited Sweden after the Swedish–Tripolitan peace of 1741. Kreüger says nothing about the flag, but when carrying a foreign representative on board, the frigate likely would not have flown any other than the naval flag, as it was the state's symbol. Since *Fama* was transporting an important guest rather than escorting a convoy, it would probably be left alone anyway. From 1755, a new intense period of naval expeditions began for the Convoy Office, prompted by the Moroccans seizing Swedish ships. Kreüger has a tally of thirteen Convoy Office expeditions between 1755 and 1760, but the minutes of the Convoy Office mention only eight.[40] All Swedish ships that were heading further than Cape Finisterre in Spain were required to get 'Algerian sea-passes' from the Swedish Board of Trade that guaranteed that they were Swedish ships and therefore protected by the treaties with the Barbary States. In the sea-pass register from those years, as many as 24 expeditions with warships can be found.[41] The exact number of expeditions to protect Swedish shipping may therefore have been higher than the thirteen Kreüger mentioned, and the involvement of the Convoy Office may have been less than he claimed, but it was undeniably a busy period for the protection of Swedish shipping.

In Kreüger's account there is evidence of the navy using the merchant flag in certain waters. In 1758, Captain Barfeldt on the frigate *Svarta Örn* had orders similar to Nilsson's thirty years earlier. In 1759, however, a ship of the line and three frigates were ordered to fly the naval ensign and pennants in all waters. After the peace treaty with Morocco in 1763, the need for convoy escorts dwindled. In 1771, however, the Secret Committee of the Diet thought that managing its expensive treaties and the ever-increasing demands of the Barbary States could be best achieved if one or two naval ships sailed in their waters every year 'in such a way as to inspire proper respect of the Swedish flag'. The following year another frigate was sent out.[42] Evidently, the concept of showing the flag was important. It was how the flag gained respect. If no Swedish warships showed themselves in North African waters, the Barbary States would not fear retaliation for attacking Swedish ships. It is important to note that the flag to show was the naval flag. Swedish merchantmen entered the Mediterranean all the time.

Gunnar Unger provides an explanation for why the Swedes went back to flying the naval flag everywhere after 1758 that also shows the importance of showing the naval flag. In April 1759, the frigate *Hök* under Captain Carl Treutiger had put in at Sheerness while on a convoy expedition to the Mediterranean. Providing more details than Kreüger, however, Unger claims that *Hök* was still flying the merchant flag. Upon saluting the British flag, *Hök* was informed by British authorities that such a salute could only be accepted if the saluting ship was itself flying the king's colours. Unger writes that it was probably Captain Treutiger's report later that year which prompted the Swedish admiralty to propose to the government that Swedish warships go back to flying the naval ensign everywhere, since it was 'unworthy for the kingdom' that the escort ships flew the merchant flag, and they should 'rather defend themselves to the last man than be forced by the English to strike the flag'. The government approved the proposal.[43]

Sweden by then was involved in the Seven Years War, increasing the need for convoys to the Mediterranean.[44] In 1757, it had entered the war by invading the Prussian parts of Pomerania, so it now had to keep an eye on Prussian privateers, both at home and in the Mediterranean.[45] Britain was Prussia's ally, complicating the Swedish strategy of avoiding confrontation with the British. In such a situation, flying the flag in northern waters would be more important than ever. The fact that *Hök* could put in at a British dockyard in 1759 shows that neither Britain nor Sweden were particularly interested in fighting each other, however. In fact, Sweden's loss of neutrality did not change its situation much outside the Baltic. Sweden continued to trade, and British privateers continued to attack Swedish ships.[46] As the example of *Prince Ferdinand* above shows, the privateers also knew how to take advantage of the system of alliances in the war. This complex situation could also explain why the orders were changed in 1759.

The French Revolutionary Wars (1792–1802) were another busy period for the Convoy Office. The Swedish merchant marine was vulnerable to British and French privateers, so by 1793 Sweden began an ambitious, if short-lived, convoy service to the Mediterranean. This was followed by a League of Neutrality with Denmark in 1794. Both countries were each to keep eight ships of the line and four frigates ready to protect their neutrality. Maintaining this force quickly became expensive, however, and from the start they only patrolled the North Sea, if at all, while no further convoys were arranged until 1798.[47] All the while, the problems with the Barbary States continued and the Swedes had to send naval ships to deliver gifts to North Africa.[48]

In 1798, the threat from European privateers grew worse, and Sweden once again decided on a more ambitious convoy service, this time organizing four convoys. One of them did not make it beyond the North Sea before being dispersed by a storm, and two were captured by the British in the English Channel. Only the fourth made it safely to the Mediterranean by navigating around the British Isles rather than through the Channel. West of the Shetlands, however, the escorting frigate lost sight of all the ships in its convoy and therefore continued to Gibraltar alone. The commanding officers of the captured convoys were Lieutenant-Colonel Anton Johan Wrangel and Major Olof Ceder-ström. Having lost their convoys without a fight to the British, and under the naval flag no less, they were court-martialled and condemned to death, but were in the end only demoted and imprisoned for a while. The captured convoys and the increasingly hostile behaviour by British and French privateers and naval ships towards neutral shipping pushed Sweden into armed neutrality with Denmark and Russia. The tense relations with the British worsened.[49]

Sweden at this point was also in a conflict with Tripoli. Though a sideshow in the great European conflict, it can tell us interesting things about the meaning of the flag and the pragmatism shown by a small power like Sweden. There were other ways to avoid problems than flying the merchant flag or choosing not to fly pennants, and one was to reinterpret what the ships were doing rather than changing flag. The conflict with Tripoli (1796–1802) led Sweden to send several warships to Tripolitan waters to protect Swedish shipping and negotiate new peace treaties. In 1797, Major David Gustaf Blessingh left Sweden with the frigate *Thetis* and the brig of war *Husaren* to settle the conflict. The new treaty of 1798 was rather unstable, however, and Yusuf Karamanli declared war on Sweden again in 1800. *Thetis* returned to Tripoli, this time under the command of Lieutenant-Colonel Carl Gustaf Tornquist, who negotiated a new peace treaty in early 1801, one that the Swedes chose not to ratify because of what they viewed as excessive Tripolitan demands. Only on the third attempt in 1802, after the dispatch of another three frigates and a brig of war under Rear-Admiral Rudolf Cederström to join *Thetis*, did Sweden negotiate a new peace treaty that would last.[50] After the convoys of 1798, there was a change in the orders to the Swedish commanders dealing with Tripoli.

Major Blessingh's orders were dated 12 October 1797, that is from before the convoys of 1798 and the subsequent worsening of British–Swedish relations. The first paragraph ordered the frigate or the brig to escort the ship carrying gifts to Tripoli. They should also escort all Swedish merchantmen headed for the Mediterranean or those they found in the Mediterranean until a new peace treaty had been negotiated. Blessingh should only do this if it would not slow his arrival to Tripoli, however. The rest of the orders detailed how Blessingh should handle negotiations, but ended by stating that the king expected Blessingh to seek to achieve the king's will 'so that trade and navigation are protected, the King's and Realm's glory and the Swedish flag's honour are upheld etc.'[51] These orders were straightforward. Although not as detailed on what it meant to uphold the flag's honour as Psilander's orders from 90 years before, the meaning was much the same. The naval ships, if time permitted, were to escort merchantmen and not accept questionable behaviour from foreign naval ships. In subsequent years, however, the Swedes would be far more careful.

After much of the conflict with Britain had been settled in 1801, the king on 3 July sent additional orders to Tornquist, who had remained in the Mediterranean after the negotiations for the second of the peace treaties with Tripoli. He was now ordered to patrol against the Barbary States and to protect and defend all Swedish merchantmen from their attacks. He was to inform Swedish consuls in Mediterranean ports when he thought he would pass so Swedish ships could join him. However, the ships that wished to sail with him should be ordered to gather and keep themselves at a distance from the frigate so it could protect them without it looking as if they were in convoy. The frigate should sail at a speed so the merchantmen could keep up, and sail with them until they had left the Mediterranean. The orders continued:

> When patrolling, the Lieutenant-Colonel may not allow himself to be drawn into any kind of dispute with any Christian power's warships he may meet, always remembering that the Lieutenant-Colonel is not convoying, but only cruising to prevent any tricks from the Barbary corsairs. But in the unlikely event that anything be required of the King's frigate that goes against the Swedish flag's honour, the Lieutenant-Colonel should answer in such a way that befits the Realm's dignity and a brave and daunting commander.[52]

There was a certain ambiguity in Tornquist's orders. He was not to engage any European naval ship, yet he was expected to uphold the honour of the flag. This was achieved by redefining what the frigate was doing. Unlike Blessingh, Tornquist was only cruising close to friendly merchantmen to protect them from Barbary corsairs; he was not escorting a convoy. This meant that if a European naval ship wanted to search and even capture a merchantman, Tornquist was not supposed to stop it. Since he had not officially formed a convoy, such behaviour was not dishonourable to the flag. If European naval ships attacked the frigate, however, the flag was to be defended. This was more than anything a question of wording. It is hard to believe that the merchantmen were comfortable with this change. But for the state, it made possible a more careful behaviour towards the warring European states while preserving the honour of the flag. Later in 1801, the Swedes went even further in this careful direction.

Rear-Admiral Cederström's orders were dated October 1801. He was ordered to organize convoys, patrol against the Tripolitan corsairs, and take the necessary offensive steps to damage Tripolitan interests as much as was necessary to force the Tripolitans to negotiate. If Tripoli and the US were at war when he arrived in the Mediterranean, he should also try to coordinate operations with the Americans. The king was happy the American frigates in the Mediterranean had protected Swedish merchantmen, and Cederström was also to protect both the American and Swedish merchant flags. Even if the American commander would not agree to coordinate with the Swedes, Swedish naval ships would still protect American shipping. If other neutrals' merchantmen wanted to join the convoys, they were free to do so, but the Swedish navy was there only to deal with Tripolitan corsairs. If any European men-of-war wanted to stop the merchantmen, whether Swedish or otherwise, to search for contraband, the escorting frigate should not try to stop it. Contraband was anything that could be used in war, such as weapons or naval stores. Neutrals were not supposed to supply such goods to belligerents in time of war, but different states had different – and changing – notions of what constituted contraband and whether or not neutral states could trade such goods with other neutrals. These differences were the cause of many of the conflicts over neutrals' rights in wartime. According to Cederström's orders, if any contraband were found, the escorting ship should only ask for the man-o'-war's name and where she was taking the merchantman, and then report this to the Swedish government. Cederström should always maintain the Swedish naval ensign's honour and reputation, and if necessary defend it with courage and bravery. However, he should be polite towards all other European men-of-war and not take part if they engaged one another. Any officer who behaved unworthily and brought dishonour to the Swedish name should be put ashore to fend for himself.[53]

The ships in Cederström's squadron could once again officially convoy neutral ships, even other countries', but only against Tripolitan corsairs. If European men-of-war wanted to search the convoy, the Swedish escorting ship had to allow it, leaving it to the diplomats to resolve by informing the government of the ships' identities and the ports where they were taken. This would have been unthinkable just a few years before. Even in Tornqvist's orders a few months earlier, there was a reluctance to use the word 'convoy' in situations when the escorting ships were not supposed to intervene against European men-of-war. The pressure Sweden had been under in the years before Cederström's expedition had changed the way it handled the flag's honour. Cederström should stay out of the warring European powers' business and focus on ending the conflict with Tripoli. Frigates flying the naval ensign were still supposed to defend their honour, but an honour redefined so it no longer extended to the ships under their protection.

During the conflict with Tripoli, then, because of the simultaneous conflict with Britain, the way the Swedes in practice perceived the flag's honour changed dramatically. Early on, the honour of the naval flag required a ship to protect any ship it was escorting from attack. Later, the honour of the flag was only connected to the escorting ship itself. The honour of the flag was as important as ever, but the Swedes had redefined what was included in the concept of the flag's honour. The direction of this development was not constant, however. After the conflict with Tripoli had been settled in 1802 and relations with Britain and France relaxed, especially after 1815, the traditional view of the flag's honour returned. The unusual way to handle its honour in 1801 therefore reflected the extremity of the situation rather than a new way to view the issue. This much was evident as late as the 1940s.

The notion of the naval ensign's honour survived well into the twentieth century. Sweden was neutral in the Second World War, but began a massive build-up of its armed forces. For the navy, this meant both building new ships and modernizing old ones. To bolster the increase even further, the Swedes also looked to buy ships from other countries. In 1940, Sweden therefore purchased weapons, torpedo boats, and four small destroyers from Italy. The destroyers were from the 1920s and early 1930s. The Swedish navy named the two larger, older destroyers *Puke* and, funnily enough, *Psilander*, and the more recent ones *Romulus* and *Remus* as a diplomatic move to encourage the Italians to go through with the sale. The Italians did not even class the latter as destroyers but as torpedo boats. Small but ideal for Swedish purposes, they became known as 'coastal destroyers' in Sweden.[54]

The Swedish crews arrived at the Italian naval base of La Spezia on the Swedish steamer *Patricia* on 19 March 1940. Torsten Hagman, the Swedish naval officer to command the squadron on its journey home, and several officers and non-commissioned officers, had been in Italy since 31 January to oversee the outfitting of the ships. On 27 March, the crews hoisted the Swedish flag.[55] Before leaving Italy, Hagman received orders for the journey from the commander of the navy, Vice-Admiral Fabian Tamm. He ended with these words: 'Otherwise, I expect that you, in response to upcoming situations, shall carry through your mission in a way that reflects the Swedish Navy's reputation and the Swedish flag's honour.'[56] The wording had changed little since the eighteenth century.

After first heading to Naples for victuals and repairs, the little Swedish squadron left Italy on 18 April 1940. It was a hazardous journey. One of the steam turbines on *Puke* broke down only a day out of Naples, which resulted in a collision when *Psilander* did not see the lead ship was losing speed. The ships put in at Cartagena to make necessary repairs before moving on to Lisbon. There they spent a month waiting for news that their onward journey had been agreed with both Britain and Germany. They also docked *Puke* for final repairs.[57] On 19 June they reached the Faroe Islands – Danish territory – where they were supposed to refuel and take on water. This was in June 1940, however. Since Sweden had taken delivery of the destroyers, Nazi Germany had attacked Denmark and Norway on 9 April, prompting a British occupation of the Faroe Islands on 13 April. The German invasion of Denmark considerably worsened Sweden's strategic position, Italy had also joined Germany in the war, and France was on the brink of surrender. Britain's situation was desperate. They had fallen back from Norway and France, and were becoming increasingly isolated as the last great power opposing Nazi Germany. This was before the USSR had changed sides or the US had entered the war. It was hardly surprising the British decided to intervene when the Swedish ships arrived in the Faroe Islands: the British did not want to risk the destroyers ending up in the Kriegsmarine – the Germans needed new destroyers having lost 10 of their 22 during the attack on Norway.[58]

On 20 June, Captain Clifford Caslon, commanding three Royal Navy Tribal-class destroyers, much bigger and more heavily equipped than the small Swedish ships, came aboard *Puke* and informed Hagman he had to surrender his ships to the British. Any attempt to flee or to contact Stockholm would be answered with force. Hagman had only two 10 cm guns bearing on the opening of the fjord where the three British destroyers were waiting. The Swedes had not yet had time to resupply, meaning they could not reach Sweden even if they tried.[59] Much like Psilander two centuries before him, Hagman was in for a fight he could not hope to win, something he himself recognized. According to Lieutenant Bengt Hellsten, Hagman told him that 'Here I have an opportunity no Swedish naval officer has had in 200 years, to join Munthe's *Swedish Naval Heroes*'.[60] An officer should fight and defend the honour of the Swedish flag rather than surrender his ships. Hagman knew this very well.

Hagman chose not to fight, however, leaving the destiny of the destroyers in the hands of the diplomats. If they were to reach Sweden, it was his only choice. The other commanding officers in the squadron agreed with him. He left the destroyers with flags and pennants flying, though, and refused to formally surrender them – an action similar to Psilander's. After a few days of intense diplomatic negotiations, the British agreed to hand back the destroyers, and on 30 June the Swedes were allowed to inspect them.[61] In July, the ships finally reached Sweden. Hagman's decision meant Sweden remained outside the war and its navy received much-needed reinforcements. It was what Sweden's leaders had wanted. Still, in the navy itself not all were convinced Hagman had handled the situation correctly.[62] It was the commander of the Swedish navy, Vice-Admiral Tamm, who met the destroyers when they arrived in Gothenburg on 10 July, not the prime minister Per Albin Hansson nor the defence minister Per Edvin Sköld. Tamm gave a speech, but according to the officers and conscripts who heard it there was a cold tone to it.[63]

Hagman had given up his ships without a fight, which meant a court-martial had to investigate the case, and in due course it decided he would not be prosecuted. The day the decision was made public,

Figure 5.6. The former Italian destroyers in Gothenburg. A naval ensign flying from the stern of another ship obstructs the view of the destroyer on the left. It is difficult to believe this was a mistake. The distinctive Swedish naval ensign spells out that the destroyers were now Swedish even in a black-and-white photo. Photo: Swedish National Maritime Museum/SMTM.

however, the commander of Kustflottan (the main fleet, lit. 'Coastal Navy'), the part of the Swedish navy with the most modern ships, Rear-Admiral Ehrensvärd, issued a secret order: 'I forbid my subordinate commanders from, under any circumstances, giving up their ships to foreign powers. The flag's honour comes first.'[64] The following day, the Swedish supreme commander, General Olof Thörnell, sent a secret message to Vice-Admiral Tamm, informing him that no officers or non-commissioned officers should take any heed of political matters when performing their duties. They should follow orders, and if no orders were given, they should do their duty in accordance with Sweden's and its military's honour and reputation.[65]

The response from Sweden's military leadership might seem odd, especially today when most agree Hagman handled the situation correctly. But in 1940, Sweden was surrounded by warring and occupied powers. As historians have since pointed out, the command could not be seen to tolerate officers who chose not to fight, because they could not risk damaging military morale.[66] If Sweden were invaded – a threat all too real at the time – all officers should be certain they were expected to defend their positions. Giving up without a fight was not an option.

Gunnar Unger, by then retired from the Swedish navy, had the freedom to take another view, however. In his 1941 history of Swedish convoy expeditions, he commented that what he considered the unfair treatment of Wrangel and Cederström after the 1798 convoys had parallels in his own time. In his opinion they had not acted in a way that dishonoured the flag, because the British demands had not been to strike the flags or sails, but simply to search the Swedish merchantmen for contraband. Unger's views were close to those in Cederström's orders: the honour of the flag only concerned the escort ship itself, not the merchantmen under its protection. Therefore, Sweden's honour had not been at stake and the officers should not have been punished. As we have seen, however, Cederström's orders were an exception, and eighteenth-century notions of national honour were usually different to Unger's. His comments – made less than a year after Torsten Hagman had returned with the destroyers in July 1940 – are interesting because he seems to have been writing in Hagman's defence. He did not mention Hagman specifically, but he made it clear that officers sometimes had to act in a way that they knew would be criticized by 'brothers in arms and their collaborators' back home. But as long as the honour of the flag was not at stake, officers should be able to decide to negotiate and avoid a fight they could not hope to win, without being accused of cowardice.[67] Like other officers, Unger was concerned with the honour of the flag, but he was more nuanced in his views than his active colleagues.

The descriptions of the duties of a naval officer were much the same in 1940 as in the eighteenth century. Officers should first and foremost protect the flag's honour. Under no circumstances should they allow foreign powers to take control of their ships. At the same time, we also see the same pragmatism as in the eighteenth century. Hagman was never prosecuted, and, tellingly, he made sure that he never formally surrendered the ships under his command. The rules were clear, but in practice they left officers with room for manoeuvre to find the best solutions. Again, we can see both aspects of the flag's honour – as institution and as object – playing a part. By keeping the flags flying, Hagman reduced the dishonour to the flag.

Some things had changed, however. Sweden's political leaders in 1940 seem to have been more open to such behaviour than its military leaders were – not the case in the eighteenth century. We see a bigger difference between civilian and military leadership in 1940 than earlier. From a military viewpoint, little had changed in the 250 years covered in this essay. Officers were not supposed to consider the political consequences of their actions; they were expected to follow orders. In civilian society, hierarchies had changed dramatically. Sweden was a democracy, not an absolute monarchy, and this had consequences for how Hagman's behaviour was viewed by the political leadership. In military matters, however, ideas about the flag's honour still meant something, and had a practical function, ensuring that the Swedish armed forces would function if Sweden came under attack. As Bishop Franzén's comments in 1831 about the meaninglessness of Psilander's actions, the eighteenth-century merchants' disregard for the naval ensign's exclusivity, and Unger's more nuanced views show, however, this process of democratization and its effects on ideas of honour were slow and complex.

Two centuries of pragmatism and honour

The examples in this essay are an interesting mix of pragmatism and steely views about honour over 250 years. Notions of honour were deeply intertwined with the naval ensign as the symbol of the state and the royal sovereign. A ship flying such a flag could not accept any treatment from foreign ships that might cast dishonour on the king or queen. In theory, all kings, being sovereigns, were equal, and if a ship flying the king's colours deigned to strike its flag, pennant, or sails or, worse, surrender to a ship flying the flag of another country, it was an acknowledgement of that state's superiority. This could never be accepted, and therefore any officer commanding a ship flying the king's flag was to defend that ship to the death, even if the cause of the fight was something as 'meaningless' as a formality. This was also why the capture of an enemy flag was such an honourable feat. It meant that the enemy had been forced to acknowledge the superiority of your own forces and sovereign. Both Psilander and Hagman, almost 240 years apart, chose not to lower their ensigns, flatly refusing to acknowledge the right of the Royal Navy to seize their ships.

On the other hand, the theoretical equality between heads of state often carried less weight in reality. Often, the Swedes were simply not powerful enough to uphold this rather static view of honour while at the same time successfully achieving their goals. We have seen examples of how the Swedes manoeuvred between this theoretical equality between sovereigns and real discrepancies in power. They used pragmatic methods to avoid having to suffer these dishonourable situations. If they flew no pennants, no one could ask them to lower them; if they were not formally escorting a convoy, foreign naval ships could search merchantmen in front of them without it reflecting badly on the flag. If men-of-war flew a merchant flag it did not sully the naval flag to allow British ships to search the convoy, and all was well.

All these examples show that while questions of honour were important, so was the desire to achieve safety for Swedish ships. Relentlessly answering all slights to the naval flag with gunfire would not work if Sweden wanted to stay out of conflicts. While the Swedes were concerned with their reputation, it was not in their interest to enter wars willy-nilly. This was just as true in the 1700s as in 1940. In the eighteenth century, Sweden wanted to use its neutrality to claim a share of the tramp trade. The safety of Swedish ships was key here. In 1940, Sweden needed more ships for its navy to protect shipping around its coasts. Even if the goals were different, the need for safety was similar.

All the talk of the honour of the flag has survived down the centuries and through the long process of democratization because it serves a military purpose. To function properly, a military organization like the navy cannot allow its officers to take politics into consideration when deciding what to do when attacked. This would risk the organization's effectiveness and ability to meet the enemy. Because it is about life and death, and because it concerns the country's sovereignty, decisions have to be made quickly. Individual officers should not have to doubt what their response should be. This is of course an ideal. In reality, officers have often been forced to consider politics. The success of their missions has depended on their ability to handle the paradox. Torsten Hagman handled it in a way that meant the success of his mission in 1940. The officers in his squadron and the political leadership in Sweden supported his decision. The military leadership, however, had no choice but to make sure his actions did not become a precedent for other officers, so if Sweden were attacked, its armed forces would defend the country with determination.

By constantly redefining the situation, rather than renegotiating the meaning of the flag itself, Sweden could create room for manoeuvre for the naval officers on their missions. An officer should fight to the death, but anyone could end up in distress. Calling for help when the ship was about to sink was not dishonourable. Just as the navy used merchantmen in wartime, there was nothing stopping naval ships from assuming the identity of merchant ships when it suited them, as long as they did not engage in battle without hoisting the naval ensign. This fluidity of identity was made possible through the widespread and accepted practice of disguising the true identity of ships, and by redefining what was happening rather than by renegotiating the importance of the flag. The honour of the naval flag, as the symbol of the king and the state, had to be protected. Using such pragmatic tactics, from the exact wording of orders to changing flags in certain waters, the Swedes could create a surprising amount of room for manoeuvre without risking the flag's honour. By isolating the meaning of the flag's honour from the shifting realities faced at sea, it was possible for the language of the flag's honour to remain largely unchanged despite the massive changes in society between 1700 and 1950.

Notes

1 Leif Törnquist, *Svenska flaggans historia* (Stockholm 2008), 100–105.
2 Törnquist 2008, 110–119.
3 The evolution of the Swedish flag is too complicated to go into here, but Törnquist 2008 is an excellent account of its history in Swedish.
4 Törnquist 2008, 22–3, 46.

5 Philip J. Stern & Carl Wennerlind (eds.), *Mercantilism Reimagined: Political Economy in Early Modern Britain and Its Empire* (Oxford 2013), 5. Awareness of the limits of state power in the early modern period was not limited to the elite – the common sailors, operating the ships that bound empires together, also knew this. Marcus Rediker, *Pirater: Sjöröveriets guldålder i Atlanten och Karibiska havet* (Stockholm 2006), 37–8.

6 For the early history of the Swedish flag, see Torsten Lenk, 'Svenska flaggans uppkomst och äldsta historia', in Otto Lybeck (ed.), *Svenska flottans historia: Örlogsflottan i ord och bild från dess grundläggning under Gustav Vasa fram till våra dagar*, i: *1521–1679* (Malmö 1942), 476–89; Törnquist 2008, 46–62.

7 Törnquist 2008, 51, 60–4.

8 For a recent discussion of the meaning of the flag to the Swedish navy in the early eighteenth century, see Lars Ericson Wolke, *Sjöslag och rysshärjningar: Kampen om Östersjön under stora nordiska kriget 1700–1721* (Stockholm 2011), 91–2.

9 Torsten Lenk, 'Svenska flaggan efter 1700', in Otto Lybeck (ed.), *Svenska flottans historia. Örlogsflottan i ord och bild från dess grundläggning under Gustav Vasa fram till våra dagar*, ii: *1680–1814* (Malmö 1943), 530–2.

10 Törnquist 2008, 86–91.

11 Törnquist 2008, 106–108.

12 Törnquist 2008, 90.

13 Lenk 1943, 534, 537 (picture).

14 Cornel Zwierlein, *Imperial Unknowns: The French and British in the Mediterranean, 1650–1750* (Cambridge 2018), 23.

15 Zwierlein 2018, 35–6.

16 Zwierlein 2018, 43–4.

17 Leos Müller, *Consuls, Corsairs, and Commerce: The Swedish Consular Service and Long-distance Shipping, 1720–1815* (Uppsala 2004), 61–2.

18 Steve Murdoch & Leos Müller, 'Neutral före neutraliteten: Svensk sjöfart i krigens skugga cirka 1650–1800', in Simon Ekström & Leos Müller (eds.), *Angöringar: Berättelser och kunskap från havet* (Stockholm 2017), 197–8.

19 Frank Lambert, *The Barbary Wars: American Independence in the Atlantic World* (New York 2007), 128–30.

20 Fredrik Kämpe, 'Neutralitetens pris: Handelsflottan och folkförsörjningen', in Mirja Arnshav & Andreas Linderoth (eds.), *Sverige och första världskriget: Maritima perspektiv* (Lund 2017), 108.

21 Kämpe 2017, 99.

22 For different types of trophies and their meanings and histories, see the excellent Fred Sandstedt, Lena Engquist Sandstedt, Martin Skoog & Karin Tetteris (eds.), *In Hoc Signo Vinces: A Presentation of the Swedish State Trophy Collection* (Stockholm 2006); for the importance of banners, public display, and the trophies' changing meanings over time, see Karin Tetteris, 'Att skapa ett kulturarv: Om troféfanor och segerparader', in Klas Kronberg & Anna Maria Forssberg (eds.), *Minnet av Narva: Om troféer, propaganda och historiebruk* (Lund 2018), 53–78.

23 Lars Ericson Wolke & Martin Hårdstedt, *Svenska sjöslag* (Stockholm 2009), 167–8.

24 Lars Ericson et al., *Svenska slagfält* (Stockholm 2003), 402–403.

25 Hans von Hofsten, *Ulven: Redovisning av de faktiska omständigheterna kring ubåten Ulvens förlisning* (Stockholm 1989).

26 Tetteris 2018, 54–5.

27 Otto Lybeck (ed.), *Svenska flottans historia: Örlogsflottan i ord och bild från dess grund-läggning under Gustav Vasa fram till våra dagar*, i: *1521–1679* (Malmö 1942), 8. The index was published as a slim fourth volume in 1949. All translations are my own unless otherwise noted.

28 Arnold Munthe, *Svenska sjöhjältar*, i: *Gustaf von Psilander* (Stockholm 1922), 8–33.

29 Munthe 1922, 38–48.

30 Munthe 1922, 51.

31 Munthe 1922, 12–13.

32 Munthe 1922, 21.

33 Gunnar Unger, *Illustrerad svensk sjökrigshistoria: Senare delen omfattande tiden 1680–1814* (Stockholm 1923), 43.

34 Ericson Wolke 2011, 92; Gunnar Unger, 'Bilder från svenska flottans konvojtjänst i avlägsnare farvatten', *Tidskrift i Sjöväsendet* 1 (1941), 39.

35 Ernst Holmberg, 'Konvojexpeditioner under Karl XI:s regeringstid', *Tidskrift i Sjöväsen-det* 5 (1929), 268; Unger 1941, 44–52. See also Ericson Wolke 2011, 91–2. Holmberg states that Lieutenant Gustaf Klöfversköld was pardoned and died in Karlskrona in 1706, and Unger that his death sentence was commuted to six months' suspension; however, Ericson Wolke, without specifying why, says he was executed in 1696.

36 Ericson Wolke 2011, 92.

37 For Swedish eighteenth-century neutrality, see Leos Müller, 'Svensk sjöfart, neutralitet och det väpnade neutralitetsförbundet 1780–1783', in David Dunér (ed.), *Sjuttonhun-dratal: Nordic Yearbook for Eighteenth-Century Studies* (2012), 39–58; for the peace treaties with the Barbary States, see Johan Henrik Kreüger, *Sveriges förhållanden till barbaresk staterna i Afrika*, i (Stockholm 1856); Eskil Olán, *Sjörövarna på Medelhavet och Levantiska Compagniet: Historien om Sveriges gamla handel med Orienten* (Stock-holm 1921), 49–58.

38 Kreüger 1856, 42–4.

39 Unger 1941, 40–1.

40 Kreüger 1856, 45–8; Riksarkivet (Swedish National Archives), Stockholm (RA), Kon-vojkommissariatets arkiv, Protokoll, vol. 4 and 5.

41 RA, Kommerskollegium, Diarier, Utgående diarier, Sjöpassdiarier, vol. 1; in the biog-raphies of Swedish naval officers in Lorentz Leopold von Horn, *Kommendörkapten L. L. von Horns biografiska anteckningar*, ii: *Officerare, som tjenat vid Örlogsflottan åren 1721–1824* (Hjelmarsnäs 1937), ii. 69–70, 108 two of the expeditions of 1760 were said to have lasted until 1763 and 1764.

42 Kreüger 1856, 46–9.

43 Unger 1941, 41.

44 Unger 1941, 42.

45 Unger 1941, 35.

46 Murdoch & Müller 2017, 195–6.

47 Gunnar Unger, 'Svenska flottans sjötåg åren 1771–1814', in Otto Lybeck (ed.), *Svenska flottans historia: Örlogsflottan i ord och bild från dess grundläggning under Gustav Vasa fram till våra dagar*, ii: *1680–1814* (Malmö 1943), 526.

48 Kreüger 1856, 63–5, 68–70.

49 For the 1798 convoys, see Kreüger 1856, 65–8; Unger 1941, 49–52; for Swedish trade policy and the complicated relations with Britain at the time, see Leos Müller, 'Swedish

merchant shipping in troubled times: The French Revolutionary Wars and Sweden's neutrality 1793–1801', *International Journal of Maritime History* 28/1 (2016), 147–64.

50 For the conflict, see Fredrik Kämpe, 'Cooperating with Competitors: Swedish Consuls in North Africa and Sweden's Position in the World, 1791–1802' (MA diss., Uppsala University 2014), 50–76; Kreüger 1856, 415–29.

51 RA, Konvojkommissariatets arkiv, Ankomna brev, No. 52, 1797.

52 RA, Konvojkommissariatets arkiv, Ankomna brev, No. 10, 1801.

53 RA, Konvojkommissariatets arkiv, Ankomna brev, No. 22 (incorrectly numbered as 23), 1801.

54 Kent Zetterberg & Gustaf von Hofsten, *Jagarincidenten vid Färöarna 1940: Brittiskt försök att beslagta svenska örlogsfartyg* (Stockholm 2020), 27–42.

55 Gunnar Hagman, 'Jagarepisoden vid Färöarna i juni 1940', *Tidskrift i Sjöväsendet* 1 (1986), 57.

56 Gunnar Hagman, 'Jagarepisoden vid Färöarna i juni 1940', *Tidskrift i Sjöväsendet* 1 (1971), 68.

57 Zetterberg & von Hofsten 2020, 52–7.

58 Zetterberg & von Hofsten 2020, 64–75.

59 Hagman 1986, 61–3.

60 Zetterberg & von Hofsten 2020, 65.

61 Hagman 1986, 63–5.

62 Ericson Wolke & Hårdstedt 2009, 339.

63 Zetterberg & von Hofsten 2020, 86–7.

64 Zetterberg & von Hofsten 2020, 89.

65 Zetterberg & von Hofsten 2020, 90.

66 Ericson Wolke & Hårdstedt 2009, 339; Zetterberg & von Hofsten 2020, 90.

67 Unger 1941, 50–5.

CHAPTER 6

Out of the water

Wrecks and salvage at the intersection of death, time past, and national glory

Simon Ekström

Some famed wrecks, salvaged, are considered cultural heritage and can be found in museums. Some similarly historic wrecks live on outside heritage institutions, in literature and popular culture. The fate of both is strikingly different to how other once well-known shipwrecks have virtually disappeared from collective memory.

This is the story of successful Swedish salvage projects. Likewise, it is the outline of how the recovered wrecks have become the focus of various types of public interest. Most important, however, is that the overall aim of this essay is to reveal how both the salvage and ships have been incorporated to varying degrees into collective memory as cultural heritage objects. Three ships and their respective salvage biographies are in focus here, even though the reasoning might be of interest for anyone concerned with the productive, intimate relation between sunken ships and heritage-making processes. One of the salvage projects in question is nowadays almost unknown. The second is much more recognized, largely because a famous Swedish artist died in the shipwreck. The third has gained international fame and the recovered ship is placed in a world-renowned museum, seen by paying visitors in the millions. The essay rounds off with a fourth and final example of a successful salvage operation, this time of a long-missing military plane shot down over the Baltic Sea in the Cold War, which is also now on display in a museum.

The essay's starting point is a brief description of the salvage of the three ships, emphasizing distinctive features of the operations and their historical backgrounds. Above all, it concerns (*i*) the loss of human life; (*ii*) the time elapsed between the sinking and the salvage and display; and (*iii*) the national pride extracted from the salvage. In close connection with these conditions is the ability of the ongoing projects to attract any (*iv*) royal presence. The further analysis highlights how these circumstances together have influenced the attention paid to the operations at the time, and the ways they have been represented afterwards.

It is impossible to draw far-reaching conclusions from so few observations; however, there are still good reasons to set the individual salvage projects alongside one another. As will be seen, even a rudimentary account of some few cases can provide essential keys to the understanding of why certain ships and their salvage are stuck in collective memory, while others are forgotten. Not that these findings are all that can be said of the salvage operations and their aftermath. Clearly, they were all affected by matters not included above, some of which will be returned to later. In line with this reasoning the concluding section underlines the importance of materiality – that is, things and stuff – for the recollection of events to remain fresh.

Three wrecks lost and found

In August 1895, the steamer *Södra Sverige* (South Sweden) ran aground on Franska stenarna (French Rocks) in Stockholm's southern archipelago (Fig. 6.1). The ship appeared to have survived the impact at first, but it sank shortly thereafter in 56 metres of water. All on board were rescued. Two years later, the wreck was salvaged, after which it was put on display for a few summer weeks as part of the world fair in Stockholm in 1897. The salvage operation had attracted spectators to the site, and the crowds were even greater when it was on show in the capital. The press reported on events, especially when King Oscar II himself chose

Figure 6.1. The steamer *Södra Sverige* at the world fair in Stockholm in 1897.
Photo: Swedish National Maritime Museum/SMTM.

to board the recovered steamer. Soon after it was salvaged, a book was published about the successful use of the 'Waller Tube', named after its maker, the engineer Per Aron Waller. A few items that were rescued from the sunken ship, among them a porcelain chamber pot and a picture with a biblical motif, are in the collections of the Swedish National Maritime Museum in Stockholm.[1]

The steamer *Per Brahe* sank in a gale on a November night in 1918. The sinking took place just off Hästholmen in Lake Vättern and later investigations confirm that too much cargo, badly lashed down, caused the accident. All 24 on board, both crew and passengers, lost their lives, including artist John Bauer and his family. Four years later, in the summer of 1922, the ship was recovered (Fig. 6.2). There was huge public interest in the operation, with extra trains and boat trips to Hästholmen, and a documentary film made. Later, in the autumn, the salvaged steamer was sent on tour, with stops at several cities around Lake Mälaren, including Stockholm. To the present day it continues

Figure 6.2. The steamer *Per Brahe* at the site of the salvage in 1922. Photo: Jönköpings läns museum.

to inspire books, dramas, and poetic adaptations. A number of objects from *Per Brahe* are preserved in various museums.

The newly built warship *Vasa* foundered on its maiden voyage in August 1628, after only a short voyage in Stockholm harbour. After being underwater for over three centuries, the royal wreck was salvaged in 1961, attracting great national and international attention (Fig. 6.3). The number of deaths when it sank is still uncertain, but the remains of nearly twenty people were later recovered during repeated excavations at the site. It was not an easy task to raise *Vasa*, and in the media the operation was described as a spectacular triumph, which owed everything to Swedish engineering skills. Once the salvage was complete it was followed by a similarly innovative preservation of the ship's wooden structure. Today, the Vasa Museum is Sweden's most visited museum and tourist destination. The Museum has a special section detailing the salvage operations, displaying models of the vessels involved, a selection of the equipment used, and portraits of people who were important for

Figure 6.3. *Vasa* in the dock at Beckholmen in 1961. Photo: Swedish National Maritime Museum/SMTM.

the successful outcome, such as *Vasa*'s 'discoverer', Anders Franzén, and the head of the diving team, Per Arvid Fälting.[2]

The afterlife of a shipwreck

The fact that these three events were salvaged wrecks means that the ships have undergone several transmissions from one functional condition to another. To varying degrees, and in assorted ways, they have all in different periods obtained the status of newly built, in traffic, sunken, ongoing salvage project, and either floating or dry-dock objects of display. Two of the vessels (*Södra Sverige* and *Per Brahe*) were reinstated after the they were salvaged. The three operations will first be considered looking at the loss of human life and the time elapsed between the sinkings and their salvage and display.

Each salvage biography has its distinguishing features. They also have things in common. One similarity is a strong element of public display, yet that is pretty much the only quality that unites them all. Two of the ships were salvaged relatively near to the time of their sinking, the third several hundred years later. Two of the shipwrecks ended in the loss of human lives, one of them did not. One event, the sinking of *Södra Sverige*, has left only the sparsest of traces in museum collections and other memory practices. Another, *Per Brahe*, is more richly represented, but over time has become closely associated with a few of those who died. The ship recovered in the third salvage operation, *Vasa*, now has its own museum, an unchallenged position as a valuable cultural heritage object, and profound tourist interest.

The salvage and display of each wreck are thus the two constants of the discussion. In addition, there were significant differences in the severity of the shipwrecks, the extent of subsequent memory work that helps keep the events in mind, and, as outlined here, eventual criticism of the more public features of the salvage operations and their aftermath. The term memory work is used here primarily to point out how the accidents are now represented and exhibited in museums, but there will also be a focus on what the media reporting and other forms of storytelling have favoured, and so preserved as specific versions of events. It is important, though, to once again underline the great divergence between the examples. The Vasa Museum is today Sweden's most visited attraction bar none. From this perspective, the interest in the other two ships seems almost negligible.

This has not always been the case. The salvage of *Per Brahe* was a major public event. Tens of thousands of people followed the process from the nearby harbour at Hästholmen, and for a couple of weeks the media reported on a daily basis, telling their readers about the latest advances or sudden complications.[3] Over the years, a long-lasting bond has been created between Lake Vättern, the steamer *Per Brahe*, and the artist John Bauer, singling out the Bauer family from the rest of their unfortunate companions. Compared to the other vessels, *Södra Sverige* made the smallest mark. After being displayed at the 1897 world fair, the steamer's dramatic fate essentially disappeared from public awareness. Apparently, there was something about the story that effectively blocked a successfully salvaged ship from qualifying as an attractive cultural heritage object. Still in traffic for decades to come, clearly it was not the right stuff for museums and other influential actors in the memory production field. How best to understand the variations in what can be considered the commemorative afterlife of a shipwreck?

Time and tragedy

One lesson that can be learnt from the salvage stories is that at times it could spark widespread criticism to display a salvaged vessel, while at other times it passed off without objection. When, after the costly recovery of *Per Brahe*, the public was given the opportunity to pay to board the steamer, the initiative was thought by several commentators to be highly inappropriate. This was not the proper respect for the dead, they said; it was a disgusting, not to say morbid, spectacle.[4] Still, no such protests were voiced against the public display of *Södra Sverige* or *Vasa*, even though the latter has been a tourist attraction in Stockholm since 1961, the same year as the salvage. Arguably, the lack of criticism was closely knit to the intimate relationship between time and death.

In the case of *Per Brahe*, there were four years between the shipwreck and the public presentation of the salvaged steamer, for *Vasa* it was instead over three centuries. *Södra Sverige* was only two years underwater, but no one was killed when it sank. *Per Brahe* and *Vasa*, though, cost numerous lives. When *Per Brahe* sank 24 people died, and after the sinking of *Vasa* the remains of nearly 20 people have been found, even though the historical sources give the record of approximately 30 lives lost.[5] Within the parameters of time and death, a distinctive pattern took shape: *Per Brahe* was put on display close in time to the fatal accident and the initiative gave rise to strong criticism; *Vasa*, with about the same number of deaths, was shown several hundred years after the sinking, and provoked no criticism; *Södra Sverige*, with no casualties, was on show shortly after the accident, and faced no criticism.

When there was only a short time between wreck and salvage, and when that elapsed time was moreover combined with loss of life, that was when critical voices were most likely to be heard. The compilation of the three examples shows that elapsed time can act as a counterweight, which reverses or dampens the tragic dimension of the accident. *Vasa* avoided the blame noticed in connection with the display of *Per Brahe*. It all came down to how the salvaged and then displayed ship was positioned relative to time past and to the fatal outcome of the shipwreck. The negative reaction that greeted the *Per Brahe* tour, together with the non-existent disapproval at the similar display of the other two salvaged ships, can thus be understood with reference to the conceptual dyad of push and pull.

Borrowing from migration studies, where the concepts are used to explain why individuals, groups, or whole communities choose to move, I however take a more literal approach. Hence, the concepts are utilized to identify a set of factors that act in two opposite directions, with 'push' meaning to repel or to thrust something away and 'pull' to attract or to drag something closer. In such a conceptual frame, the likelihood of incurring criticism for displaying a ship soon after it was shipwrecked with lives lost can be considered a pull factor, while a substantial time between accident and display works in the other direction, and is thus a push factor, as is the absence of deaths.

With time and death considered, we now move on to the circumstances of national pride and royal presence. The public display of the salvaged ships will be related to shipwrecks' ability to tap into a national rhetoric – and to attract royal interest.

National glory and royal presence

The steamer *Södra Sverige* could be salvaged because of the Waller Tube (Fig. 6.4). A Swedish invention, it was a long metal pipe down which a worker could be lowered to a greater depth than was previously possible. In fact, when the steamer was finally raised from a depth of 56 metres, it set a new (unofficial) world record for deep-water salvage, thought all the more notable because it was achieved with a Swedish invention. In fact, it was a record that took the salvaged vessel all the way to a world fair.[6]

The nationalist aspect of the operation was thus a vital part of events. When the newspaper *Dagens Nyheter* told its readers of the moment when the King went aboard the salvaged steamer, the headline exclaimed,

Figure 6.4. The upper part of the Waller Tube with one O. Jensen about to be lowered down the tube to the wreck. Photo: Swedish National Maritime Museum/SMTM.

'Our proudest rescue. *Södra Sverige*'s entry into Stockholm', and the article continued in the same vein:

> A great deed has been done in the realm of ship salvage. The mighty steamer *Södra Sverige*, which has been hidden in the deeps for 20 months, buried in the seabed, has been brought to light and is now afloat as before on the surface. Yesterday it was brought in triumph into Stockholm and is now in our harbour, a silent witness to what inventive genius, drive, and energy together might achieve.[7]

When *Södra Sverige* was given its own place at the exhibition it was purely because of the successful use of the new gear. As the headline 'Our proudest rescue' frankly declared, it was indeed the salvage and the Swedish record that were on show. The steamer itself was mostly a material excuse or necessary prop.

When *Per Brahe* was raised there was no such new Swedish technology to give it a positive spin. Instead, it was down to proven methods, hard work, and heavy machinery. The newspapers reported about the tough working conditions rather than innovative solutions and Swedish engineering skills. The two divers, who worked in shifts on the sunken steamer, were depicted as strong and fearless, and with nerves of steel because they endured working in confined spaces surrounded by dead bodies in various stages of decomposition. In the ensuing tour, however, its salvage played a much more obscure role. There was a small exhibition on board, with a model meant to show how it was salvaged, and it was even possible to see parts from one of the diving suits. But, no doubt, what attracted interest on the tour was the fact it was the real *Per Brahe*, the infamous steamer that sank four years before and no one survived. The fierce drama of the salvage project was by then overshadowed by the authentic tragedy.

Vasa was raised from the water thirty years after *Per Brahe*, in an operation which took place in a fundamentally different media climate. The events in the depths off Hästholmen where *Per Brahe* was salvaged were considered a significant news story, scrupulously reported by the national press. All the same, it was a news event in Sweden and Sweden only. *Vasa*'s news value stretched far beyond the country's borders.

However, the fact that the salvage soon became an international event did not prevent it from having an apparent national aspect. The discovery of the uniquely well-preserved seventeenth-century ship brought twofold glory to the Swedish nation. First, it allowed Sweden to show itself as a powerful 'historical' player on the early modern European stage, and, second, it was an opportunity to demonstrate its 'modern', cutting-edge know-how.[8] The salvage operation was technically and logistically advanced, and when finished was followed by the innovative preservation of the hull to prevent it from drying out and falling apart in the air.[9] This modern expertise meant that *Vasa* (for which read Sweden) was of some interest to the outside world.

What, then, of the royal presence at the three salvage operations? The visit the then Swedish king, Oscar II, paid to *Södra Sverige* when it was on display has already been noted. Besides that one-off occasion, it seems there was no other direct royal participation in the salvage or the wreck's subsequent display. *Vasa*, on the other hand, was closely associated with such a presence from the start. There was a royal continuity which extended all the way from the king who commissioned it, Gustav II Adolf (Gustavus Adolphus), to Gustav VI Adolf, king when the ship was raised, and ultimately to the present king, Carl XVI Gustaf.

Gustav VI Adolf was himself part of the network that contributed to the financing, and marketing, of the Vasa salvage project.[10] Thereafter the royal family was involved in subsequent events, such as the realization of the first museum, Wasavarvet, in 1961. Their commitment might have something to do with Gustav VI Adolf having trained as an archaeologist.[11] Or perhaps this was too ready an explanation. In his account of the preparations for the museum, Henrik Arnstad notes that Gustav VI Adolf seemed more interested in the spectacular salvage operation than with any of the archaeological finds retrieved from the sea bottom.[12]

Regardless of which explanation was the most accurate, one thing is clear: compared to the two other salvage operations the case of *Per Brahe* stood out by not attracting any royal presence. The single instance was of a possible, but unconfirmed, visit by Prince Eugen to Hästholmen during the salvage. Thus the following sequence presents itself. The record-breaking salvage of *Södra Sverige* was carried out with the help of a new Swedish invention, and then King Oscar II toured the steamer at the world fair. The salvage of *Per Brahe* was achieved by relatively simple means, and was written up as man's struggle with the elements. The contemporaneous writing was not noted for its national rhetoric and with one possible exception, no royal presence was noted at any point after the sinking. *Vasa*, a uniquely well-preserved Swedish warship from the seventeenth century, was a technically complex salvage operation, and later the innovative preservation of the hull was also international news. The salvage and even the ship's wider fate elicited a significant royal commitment.

Given this pattern, I would suggest it was thought acceptable to put *Södra Sverige* on public display, and even be visited by the king, because there had been no loss of life when it sank, and its salvage was an example of the successful application of new Swedish technology. Conversely, those responsible for the salvage of *Per Brahe* were criticized for attempting much the same kind of display, because the steamer was still very much associated with the tragedy of the shipwreck. The salvage of *Per Brahe*, like that of *Södra Sverige*, could reasonably be described as a feat, but it lacked a national subtext and was achieved with brute strength and fairly simple techniques. *Per Brahe* also lacked the documented involvement of the royal family. That was not true for the raising of *Vasa*. On the contrary, there was plenty of both national rhetoric and royal commitment. Its sinking in Stockholm harbour entailed considerable loss of life, but by the time it was salvaged over three hundred years had passed.

Now, one might ask if it is possible to find any reasons justifying the royal presence or absence at the salvage operations. To answer that question, I would like to return to the two strands of death and national pride. In terms of royal participation, they can be analysed using the push and pull model. The framing of *Södra Sverige* can be described as a combination of an apparently strong pull factor (the application of new Swedish technology, which was good grounds for national pride) with no corresponding push factor (loss of life); *Per Brahe*'s profile was characterized by the opposite, where circumstances were dictated in a

Figure 6.5. The Vasa Museum's description at DigitaltMuseum of this photo from the raising of *Vasa* states that the group of divers were responsible for the most pressing and complicated part of the salvage, namely making the six tunnels necessary to lift the ship, 'Without a doubt, some of the most advanced diving work ever completed.' Photo: Swedish National Maritime Museum/SMTM.

push-like manner (a large number of recent deaths), but there were no corresponding forces to increase the pull of the salvage operation (no new Swedish technology, no real scope for national rhetoric). *Vasa*, meanwhile, was subject to several strong pull factors. A uniquely well-preserved ship from the Swedish Empire, when Swedish power was at its zenith, partnered with modern Swedish engineering expertise and innovative preservation methods: these were good conditions for national rhetoric. At the same time many deaths long preceded the raising of *Vasa*, which, considering the setting, gave it a low push effect.

Nevertheless, it is important to keep in mind that this reasoning concerns tragic accidents without clear elements of heroism. When such circumstances as heroism are part of the events, other rationales arise. This was often the case with military losses in both wartime and peace, when the aftermath was directed towards the idealized sacrifice of one's life for the nation, and other extreme or heroic situations.[13] Military sacrifice had a strong impact on what was considered an appropriate way of displaying the dead, and the settings and items used to call to mind the fatal incident.[14]

The personal engagement of the royals, and in wider terms the overall royal presence in the salvage projects, was predicated on minimizing royal contact with things or events that could attract criticism, while maximizing the connection between the royal family and the successful nation.[15] This meant that royal appearances at the salvage operations were dictated by a desire to take part in the national values found in, for example, a successful innovation, offset by their wariness of being associated with disrespect to the dead and other vulgarities.

From wreck to state of the art

When you look at the public afterlife of the three wrecks, they have to varying degrees become part of Sweden's history and cultural heritage. The successful salvage of *Södra Sverige* was something of a sensation, which explains why it could qualify as a visitor attraction at the world fair in 1897. The immediate interest in the steamer, however, was not a currency that could be exchanged for extended status as a cultural heritage object. In other words, the event was not memorable enough to be included in the historical narratives that inevitably would be preserved for future generations.

With *Per Brahe*, things were different. Both the severity of the accident and the later tour with the salvaged vessel contributed to give the steamer a stronger grip on collective memory in Sweden. The process was fuelled by the crowds who went to Hästholmen to see the salvage operation. But more than anything else, it was the death of the Bauer family that made the shipwreck memorable in the longer term.

In biographical accounts in encyclopaedias and art history books the story is told of the fateful journey when John Bauer, his wife, the artist

Esther Ellqvist, and 3-year-old son Bengt, known as Putte, tragically lost their lives in the waves. This scholarly approach is paralleled in a more vernacular public form when Swedish newspapers regularly mark the anniversary of the accident – effective reminders of the incident as well as the deaths, often giving clear priority to the celebrity family. Several books have been written about the sinking and its aftermath, and it has been commented on in the performing arts and poetry. Lake Vättern, the steamer *Per Brahe*, and the artist John Bauer have over time been spun together into an intrareferential memory, where the mention of one element immediately recalls the others.[16]

No doubt, *Vasa* is the salvage project that has become part of Sweden's cultural heritage most profoundly. There are too many reasons to go into here, so to pick one crucial factor there was the strongly national character of the salvage operation. Of course, one should not underestimate the strength of a good story or eloquent personal portraits. This was definitely the case with the ship's rediscoverer, Anders Franzén, and the head diver, Per Edvin Fälting. They were both well suited to fit in with the media quest for strong personalities and exciting narratives.

In an astonishing way, *Vasa* has gone from being an almost epic military failure to much later gaining new life as a highly sought-after cultural heritage object. From that perspective, the salvage seems a welcome opportunity to put things right. The ill-fated maiden voyage was ultimately converted into an outstanding national success. Or as the marketing department at the Vasa Museum often summarizes it, 'From wreck to state of the art'.

The sinking or the salvage?

As regards the continuing memory work, there is a tension between what has attracted the greatest media attention in the long run and the interest at the time of the event. Put at its simplest, was it the sinking or the salvage that mattered most? *Södra Sverige*'s presence at the world fair can be perceived as a way of exhibiting the salvage rather than the recovered ship. In one respect that claim is a simplification, though: at the end of the nineteenth century, the salvage of ship at 56 metres depth was a high-risk project. When the steamer was put on display its tarnished exterior therefore visually reinforced the sense of great depth, and, accordingly, the technical achievements of the salvage operation.

Turning to *Per Brahe*, things were more complicated. The shipwreck itself, shortly after the end of the First World War and in the midst of the Spanish flu pandemic, was immediately front-page news. But soon the newspapers' interest shifted to the official inquiry, appointed to establish who was responsible. The key issue was to determine whether the shipping company's routines were behind the overloading of the steamer, which seemed to have contributed to the wreck. The accident itself and its over twenty deaths soon disappeared from news reports, however. When looking back at the press coverage, it was the salvage, carried out four years after the accident, that created the greatest interest. The media were fascinated by both the crowds that descended on Hästholmen to watch and the uncertain struggle to salvage the steamer out in the lake. The operation was portrayed as a sporting achievement, and the focus was directed at the salvage operation's ability to overcome a seemingly overwhelming opponent with simple means and determination. This was an account of an epical relation between man and nature, and likewise a media narrative with strong references to gendered issues involving men and masculinity.

However, as the memorial work of the event progressed in subsequent decades, *Per Brahe*'s sinking was eventually reduced to the death of the artist John Bauer. Over time, the salvage operation, once the primary focus, lost its defining ability. Now when the *Per Brahe* accident is written about it is usually the fatal shipwreck, not the later salvage. Aside from that, there are those commentators who continue to point out that putting the recovered steamer on show was a somewhat macabre and inappropriate business – in many respects similar to some of the press reactions of the time, when the worn exterior of the ship was understood as an expression of the tragic nature of the event. The same kind of evident damage which in the case of *Södra Sverige* put a national gloss on the salvage project, was for *Per Brahe* an ominous sign of anguished death.

The association with death which was considered a real problem (a push factor) for the public display of *Per Brahe* during the tour in 1922 thus proved to be an asset (a pull factor) in the continued memory work surrounding the shipwreck. It was because of the loss of life in Lake Vättern that the shipwreck had a mark to make in the memory work of the media and in other memory practices. What has happened since, however, is that both deaths and memories have narrowed down over time, reduced to just the artist John Bauer and his family. In other words, the same death that was an obstacle to the salvaged steamer first being put on public show has become the circumstance that continually keeps the memory of the accident alive in a variety of contexts.

The steamer *Södra Sverige* was the reverse. Here, the absence of death meant that the recovered vessel could be displayed at a world fair and visited by King Oscar II. Ironically, with no loss of life and no prominent death such as the artist John Bauer, it is no surprise that *Södra Sverige* has no place in collective memory. Not everything can be put down to everyone surviving the shipwreck, however. The cancelled memory work also includes the information that the Waller Tube never became the epoch-making Swedish invention that many expected after the successful salvage. With hindsight, it is plain that the salvage of *Södra Sverige* was the one and only occasion when the pipe was put into service.

With *Vasa* things are again somewhat different, as the wreck and salvage are so separated in time. One might even claim that what makes *Vasa* famous today is not the actual sinking, but that the richly decorated ship three hundred years later was successfully lifted from the bottom and raised intact to the surface. It is the salvage project, with the subsequent preservation of the wooden structure, that has attracted the attention of the outside world. *Vasa*'s widely acknowledged fame today rests heavily on the fact that she was salvaged and, even more, made available for visitors.[17] It is also true that its fame has been propelled by its royal associations, just as royalty has benefited from the national pride that could be extracted from the salvage operation. The ongoing musealization of *Vasa* has much in common with another high-profile national event, the annual Swedish Nobel banquet. At this exclusive

Figure 6.6. State visit by members of the British and Swedish royal families to the old museum, Wasavarvet, in 1983. Photo: Gunnel Ilonen, Swedish National Maritime Museum/SMTM.

occasion too one can spot a great deal of performative royalty, both in the extensive media coverage and at the banqueting tables.[18]

In short, *Vasa* is associated with a striking royal continuity (Fig. 6.6).[19] However, it is important to stress the double-sided character of that observation. Gustav II Adolf's role in commissioning the ship and Gustav VI Adolf's personal importance for the salvage project have already been commented on. The relationship between *Vasa* and the royal family has continued since. At the burial of some of the human remains from *Vasa* in 1963, the king's brother, the author Prince Wilhelm, read one of his own poems, which was also inscribed on the gravestone. Another example was the two commemorative coins produced for the opening of the current Vasa Museum in 1990. Both the 1000 kronor gold coin and 200 kronor silver coin were minted with the portrait of Carl XVI Gustaf, the present King of Sweden, who inaugurated the museum.

Figure 6.7. State visit from Luxemburg on board *Vasa* in 2008. Just like the royal ship itself, the Swedish King and Queen are part of the occasion. Photo: Maria Ljunggren, Swedish National Maritime Museum/SMTM.

As pointed out in the literature, the entrepreneurs behind the *Vasa* salvage project and afterwards the two museums where the ship was on display had much to gain from such royal connections (Fig. 6.7). Like Arnstad, one could therefore speak of a distinct royal capital, akin to Bourdieu's widely accepted concept of social capital.[20] Yet if entrepreneurs and museums had strategic reason to form alliances with the monarch and his entourage, so royalty had reason to interact with the *Vasa*. It certainly bears out what the historian Peter Burke has said: that for the king to be the king, royalty needs repeatedly performed acts of recognition.[21] Such acts may take the form of ceremonies, such as coronations, but can also have the materiality of things.

I have outlined how that might well include new technology, such as salvage equipment and methods, not to mention successfully salvaged wrecks. Still, it is not enough. To maintain, even enrich, the royal aura, there must also be an element of national glory involved. Therefore, both the event and its materiality have to be imbued with national meaning: a Swedish innovation, and a uniquely well-preserved Swedish warship. The argument is also valid the other way around, meaning that the royals have good reason to avoid participating in events and material settings that might be considered inappropriate to their royal status. As we have seen, salvage projects and wrecks put on public display have the ability to function in both ways.

A DC-3 in the Air Force Museum

Finally, there is a fourth and rather different example of a salvage operation and its subsequent memory work. This time, however, the recovered vessel was a plane and not a ship, namely a DC-3 military aircraft that disappeared, with its entire crew of eight men, when on a routine mission over the Baltic Sea in the summer of 1952. Their assignment was highly classified as the plane carried sophisticated intelligence-gathering equipment. It was not until 2003 that the fuselage was located on the seabed, some ten nautical miles east of Gotska Sandön. The following year much of the plane was salvaged, and since 2010 it has been the central object in the permanent exhibition at the Air Force Museum, just outside Linköping (Fig. 6.8).

This is how the museum presents the plane online:

> The crown jewel in the Swedish Air Force Museum's collections is the Swedish DC-3 that was shot down by a Soviet fighter aircraft over the Baltic Sea in 1952. After more than fifty years of speculation, the wreck was found at the bottom of the sea, salvaged and laid to rest in the museum. The exhibition *Acts of Secrecy – The DC-3 that Disappeared* is a story full of mystery.[22]

Key parts of the exhibition are thus occupied with an attempt to document and confirm the course of events when the aircraft was shot down, based on extensive damage to the fuselage. Above all, though, the visitor is presented with an elaborate Cold War narrative focusing on how the Swedish state and its agencies had to withhold the political and military background to the shooting – secrets kept for over half a century.

Figure 6.8. The salvaged airplane is exhibited in a huge showcase, where the dim blue light adds to the sense of being underwater. Photo: Stefan Kalm, Swedish Air Force Museum.

The real point of the exhibition is therefore to describe how several senior military and political officials in more than one government have withheld information that could have clarified both the nature of the plane's mission and why it might have provoked a hostile response from the Soviets. In other words, the Swedish state had actually known, but preferred to remain silent, despite the suffering this caused the families of the missing crew members.

From this it follows that even if the salvaged aircraft is the obvious centre of the exhibition, and the museum's 'crown jewel', it is the secrecy, all the shady goings-on, that give it its ethical nerve. Critic and journalist Dan Jönsson pinpointed it in a review:

That's what a monument to a public lie might look like. The story of Swedish double-dealing and the tragedies it gave rise to are objectively told just as it is: a key to understanding Swedish post-war history. A visit here should be a compulsory part of public education.[23]

Unlike the record-breaking salvage of *Södra Sverige* with the innovative Swedish Waller Tube, or the highly impressive engineering work behind first the salvage and later the preservation of *Vasa*, there are no such elements of national pride to be found in this case. On the contrary, it was years of secrecy about the shooting, and its causes and strategic aftermath, that was brought to the surface just as much as the wrecked aircraft itself. As memory work, the exhibited DC-3 can hardly be said to glorify the Swedish nation. Rather, the museum explicitly wants to highlight that the authorities and the military, in the face of the Cold War and for political reasons, scrupulously avoided doing what is solemnly presented as 'the right thing'. It is not so very different, one may add, from how the Vasa Museum has turned a disaster into a vibrant heritage object and tourist destination.

The importance of things

The lost, rescued, and publicly displayed DC-3 illustrates a relationship easy to overlook, namely that the wrecks have left clear material traces in collections and museums that also remain in the collective memory. Here, we need do no more than think of famous ships as *Titanic*, *Vasa*, and *Mary Rose*. They are all well known to the world as iconic maritime accidents – and to a certain degree they all defend their place in the collective memory because they can be visited in exhibitions and museums. For the same reason, the presumably shameful history of the long-lost DC-3 was only given its own museum exhibition until after the plane was salvaged and acquired by the museum. Subsequently, it was when the materiality of the tragedy was in place that the memorial work could begin at the Swedish Air Force Museum on a public scale.

The archaeologist Mirja Arnshav has suggested that objects often do function as prerequisites for memories.[24] Her wording points to how objects facilitate the process that sees a past event transform into a memory, which can be both personal and upheld by institutions such as museums.[25] Of course, it is also possible to remember events not preserved in objects, but it is not as easy.[26] Things are, as Arnshav also stresses, simply very good at anchoring both stories and remembrances.[27] Their materiality, the preserved and stored traces of events, can thus contribute to an understanding of why some accidents and salvage operations are better remembered than others. Objects have an ability to speak to us through their own materiality.[28] The anthropologist Claude Lévi-Strauss once famously remarked that animals 'are good to think with'.[29] Objects, in much the same way, are good to remember with. Their sheer presence in the physical world keeps our dearest, or most frightening, memories from vanishing.

However, as this brief inventory has shown, some of Sweden's salvage projects have not only been remembered, but also for a varying amount of time celebrated, with the help of objects alone. It is equally clear that no maritime accident or salvage operation will automatically be memorable, however many material objects survive to back it up. By highlighting the commemorative work associated with three shipwrecks and their salvage, this essay therefore has another theme. How is it that the results of some once famous salvage operations are regarded as so memorable they end up in museums, or in other ways are strongly preserved in collective memory, while others slip away without leaving much trace? There remains much to be said on the topic, but with this initial offering of four examples I hope to have fuelled the discussion.

Some concluding remarks. Certain wrecks that have been salvaged, such as *Vasa* and the long-lost military DC-3 aircraft, are considered unambiguous cultural heritage and accordingly have a self-evident place in a museum. Other similar events live on outside heritage institutions. Every year, on the anniversary of the accident, the steamer *Per Brahe* sinks to the bottom off Hästholmen along with its human cargo: in brief reports in the local and national press the memory of the deaths of the Bauer family is thus kept alive; the tragedy on Lake Vättern is continually repeated in biographies, encyclopaedias, literature, and drama. It is a striking difference, remembering that some other once well-known shipwrecks have almost disappeared from collective memory. Today there are few anchoring points left for those who want to remember the salvage of the steamer *Södra Sverige*.

Perhaps it is also a question of how both wreck and salvage, in order to register in the collective memory, must have some leeway to attach themselves to culturally established forms of meaning, reaching far beyond the arena of the usual heritage institutions. It would seem so, given the observation that there are few accidents at sea with such affectivity and materiality that they are capable of occupying the entire spectrum of the memory-bonding processes for any length of time. As in the countless exhibitions, features, books, and films in which the passenger liner *Titanic* continues its fateful maiden voyage.

Notes

1 See 'Wallerska tuben', digitaltmuseum.se/.

2 Franzén's discovery of the wreck in 1956 was rather a rediscovery. *Vasa*'s position had in fact been known for several hundred years, see Carl Olof Cederlund, 'Ett oskrivet kapitel i Vasas historia', *Forum Navale* 68 (2012), 9–63; Niklas Eriksson, *Riksäpplet: Arkeologiska perspektiv på ett bortglömt regalskepp* (Lund 2017); Georg Hafström, 'Äldre tiders bärgningsarbeten vid vraket av skeppet Wasa', *Tidskrift i Sjöväsendet* 121 (1958), 771–844.

3 Sven Jerring, *Ångfartyget Per Brahes undergång och bärgning: Tillägnad de män, vilkas sega energi efter fyra år förde olycksskeppet i hamn* (Linköping 1976, first pub. 1922); Claes-Göran Wetterholm, *Skrufångaren Per Brahe* (Skärhamn 1989).

4 See Wetterholm 1989, 105–112.

5 Ebba During, *De dog på Vasa: Skelettfynden och vad de berättar* (Stockholm 1994).

6 Claes-Göran Wetterholm, *Vrak i svenska vatten* (Stockholm 1994), 81–93.

7 *Dagens Nyheter* (*DN*) 4 June 1897: 'Vår stoltaste bärgningsbragd. Södra Sveriges infärd till Stockholm'; 'Ett stordåd har utförts på fartygsbergningens område. Den stora ångaren Södra Sverige som i 20 månader legat dold i djupet, nedgräfd i havsbottnen, har bragts upp i dagen och flyter nu som förr på vattenytan. Den fördes i går i triumf in till Stockholm och ligger nu i vår hamn, ett stumt vittne till hvad uppfinnarsnille ihärdigt arbete och drifvande energi samfällt förmå'.

8 See Klas Helmerson, *Att fånga tillfället: Hur ett fiaskobetonat ettföremålsmuseum blev världsberömt* (Stockholm 2013); see also Henrik Arnstad, *Varför bärgades skeppet Vasa? Studie angående nätverk och historiekonstruktion under slutet av 1950-talet* (BA diss., Dept. of History, Stockholm University 2009).

9 Anders Wahlgren, *Vasa 1628: Människorna, skeppet, tiden* (Stockholm 2011), 174–8.

10 See Arnstad 2009; Henrik Arnstad, 'Royalismen lyfte "Vasa"', *DN* 23 Apr. 2010.

11 See Helmerson 2013, 36.

12 Arnstad 2009. Nonetheless, there is no doubt that Gustav VI later took a great interest in the excavation and was a frequent visitor to the Vasa Museum (see Helmerson 2013, 36–8).

13 Cecilia Åse & Maria Wendt (eds.), *Gendering Military Sacrifice: A Feminist Comparative Analysis* (London 2019).

14 Mirja Arnshav, 'Risker och olyckor: Minnen av Ulven', in Andreas Linderoth (ed.), *Det dolda hotet: 12 forskare om ubåtar* (Karlskrona 2014), 11–29. Another relevant focus too lengthy to squeeze into the discussion is how collective memories and public displays of wrecks and rescues are connected to other kinds of historical exposés. For such an analysis, figuring once well-known disasters and heroic initiatives, see, for example, Anders Ekström, 'Exhibiting Disasters: Mediation, Historicity and Spectatorship', *Media, Culture & Society* 34 (2012), 472–87; see Mirja Arnshav, 'Fröken Allards förmenta skor: Marina katastrofer och arkeologiska berättelser', *Marinarkeologisk Tidskrift* 35/4 (2012), 4–10.

15 See Mattias Frihammar, *Ur svenska hjärtans djup: Reproduktion av samtida monarki* (PhD thesis, Stockholm 2010).

16 See Maria Bäckman, 'The Contract-labour Photographs of Gunnar Lundh: A Media History Study of a Photo Archive in Motion', *Culture Unbound* 12/1 (2020), 36–64.

17 At the same time, of course, sinking is the prerequisite of salvage, and even a museum. The shipwreck itself is, therefore, an important feature of the museum that holds *Vasa*, where texts, models, and films attach great importance to explaining both the actual events of the tragedy and the historical background to why *Vasa* was so unstable.

18 See Simon Ekström, *Humrarna och evigheten: Kulturhistoriska essäer om konsumtion, begär och död* (Gothenburg 2017).

19 This prolonged royal presence in relation to *Vasa* as a ship, rescue project, and museum is also recognised by Helmerson 2013, 36–8.

20 Arnstad 2009; See also Pierre Bourdieu, *Homo Academicus* (Cambridge 1988).

21 Peter Burke, *The Fabrication of Louis XIV* (New Haven 1992); See also Cecilia Åse, *Monarkins makt: Nationell gemenskap i svensk demokrati* (Stockholm 2009); Frihammar 2010.

22 https://www.flygvapenmuseum.se/languages/engelska/.

23 Dan Jönsson, 'Svenska lekar, lögner och luftfärder', *Utställningsestetiskt forum* (2010), https://utstallningskritik.se/2010-5/svenska-lekar-logner-och-luftfarder/: 'Så kan ett monument över en offentlig lögn se ut. Historien om det svenska dubbelspelet och de tragedier som det gav upphov till berättas sakligt, just som det den är: en nyckel till förståelsen av den svenska efterkrigshistorien. Ett besök här borde vara en obligatorisk del av allmänbildningen'.

24 Mirja Arnshav, *De små båtarna och den stora flykten: Arkeologi i spåren av andra världskrigets baltiska flyktbåtar* (PhD thesis, Lund 2020).

25 On a personal level, an obvious example of how objects have the capacity to support memories is souvenirs. For the museum as a locus of materiality, see Barbara Kirshenblatt-Gimblett, *Destination Culture: Tourism, Museums, and Heritage* (Berkeley 1998); Camilla Mordhorst, *Genstandsfortællinger: Fra Museum Wormianum til de moderne museer* (Copenhagen 2009); Sandra Dudley (ed.), *Museum Materialities: Objects, Engagements, Interpretations* (London 2010); Anna Maria Forssberg & Karin Sennefelt (eds.), *Fråga föremålen: Handbok till historiska studier av materiell kultur* (Lund 2014).

26 As is the case in oral cultures used to relying on songs and other verbal narratives to communicate memories between generations.

27 See also Katarina Ek-Nilsson & Birgitta Meurling (eds.), *Talande ting: Berättelser och materialitet* (Uppsala 2014).

28 Hans Ulrich Gumbrecht, *Production of Presence: What Meaning Cannot Convey* (Stanford 2004); Margrit Wettstein, *Liv genom tingen: Människor, föremål och extrema situationer* (Eslöv 2009). To be more specific, I do not mean that objects have either meanings or cultural values in themselves, but rather that they are imbued with meaning, and it is people or museums (curators and such) who are doing the ascribing. In that sense an object's meaning is really 'in the eye of the beholder', as said in a very different context by the anthropologist Mary Douglas, *Purity and Danger: An Analysis of Concepts of Pollution and Taboo* (London 1966): once given and explained, the object has the capacity to evoke that particular meaning.

29 Claude Lévi-Strauss, *Totemism* (London 1964).

CHAPTER 7

Swedish naval officers and the nation

The discourse of national identity in the magazine *Vår Flotta*, 1905–1920

Andreas Linderoth

National identities can be analysed as discursive constructions. Many versions, or discourses, of a certain national identity exist simultaneously and compete for influence. One discourse where the sea was given profound importance was the one constructed in *Vår Flotta*, a naval monthly in the early twentieth century.

National sentiment continues to keep its grip on people's hearts and minds. Even though tendencies in the late twentieth and the early twenty-first centuries seemed to indicate that national identities might be on their way to losing some of their meaning for individuals, events in the last ten to fifteen years have shown that nations and national identities are still important. Strong nationalist sentiment was very obvious in the European migrant crisis in 2015 and the COVID-19 pandemic. Nations have focused on their own perceived needs rather than cooperation with other nations. National identities – their creation, their effects, how they develop – are therefore still important phenomena and essential to be understood. Studies of national identity usually start from the assumption there are many versions, or discourses, of national identity in a society. The discourses compete for influence and one of them is normally dominant. Here we are interested in a discourse of Swedish national identity, one set in a maritime context. Through an analysis of the monthly magazine *Vår Flotta: Tidskrift för Sjövapnet* ('Our Fleet: Magazine for the Navy') in the period 1905–1920, the role played by the sea and other maritime components in the national identity constructed in the magazine is discussed. How did maritime factors come into play in the magazine's reporting on Sweden, Swedes, and how Swedes ought to be? How did the discourse of Swedish national identity in *Vår Flotta* relate to the dominant discourse of Swedish national identity?

National identities are a common object of research in the social sciences and humanities. There are a plethora of theories and perspectives focused on national identity, an identity which is seen as more pressing than all others. But national identity as a concept is often vague. As the historian Peter Mandler has stated, '"identity" has an important but elusive quality, and "national identity" even more so'.[1] National identities are often regarded as neither fixed nor stable. They can change. As the media scientist Sanna Inthorn states in *German media and national identity:* 'Nation and national identity are constructs, built from a selective choice of defining elements. This choice may vary, depending on who tells the story of the nation.'[2] A national identity is open to be contested and reinterpreted, and hence there are many versions, or discourses, of national identity in a society, all competing for influence. Normally one of them is dominant.[3] Previous research has often stressed the importance of the mass media for the creation of national identities. The historian Benedict Anderson, in his influential work on nations as imagined communities, strongly emphasizes the importance of newspapers for the creation of imagined communities in the nineteenth century.[4] Many researchers interested in national identities have since analysed newspapers, journals, television, radio, and the internet to get a better grasp of the phenomenon. The mass media are seen as promising objects of analysis, because their reporting contributes to their readers', viewers' or listeners' construction of what it means to be part of the nation and to embrace a certain national identity.

Even though national identities have attracted a great deal of attention from historians and social scientists, research on how they relate to the maritime sphere and the way maritime phenomena might have influenced national identities is rare. That is certainly the case for Sweden and the other Nordic countries. Research on the UK has, however, shown that maritime phenomena have been important in developing the British national identity, underlining the importance of giving greater attention to the maritime dimension and how it affected the shaping of identities, especially national identities.[5] The fact that the UK is an island nation where the sea has been of paramount importance for the existence of the state and the livelihood of many of its inhabitants does perhaps make it less than representative, but research has shown that the sea has affected national identities in other countries, at least in certain periods. One example is Germany in the early twentieth century, when the sea and Germany's role on the oceans were important for the construction of German national identity.[6] It is useful, then, to analyse in what ways the sea and maritime matters have affected national identities in other countries, and Sweden is a rewarding case to study. It is a nation where the maritime sphere can have been important for the formation of national identity. It has a long coastline and the sea has historically had great importance as a means of transport between different parts of the country. From the perspective of national security, a military invasion from the sea has been regarded a threat since at least the sixteenth century, at the time when the full apparatus of state was first established. Today, most of the Swedish population live in cities and villages along the coast, and therefore come into contact, albeit indirectly, with the sea and maritime matters more or less daily. Research on the discourses of Sweden's maritime national identity or how maritime matters may have influenced the Swedish national identity is extremely limited, however.[7] This essay contributes to changing that by studying one specific maritime discourse of national identity: the one found in the magazine *Vår Flotta*.

Vår Flotta was published by Sveriges Flotta, Förening för sjövärn och sjöfart (Sweden's navy, Society for Naval Defence and Shipping). The purpose of the society was to inform and influence public opinion on naval and maritime matters: it wanted to convince the general public of the importance of the sea and shipping for Sweden, and show the

Figure 7.1. Erik Hägg (left) started *Vår Flotta* in 1905 and was its editor until 1919. When the picture was taken in 1936 Hägg was director-general of a Swedish governmental agency in charge of lighthouses and maritime pilots. Photo: Statens Maritima och Transporthistoriska Museer.

importance of a strong Swedish naval defence.[8] As would seem natural considering the aim of the society, many of its most influential members were naval officers. The national identity expressed in the magazine therefore ought not only to have been influenced by maritime traditions and maritime matters, but especially by naval matters and traditions. *Vår Flotta* was a monthly magazine that mainly printed articles about the Swedish navy, Swedish shipping and shipbuilding, Swedish security policy, and Swedish history. But it also carried fictional naval stories, debate articles, letters from its readers, and sometimes poems. The reach of the magazine was limited – the society had between 5,000 and 8,000 members and its usual print run was 9,000 copies (Fig. 7.1).[9]

The Swedish national identity constructed in *Vår Flotta* was possibly not the dominant Swedish national identity in the early twentieth century, but it is still worth studying as it can give us a more nuanced view of Swedish society and national sentiment in the early twentieth century – and the various discourses of national identity. It can also be seen as a contribution to Swedish naval history by giving us a glimpse of a national identity that was relevant to many naval officers. And naval matters could be of interest to a much greater part of the Swedish population than those who normally read or were otherwise reached by *Vår Flotta*'s message. As we will see, that much was shown by Pansarbåtsinsamlingen, a hugely successful public campaign to raise money to equip the Swedish navy with new ships in 1912.

Political upheaval, 1905–1920

The early twentieth century in Sweden was characterized by an intense political struggle between conservative and more radical forces regarding the direction of Swedish democracy. The Swedish nation and what constituted it were key questions, and all political forces positioned themselves in relation to the nation.[10] The period saw a surge in naval rearmament in Europe, and military questions were debated not only in Sweden but in many European countries. In these debates different views on the nation were expressed and contested, and even though they were mainly matters of interest for politicians and military men, there were times when the Swedish navy and how it was to be equipped engaged large parts of the Swedish population. This was especially the case in 1912 when the liberal government had cut the budget of the Swedish armed forces to be able to finance social reforms. The strength of feeling was such that a campaign, Pansarbåtsinsamlingen, was started to raise money from companies and private citizens to build a coastal defence ship. Such a ship was seen as a much-needed addition to the Swedish navy. The campaign, however, was not only about raising money, but plainly objected to the liberal and social-democratic forces that in the preceding 10–15 years had become more and more influential in Sweden. The coastal defence ship, the *F-båten*, became something of a symbol for all concerned. For the conservatives, it represented Swedish national ideals. Liberals and social democrats saw it as a symbol of the groups who were against democracy, parliamentarianism, and social reforms. But for most people who donated money, and there were a great many of them as the campaign was a stunning success, their contributions were probably rather an expression of their worry about the fate of Sweden in a future war.[11]

Sweden, a nation under threat

The most important international events in the years 1905–1920 – the start of the First World War in 1914 and its end in 1918 – had strong repercussions on Swedish society even though Sweden was not one of the warring parties. But neither the tense situation leading up to the war, nor its start, nor its end, seem to have affected *Vår Flotta* and its views of Sweden and the international situation to much extent. *Vår Flotta* took a very consistent position on Sweden and its position in the international political system. The magazine described the world as a hostile environment where peoples and states fought for power and the stronger powers tried to gain the upper hand, to the disadvantage of the weaker powers. So it had been historically and so it was then. Even if Swedish relations with other nations were peaceful at that stage, the magazine was certain there were no guarantees the situation would remain that way.[12] Sweden was seen as being threatened by stronger states, surrounded by large, 'utterly armed and militarily prepared nations'.[13] It was said some countries would not hesitate to invade others when their own resources were not seen as satisfactory any more – or when they just want to grow bigger and more powerful or gain international prestige. Therefore, it was concluded, if smaller nations were to stand any chance of avoiding falling prey to stronger, more powerful states, they needed a military defence strong enough to command the respect of the power-hungry. According to *Vår Flotta*, one lesson from history was that a people had to be prepared to bear the heavy burden of military defence on their own, and not rely on help from other states. If they did not make the necessary sacrifices for their country's military upkeep, they would perish.[14] The smaller states therefore had to prepare for war to keep the peace.[15] One writer summed up the position of *Vår Flotta* vividly: 'Left to himself, with a free hand in dealing with the honourable victim, the stronger party knows no other policy than this: he takes! But he does not 'take' where he knows he is certain to have his fingers chopped off.'[16]

The starting point for *Vår Flotta*'s description of Sweden and its international position was the country's geographical position. According to *Vår Flotta*, Sweden should use the potential of its geographical position, and above all the fact it bordered onto the Baltic and the North Sea. *Vår Flotta* emphasized that the sea with its unlimited potential for transports played a crucial role in the economic life of nations. But it also had an inherent risk: a power that could control the sea had also almost 'unlimited opportunity to force other peoples dependent on the sea to conform to its will.'[17] Sweden therefore needed resolute protection against threats emanating from the sea, and the answer was a strong navy. Only then, according to *Vår Flotta*, could it take advantage of its geographical position and avoid being forced to take measures that went against its will and interests. The magazine said that the greatest threat to Sweden was being occupied by a foreign nation or by other military means, for example by a blockade of its ports, being forced to concede to a foreign nation against its best interest.[18] The threat against Sweden seemed imminent. Sweden, *Vår Flotta* warned continually, needed to insure itself against foreign threats by strengthening its military defences, especially the navy. And for that the Swedish populace had to be made to understand that a strong navy was necessary to prevent a war. Even if a strong Swedish navy could not deter an attack, it would be essential in hindering the aggressor from setting foot on Swedish soil.[19] Such a navy, the magazine stated, would be no problem for Sweden to finance. It was indeed emphasized that *'the strength of the navy is* the best gauge of the strength of the *kingdom'*.[20] A strong navy would signal to a hostile world that Sweden was a strong and successful nation and that it would be no easy prey for foreign powers.

Vår Flotta described the threat against Sweden as having grown because it had enjoyed healthy economic progress for almost a century, thanks to the Swedes on their own using their own domestic resources. Economic development was obviously a good thing, but according to *Vår Flotta* it could lead rapacious states to take a keen interest in Sweden. With its rich natural resources and now blossoming industry it would be so much bigger a prize than before. The magazine described the severe consequences for Swedes if its military defence were neglected:

> No one, not least a small nation, can always be certain of having a future. And a people who, so to speak, lose themselves will at the earliest convenience of course be *taken* by a mightier power, be united with it, and in time have to conform to all its rules and regulations, its traditions, language, religion, and laws. It can very easily lose it *all* – territory, independence, and freedom. Poland is an instructive example. For the people of such a – one might say lost – country would remain only remorse, self-reproach and despair. The parts of its language that remained would in every word whisper, I dare not say what; the historical memories would soon fall into oblivion and rather be forgotten, as every memory would be a reproach; its history would be forever ended as it belonged to another people, its name would only be the name of a province; its very character would disappear and with time be transformed, after [the example] of its new masters.[21]

But which states were threatening Sweden? Interestingly, considering Russia since at least the eighteenth century had been regarded the greatest threat to Sweden, the magazine rarely reported on it as the main potential enemy. Rather, *Vår Flotta* described all the great powers of Europe – Germany, Russia, and the UK – as equally threatening, excepting France which had no particular interest in the Baltic.[22] In the fiction it published about naval attacks on Sweden, in historical articles and in a few debate articles there was an obvious tendency to describe Russia as an aggressive power, however.[23] Yet the magazine's overall message was that Sweden found itself in a generally hostile and threatening environment, and the threat came from all sides.

Merchant shipping and shipbuilding

Vår Flotta reported not only on military matters and the international political situation, it published reports on merchant shipping and ship-building, all of which is worth analysing for a better understanding of how the Swedish national identity was constructed in the magazine. *Vår Flotta* stressed the importance of a strong economy for the development of the Swedish nation. Without it, Swedish society could not flourish and foreign influence be held back. The importance of the sea for the Swedish economy was emphasized. It was argued that Sweden needed to take advantage of its geographical position and long coastline, and to have extensive trading routes overseas (above all the shipping routes to central Europe) in order to be independent of foreign powers.[24] Shipping was said to make a key contribution to Swedish independence from foreign powers, as much of its trade went by sea. From time to time different numbers were quoted in *Vår Flotta* for how much Swedish trade passed through its ports: it varied from 75 to 98 per cent of all Swedish trade. But in any case it was remarkably large. For *Vår Flotta*, keeping sea routes open was a priority. It was regarded a vital prerequisite for Sweden's continued existence. Civilian shipping was compared to human lungs: 'Our coasts and our harbours are the lungs through which we breathe. A state stopped from seaborne trade has no future.'[25] *Vår Flotta* also argued that Swedish goods should be sent only on Swedish ships. Only then could Sweden be truly independent, free of the oversight of any other country. Also, ships transporting Swedish goods should be built in Sweden. In this case *Vår Flotta* looked to both the UK and Germany for inspiration, where, it said, the shipping companies' collaborations with shipbuilders were the reason for those countries' sea power. It was therefore necessary for Sweden to create similar collaborations to develop both sectors for the greater good of Sweden. But there was a problem. Even though, according to *Vår Flotta*, shipbuilding was a natural thing for a country surrounded by water, Swedish shipbuilding in the early twentieth century had lost ground to its neighbours Norway and Denmark. Once again the magazine pointed to the importance of the navy. If the navy were strengthened in the way it so strongly argued for, the new ships should be built in Swedish yards. That would improve the skills of the workforce in the shipyards and be advantageous for the civilian shipping companies, which could then order high-quality ships domestically rather than abroad.[26]

The reporting on merchant shipping in *Vår Flotta* underlined not only its importance for Sweden on its own merits, it was also a way of emphasizing the importance of the navy: shipping had to be protected by a strong navy, and only a strong navy could guarantee shipping routes remained safe for Swedish trade.[27] The magazine tried to demonstrate the consequences if Swedish trade were stopped or obstructed. What would happen if a hostile power cut Sweden's overseas connections with other states? The effects would, according to *Vår Flotta*, be devastating. Vast numbers of people would lose their jobs and 'the quays would be deserted and quiet, all dockyards that build, equip or repair ships would have to close. The workers in the ports would cry out for bread and the dockyard workers search in vain for new employment elsewhere. Wherever one went there would be only misery.'[28]

As in *Vår Flotta*'s reporting on Sweden's international position, there was little change in its reporting on Swedish shipping. Its message was largely the same in 1920 as in 1905. The merchant fleet was just as important after the war, when its strengthening was said to be the 'central ingredient of how our future destiny will turn out'.[29]

The navy as creator, protector, and saviour

Vår Flotta often turned to history to underline the importance of the maritime and naval sectors for Sweden and its future. It stated that Sweden had a great history as a maritime nation, and for the sake of a future successful Sweden, Swedes should keep their maritime traditions alive and develop a deeper understanding of the sea's importance. The navy in *Vår Flotta* was seen as a vital prerequisite for the founding of modern Sweden in the early sixteenth century, when Gustav Eriksson Vasa seized control of the country and became its king. According to *Vår Flotta*, he managed to free Sweden from foreign political and economic oppression, and in securing power he relied on a strong navy that protected Swedes from foreign aggression.[30] The naval ships Gustav Vasa organized enabled him to take Stockholm, his opponents' last stronghold. *Vår Flotta* described the sequence of events that made him king as having ended with 'the Danish garrison in Stockholm', which, cut off,

> could no longer hold out, and on 20 June 1523 the Swedes took control of their capital, after their navy had taken a direct part in the siege. The war was over for now and the foundations of a united Sweden had been laid ... sea power had with all clarity shown its influence on Swedish history ... Gustav Vasa, helped by the navy, had laid the foundations of Sweden's political independence.[31]

The navy was not only described as of vital importance in creating modern Sweden, but also as its saviour on many occasions, for example in the war against Russia in 1808–1809. That war was a bitter defeat for the Swedish armed forces as Finland was conquered by the Russians and there were no large sea battles where the Swedish navy could have had influenced the result of the war, but that did not stop *Vår Flotta* from claiming the navy had saved the day by forcing the Russian navy to stay in harbour, so preventing Russian forces from raiding Sweden.[32] In subsequent years (1809–1812) the Swedish mainland lived under the threat of a Russian invasion. *Vår Flotta* said that the British Baltic fleet then protected Sweden from being attacked, but at the same time underlined that the British fleet cooperated closely with a small but 'well-maintained' Swedish squadron. Thus, according to *Vår Flotta*, the navy once again prevented the enemy from invading Sweden, and protected Swedish merchants against privateers, saving the country from total annihilation.[33] It also claimed the navy had been an important factor in the peaceful dissolution of the union between Sweden and Norway in 1905. The navy was indeed mobilized and sent to the Swedish west coast, close to the Norwegian border, to put pressure on Norway, though the effects of that decision on the negotiations were not clear-cut. But *Vår Flotta* said that without the pressure from the navy, Sweden would have had to take a softer stance towards the Norwegians: it was thanks to the navy that the negotiations ended successfully and war could be avoided. Shortly after the First World War, *Vår Flotta* again presented the navy as saviour of the nation. Sweden had been neutral, and had managed to remain so because of the activities of the navy. It protected Sweden against attempts by the warring parties to drag it into the war, and it protected Swedish ships and fishing-boats from being attacked: without the protection of its navy, Sweden would have found it hard to stay out of the war.[34] The navy, then, was described as an insurance policy, and a very important one for Sweden's future as an independent nation. It had on several occasions saved the Swedish nation from potential extinction.

Theories of identity often stress the importance of the other, a counterpart in contrast to which an identity can be constructed.[35] There was no constant, obvious other in relation to which the Swedish national identity was constructed in *Vår Flotta*, however. Sometimes it was the UK, sometimes Germany, sometimes Russia, and sometimes Norway which was used as the counterpart to the Swedish national identity. The other was always described as aggressive – a military threat to the freedom and prosperity of the Swedish people. Yet it was rare for an identifiable state or nation to be presented as the enemy; rather it was a diffuse and threatening other in relation to which Sweden and the Swedes were constructed.

To extract the key findings about the Swedish national identity in *Vår Flotta* from the themes discussed thus far, it is safe to say the national identity constructed in the magazine had many maritime components. In terms of the national identity discourse found in *Vår Flotta*, it was maritime. It was primarily naval, at that. Even though the importance of civilian shipping was emphasized, the magazine concentrated on making the case for a strong Swedish navy. Sweden was described as having a long history as a maritime nation. But lately, however, Sweden had been weakened as a maritime power. Therefore civilian shipping and the navy needed to be given more attention and funding. The navy had saved Sweden and the Swedes from dangerous situations in the past, but now faced even greater danger in a hostile world. Sweden had turned its gaze inwards to domestic concerns, and had failed to notice the threatening international situation. The navy as it was would not be strong enough to protect Sweden, which risked obliteration as an independent nation. *Vår Flotta* stated that the future of Sweden was utterly dependent on the sea. Without a strong merchant fleet, protected by an efficient navy, it could be forced to merge with a stronger power. According to the magazine, Swedes needed to understand their nation's dependence on the sea. In order to secure an independent Swedish nation for the future, Swedes should support a strong navy that could protect its shipping and support its shipping companies and dockyards.

But why, according to *Vår Flotta*, was Sweden important to protect? Which values and characteristics were seen as Swedish, and essential to keep alive and to strengthen?

Defining elements of a true Swede

According to *Vår Flotta* many of the traits that characterized Swedes were connected to the sea. Swedes were described as always having had a close connection with the sea and as potentially very able seamen. Swedes were natural-born people of the sea, and almost every man in the Swedish coastal communities at some point longed to go to sea: 'the young boy has had his gaze drawn towards the sea and its professions. The step from cradle to boat has often been as short as it is natural – they do share a certain similarity.'[36] It was only at sea that a man's true worth would be revealed, as on land the signs of his true character were vague and often false. Success in love or wealth could make an unworthy man in many ways seem respectable and admirable, his successes proof of his good (male) nature. But that was only a façade. The true measure of a man's worth and character was only revealed at sea, against quite a different yardstick, *Vår Flotta* concluded. If a man really were of good character it would soon show in the way he handled himself at sea. If he could not cope, it would soon be cruelly obvious.[37]

Några ord om skeppsgossekåren och dess verksamhet.

Skeppsgossekårens ändamål är att utbilda dem af landets söner, som så önska, till matroser vid örlogsflottan, hvarpå de sedermera efter i sjömanskårens skolor inhämtade kunskaper och på sjön vunnen praktisk färdighet i sitt yrke befordras till underofficerare vid flottan.

Kåren har hittills varit förlagd till flottans station i Karlskrona, med undantag af ett fåtal skeppsgossar, som utbildas till hornblåsare vid flottans station i Stockholm. Den upptager för närvarande 500 nummer.

Vid innevarande års riksdag hafva emellertid medel beviljats för att å ett kasernfartyg i Marstrand för lägga en del skeppsgossar, i samband hvarmed kåren kommer att ökas till 600 nummer.

Gossarnes utbildning, som i allmänhet är tvåårig, är under 8 månader (halfva September—halfva Maj) förlagd i land samt försiggår under återstående tiden ombord å de s. k. skeppsgossefartygen.

Vid tjänstgöring i land i Karlskrona äro gossarna inkasernerade dels i skeppsgossekasernen, dels ombord å kasernfartyget Norrköping.

Skeppsgossekasernen är en stor byggnad, 4 våningar hög. Den öfversta våningen inrymmer skolsalarna, och i de öfriga våningarna äro inredda logement. I hvarje logement finnes utrymme för 40 gossar, och då logementens antal är 10 kunna alltså 400 gossar rymmas i kasernen. Logementen äro höga, ljusa, väl ventilerade och uppvärmda. Hvarje gosse har sin säng och ett bredvid sängen stående skåp för sina tillhörigheter, och förvarar han själf nyckeln till sitt skåp. I hvarje logement finnes ett å två större bord, vid hvilka gossarna under

Skeppsgosse.

Kasernen har en stor kaserngård, som användes till exercis- och lekplats. Vid kaserngårdens sidor ligga kokhusbyggnaden med kokinrättning och matsal för 400 gossar, badrum m. m. äfvensom en ny, tidsenlig gymnastikbyggnad.

Kasernfartyget Norrköping, som är förlagdt till örlogsvarfvet, har förr varit öfningskorvett och blef år 1902 omändradt till kasernfartyg för skeppsgossar. Det är afdeladt i 3 våningar. Den öfversta användes till lektionsrum och samlingsrum; den mellersta våningen är inredd till matsal och sofrum. Gossarne ligga här liksom på sjön i hängmattor. I nedersta våningen finnas tvättrum, förvaringsrum för gossarnes kläder, sjukrum m. m. Längs ned i fartyget finnes en ångpanna, som lämnar kraft att drifva såväl motorn för fartygets elektriska belysning som en fläkt för luftväxling i fartygets olika delar. Dessutom förser den värmeledningen med ånga.

Den mat, som bestås gossarna, är både god, riklig och omväxlande. Frukosten består af kaffe med smörgåsar och bullar samt en varm kötträtt med potatis. Middagen utgöres af soppa, färskt kött och potatis tre gånger i veckan, ärter, fläsk och potatis en gång i veckan, välling, stekt fläsk och potatis en gång i veckan samt välling, smörgåsar, stekt sill och potatis två gånger i veckan. Aftonvarden utgöres alla dagar af gröt och mjölk samt bröd; om söndagarna erhålles smör till brödet.

På sjön är kosten i hufvudsak lika med den nyss angifna; dock äro portionerna rikligare tilltagna på grund af den större aptit, som sjöluften framkallar.

Skeppsgossekasernen.

Logement.

fritiden kunna läsa, skrifva m. m. Bredvid hvarje logement finnes ett tvättrum med 20 st. handfat. Hvarje gosse har sin handduk, som ombytes en gång i veckan. Tvättning af handdukar, lakan och gossarnas kläder verkställes kostnadsfritt i kronans tvättinrättning. Ungefär en gång i veckan erhåller hvarje gosse ett varmt bad.

Förutom skolsalar och logement inrymmas i kasernen chefens och kompanichefernas tjänsterum jämte en del ekonomirum m. m.

I land meddelas undervisning dels i militära, dels i vanliga skolämnen, och är undervisningstiden 38 timmar i veckan, nämligen 20 timmar i militära och 18 timmar i i vanliga skolämnen.

De militära ämnena äro:

gymnastik,
militära skyldigheter, d. v. s. de skyldigheter och fordringar, som i dagliga lifvet ställas på hvarje militär,

Figure 7.2. *Vår Flotta* published articles about life at sea to promote boys' interest in the navy and shipping, such as this article about a young boy training to become a sailor in the Swedish navy. *Vår Flotta* May 1906. Photo: Andreas Linderoth.

The sea in *Vår Flotta* was not only presented as the place where men's abilities were tested and measured, it was also ascribed the power to force men to develop certain traits. And that was imperative for the development of important Swedish national characteristics. Sailing ships in particular offered invaluable experiences, as 'nowhere is a man as free and left to his own devices as on a boat at sea.' On a sailing ship, a young Swede could learn 'to be independent and alert to his surroundings. He learns to be confident, determined, and resourceful in sudden, complicated situations. The ability to take action [is learnt] and sound judgement is generated.'[38] (Fig. 7.2). *Vår Flotta* also said the sea forced people on board ship to be friends and help one another when danger loomed. People with different backgrounds and different political opinions had to unite in the shared task of fighting the elements. They had to fight the winds and the waves together, and keep a lookout for land-wash and sandbanks. According to *Vår Flotta* those were sufficient enemies and there was therefore no room for internal divisions in a ship's crew.[39] But even for *Vår Flotta*, with its strong emphasis on learning from the sea at first hand, it was unrealistic for the entire Swedish male population to work as sailors. Fortunately, there was a good substitute: sailing as a hobby. Sailing was promoted by *Vår Flotta* as 'probably the most noble national sport' and a way of nurturing the young, and above all boys. Sailing would not only strengthen the body, but also develop young boys' manliness and give them an undaunted mind.[40] That one's true colours were shown at sea also applied to entire nations, according to *Vår Flotta*. That was the reason seafaring nations had been the most successful states historically: they had been hardened by the demands of life at sea.[41]

Considering the weight given to the navy and to life experience at sea, it is perhaps not very surprising that *Vår Flotta* described sailors, especially in the navy, in a positive light. Naval men were presented as very brave and, according to the magazine, well aware of the fact there was a high risk they would see battle. Swedish naval men happily shouldered the responsibility of defending Sweden, and possibly bearing the brunt of an enemy attack, as they were convinced it was for the greater good. The magazine said traditions in the navy were such that not even a disadvantage of one to ten would make Swedish sailors quail.[42] A story printed in 1908 was typical of how naval officers were described: after a bloody battle, Swedish naval officers had wanted nothing less than to square up to the enemy again and teach them how 'Swedish steel bites'.[43] Another peculiarly Swedish trait, according to *Vår Flotta*, was the naval men's willingness to make sacrifices for the nation – sometimes described in almost religious terms. In January 1912, *Vår Flotta* printed a fundraising campaign for the navy, signed by Manfred Björkquist and Per Stolpe. This was the Pansarbåtsinsamlingen, an appeal framed to underscore the importance of active sacrifice, because actions speak louder than words: 'no one can resist sacrificing love. Sacrificial deeds speak for themselves. The willingness to sacrifice is contagious. Sacrifices reconcile and heal. Sacrificial belief wins. Let us then in a bold and enlightened faith do an awakening, uniting, and reconciling sacrificial deed.'[44]

Other Swedish characteristics that the sailors in *Vår Flotta* represented were a strong work ethic and good relationships. They were described as very hard-working, good-natured, and good comrades. One illustrative example was a description of the coaling of a naval ship in 1908:

> Now there was action everywhere! The baskets are filled and brought up with unbelievable speed; their black contents are thrown into the coal bunkers through holes in the deck and then the empty baskets are thrown back into the pram to be filled again. The work is carried out in the best of moods. The jokes come thick and fast, and woe betide the one who does not put his life and soul into the work. The mates discover that immediately and do not hesitate to choose a suitable means to drive him on. Sometimes an empty basket to the head of the erring person as if by chance. Sometimes a few abusive words that would have convinced a rock to start work.[45]

Vår Flotta also underlined that Swedish sailors were easily pleased: they did not have many opportunities to relax, but had to be content with the joys of being physically tough, body and soul steeled.[46] Seeking after pleasure and unrestricted freedom would lead to no good, the magazine was sure.[47] Sailors and their officers were also described as being frank,

Figure 7.3. Sailors on board HMS *Blenda* doing gymnastics in 1911. *Vår Flotta* liked to describe Swedish sailors as easily entertained: they had few opportunities to relax, and had to be content with the joys of being physically and mentally tough. Photo: Statens Maritima och Transporthistoriska Museer/SMTM.

smart, and always willing to lend a hand whenever needed. They were also described as role models when it came to cleanliness. They might only have a bucket of water and a piece of soap, but they still kept themselves as clean as if they had far greater resources to hand. According to *Vår Flotta*, the sailors of the navy often kept themselves as trim as the dandies seen strolling around Stockholm and other fashionable cities. Naval ships, too, were described as being notable for their order and cleanliness.[48] Another important, positive characteristic of Swedish naval men was their competitiveness, not only when carrying out their duties but also in their spare time. By participating in assorted maritime challenges, naval men, according to *Vår Flotta*, could prove their physical strength and their powers of observation and attentiveness (Fig. 7.3).[49]

Figure 7.4. Fishermen on the Swedish west coast in 1915. Like naval officers and sailors, fishermen were seen as important role models in *Vår Flotta*, and were described as calm, hardy men who focused their energies where they were needed most, even in potentially dangerous situations. Photo: Dan Samuelsson, Statens Maritima och Transporthistoriska Museer/SMTM.

Besides naval officers and sailors, *Vår Flotta* found important role models among the fishermen and those living in traditional coastal communities. They were described as calm men who used their energies efficiently and directed them where they were needed most, even in potentially dangerous situations. They were also ascribed a form of solid self-confidence, which according to the magazine only came from close contact with the sea in all its changeability.[50] *Vår Flotta* described them as 'worn and torn but tough and irrepressible, rugged not only in body but also in other respects.' Even though they need to work almost day and night 'to wrest their meagre livelihood from the ocean deep and sometimes from the air', they were said to be content with their situation (Fig. 7.4).[51]

Sailors, especially in the navy, were described by *Vår Flotta* as having a special aptitude for life at sea. They were seen as excellent representatives of Sweden, embodying key Swedish characteristics. Hard-working, honest, brave, vigilant, and clean, and happy to make sacrifices for the nation, safe in the knowledge that their strong belief in the nation would be rewarded in the end. Seamen were seen as the vanguard of the positive development, economically and culturally, that beckoned for all Swedes.

Vår Flotta thus had a very positive view of naval men, fishermen, and the coastal population, but even the sections of the Swedish population who did not fall into one of those categories were generally described in a positive tone. While willing to make the ultimate sacrifice for the nation, it is said the need to make that sacrifice often dawned on them too late. Swedes were not perfect and had their weaknesses: *Vår Flotta* sometimes described them as melancholic and given to gloom and doom, and often not sufficiently aware of the sacrifices needed. In 1913, *Vår Flotta* quoted the German general Friedrich von Bernhardi, who warned that 'A people, who will not willingly carry the costs and make the sacrifices for schools and military service, deny their will to live and sacrifice high values that safeguard the future for purely material, fleeting advantages', and *Vår Flotta* added in a similar vein, 'We Swedes would perhaps *deny our will to live!* Would our "tragic mood" really lead us all the way there?'[52] The flaws in the Swedish character needed to be counteracted by summoning up all the positive traits, and here, according to *Vår Flotta*, naval men and fishermen were important role models. The magazine put great emphasis on the need to foster Swedes' belief in Sweden's ability to defend itself against the great powers; if not, it would lead to Sweden's demise. And there would be no cultural development, as that was not promoted by downheartedness and lack of independence.[53]

National identity in focus

Bo Stråth writes in his recent history of Sweden in the nineteenth and early twentieth centuries that by 1900 there were two dominant, competing visions of Sweden.[54] One was what he terms *Punsch-patriotism* – for the Arrack spirits popular among the more revanchist-minded

– which looked to Swedish history, underlined the importance of military defence against a perceived threat from Russia and of keeping the Norwegians in the union with Sweden. The other was the workers' movement, which looked to the future and longed for a better society with freedom, justice, and no social distress. In Stråth's account, these two visions polarized Swedish society and eventually led to the emergence of a third competing vision. This vision was directed against the class-bound thinking of the workers, but also sympathized with their situation and underlined the need for social reform. It is associated with the conservative professor of political science, Rudolf Kjellén (1864–1922), the Farmers' League politician Alfred Petersson i Påboda (1860–1920), and the conservative politician Arvid Lindman (1862–1936). Socially conservative, it envisaged a future where Sweden would be a new kind of political power: peaceful, wealthy and with a society without social strife.[55] As it was Kjellén of the three who had the most elaborate and detailed vision of a future Sweden, his views are taken here as representative of the third of the approaches on Swedish national identity, which according to Stråth emerged at the turn of the last century.

Considering that the most influential men on the boards of *Vår Flotta* and its publisher the Society for Sweden's Naval Defence were naval officers, it might have been plausible for *Punsch-patriotism* to dominate. But this was not the case. True, as we have seen, *Vår Flotta* strongly emphasized military defence and the vast military threat against Sweden, but that extended to Germany and the UK and was not limited to Russia. Norway's importance to the union was not dwelt on; however, as *Vår Flotta* first came out in the year the union with Norway was dissolved (1905), there is little evidence of its position towards the union when it existed. The repercussions of the dissolution of the union are mainly dealt with in a positive way, to the point where *Vår Flotta*'s tone was almost pleased: now the Swedes could focus on themselves and Sweden's progress, and that was a good thing.[56] *Punsch-patriotism* is thus not a very good label for the national identity constructed in *Vår Flotta*. That is equally true of the social-democratic vision of the Swedish nation, which was almost absent from the magazine. But there is ample evidence of the third vision of a Swedish national identity, the one associated with Kjellén, Petersson i Påboda, and Lindman. It was heavily emphasized in *Vår Flotta* that Sweden, aided by a strong navy, must keep the peace, remain free from unwanted foreign attention, and develop into a wealthy nation – all goals emphasized by the third vision. Sweden was characterized as 'the land of freedom on earth'.[57] Since the promotion of the navy's importance permeated the magazine, the concept of freedom was key to its arguments: Sweden was one of the best countries in the world, so Swedes should be ready to fight for that freedom, especially against external powers trying to take it away from them. *Vår Flotta*'s description of Sweden as a country with a great degree of freedom can also be seen as connected to the dominant discourse of Swedish national identity, as described in previous research about the period. Sweden as a representative for freedom had been an important theme in conservative, nationalist rhetoric since the nineteenth century. As Sweden had not seen serfdom, ergo it had a long tradition of freedom – that was the claim. And that argument was still a vital part of the dominant national discourse in the early twentieth century.[58]

There were many similarities between *Vår Flotta*'s views on the international system and Kjellén's. He believed every state should strive to find its natural borders in a hostile world. For him, the international system was characterized by a fight between contending national interests with their origins in geography. It was very similar to the line taken by *Vår Flotta*. Kjellén saw the state as an organism to be filled with means of production and those means of production should be in harmony with the geographical preconditions of the state – akin to *Vår Flotta*'s heavy promotion of Sweden's maritime businesses.[59] Shipping and shipbuilding, according to *Vår Flotta*, were natural activities for Swedes because so much of Sweden had a coast. Also like Kjellén, the magazine emphasized the need for Swedes to make sacrifices for the good of the nation.

The will of the people was another important theme for Kjellén. The people's will to live was the main foundation of the nation, and also decided a nation's possibilities. The state should strive for harmonious unity at home, but though Kjellén stressed the will of the people in that too, in his view the political system did not necessarily need to be democratic. The nation and its needs, not the political system and individuals' right to vote, were the crucial factors deciding the future of Sweden.[60] *Vår Flotta*'s views on democracy and Sweden's political system was not explicit. Its priority was the strengthening of Sweden's naval defences, and all the subjects covered in the magazine spoke to that. Democracy and the political system do not seem to have been especially important to *Vår Flotta*. That fact makes it hard to spot any resemblance between Kjellén and *Vår Flotta* on that point.

Bo Stråth is not the only one to have analysed Swedish national identity in the early twentieth century. According to the historian Nils Edling, a new Swedish national identity emerged then, centred on the importance of industrial development to Sweden. Sweden was seen to be on its way to becoming a strong competitor in terms of international industrial, and scientific advances.[61] There were quite a few traces of this identity in *Vår Flotta*, with its many references to Sweden having become stronger internationally. But even though there were obvious similarities between the Swedish national identity in *Vår Flotta*, the one described by Edling, and the one promoted by Kjellén and other conservative thinkers, *Vår Flotta* had its own special take on national identity: its strong emphasis on maritime matters. The need for Sweden to have a strong naval presence and a strong merchant fleet was everywhere in the magazine. A strong maritime presence was necessary to secure, protect, and strengthen Sweden's economic development. Without it Sweden might cease to exist.

National character in focus

It was in the early nineteenth century, when national sentiment was on the rise in Sweden, that the question of a Swedish national character arose. The discussion continued for the entire century and beyond, as *Vår Flotta* showed.[62] According to Bo Stråth, late nineteenth-century Swedes saw certain values and characteristics as characteristically Swedish: to be dutiful, faithful, trustworthy, hard-working, patient, tolerant, and poor.[63] There was an evident connection between the key elements in the dominant national identity discourse and those in *Vår Flotta*. Indeed, all those characteristics were present in the discourse of national identity found in *Vår Flotta*. The naval officers and sailors, fishermen and people living in coastal communities as they were described in the magazine to a large extent embodied those values.[64]

In Sweden, nationalism was characterized by a striving to improve the character of the Swedes. Not only were they thought ignorant of national priorities, but also not healthy enough. There was therefore a tendency to look back to older, healthier ways of life. Such healthier patterns were associated with the countryside, so it was there the true Swedish qualities were thought to be found. The countryside was more genuinely Swedish than the cities.[65] It was important to the national identity constructed in *Vår Flotta*, which found many of the best and most genuine Swedish characteristics there. But whereas in the Swedish tradition, since the late nineteenth century at least, Dalarna was the province that best symbolized Sweden, *Vår Flotta* instead held up the coastal provinces of Bohuslän and Blekinge, where the harsh conditions had hardened the population and made them resilient and strong. The magazine's trope of weather-beaten Swedes, toughened by the barren land, was a common way of characterizing Swedes known since at least the 1830s. But the provinces of Bohuslän and Blekinge were rarely seen as typically Swedish.[66]

In the dominant discourse of Swedish national identity, peasants were the important role models, the backbone of Swedish society. The values associated with the peasantry were often traced to a poem by Erik Geijer, *Odalbonden*, written in the early nineteenth century. Geijer's eponymous peasant was a proud, independent man, working his own land and beholden to none. For obvious reasons, a peasant was not the best role model for a magazine like *Vår Flotta* that wanted to promote the importance of the sea and maritime matters. As we have seen, though, the nationalist discourse in *Vår Flotta* was essentially conservative, so there were other poems of Geijer's as inspiration, especially as one of his better-known poems was about a Viking. Vikings, not unlike peasants, were indeed used as role models in the nineteenth century: Swedes, it was said, should aspire to be more like them – hard on the outside, simple and sound on the inside.[67] The values associated with the Vikings would not have openly clashed with *Vår Flotta*'s notion of exemplary Swedes. And the fact that Vikings were held in high regard as seafarers ought to have been to *Vår Flotta*'s liking. Yet interestingly, the magazine rarely promoted Vikings as role models or held them up as exemplary Swedes. Perhaps it was the Vikings' recklessness – Geijer's Viking was described as an impatient adventurer, after all – which did not suit a magazine intent on promoting responsible, hard-working, and steady-going Swedes. For *Vår Flotta* it was fishermen and the men employed in the navy, naval officers and ordinary sailors, who represented true Swedish values.

The national identity discourse in *Vår Flotta* was very masculine. It was men who had agency, perhaps because it was mainly men who contributed to the magazine. Of all the maritime professions the majority were associated with men, and it was young men the magazine hoped to inspire to go to sea. The key Swedish characteristics *Vår Flotta* promoted were often regarded as male – for example, bravery.[68] Not to say women were absent from *Vår Flotta*. Women were members of the Society for Sweden's Naval Defence and some took an active part in its activities.[69] Yet they did play a very minor role in the magazine. They seldom contributed to it or appeared as independent agents.

Vår Flotta and Swedish national identity

Vår Flotta strongly emphasized the importance of the sea for Sweden, and the sea was a vital part of the national identity constructed in the magazine. Above all, the sea had symbolic meaning. According to *Vår Flotta*, Sweden had to revive its historically strong maritime traditions to safeguard its future. The sea and its control would determine Sweden's fate. The sea was where the navy had saved Sweden from being dragged into a war or being invaded by foreign powers, historically and in the present. The navy, *Vår Flotta* claimed, had once had a vital part in creating modern Sweden. *Vår Flotta* saw Sweden as a small nation, dependent on the sea, whose maritime activities had to increase if it were to thrive. Sweden was presented as an increasingly successful nation, utterly dependent on its sea lanes. Success had come at a price, though:

Sweden was subject to unwanted attention from potentially hostile powers. The only answer was to have a strong navy as a deterrent. Without it, Sweden risked annihilation as an independent nation.

Another important dimension to the sea in the discourse of Swedish national identity in *Vår Flotta* was the way it could make Swedes into true Swedes. A close connection to the sea, facing its dangers, would see true Swedish qualities develop: bravery, calmness, confidence, cleanliness, and a willingness to make sacrifices for the greater good. Naval officers, sailors, fishermen, and others living in proximity with the sea were described as representing true Swedish values. According to *Vår Flotta*, if only all Swedes were to embrace those values then the country would prosper and have a grand future.

The discursive construction of a Swedish national identity in *Vår Flotta* bore similarities to competing discursive national identities in Sweden at the time, especially a conservative one associated with the political scientist Rudolf Kjellén. It is perhaps not surprising that a conservative strand of nationalism would appeal to the naval officers behind *Vår Flotta*, including those who wrote for it. Military officers often had a conservative view of the world. But it should be stressed that the magazine did not espouse Kjellén's nationalist programme in its entirety. The discourse of national identity in *Vår Flotta* was a maritime one, or, perhaps more accurately, a naval one. It had elements of other discourses which were important at the time, but it had its own peculiarities. One was its strong emphasis on the sea, the people working in the maritime sector, and the people living close to the sea. It was in the coastal provinces of Bohuslän and Blekinge, not rural Dalarna, and among the fishermen and the naval men, not farmers, where the truest Swedish values could be found.

The discourse of Swedish national identity in *Vår Flotta* was one of many discourses competing for influence in the early twentieth century, and it was not the dominant one. But the national identity constructed in the magazine is nevertheless important in understanding the possible influences of the sea and the maritime sphere on Swedish national identity.

Notes

1 Peter Mandler, 'What is "national identity"? Definitions and applications in modern British historiography', *Modern Intellectual History* 3/2 (2006), 272, 281.

2 Sanna Inthorn, *German media and national identity* (Youngstown 2007), 3.

3 Ruth Wodak et al., *Discursive Constructions of National Identities* (Edinburgh 2009); Ariane Bogain, 'Terrorism and the discursive construction of national identity in France', *National Identities* 21/3 (2019), 242.

4 Benedict Anderson, *Imagined Communities: Reflections on the Origins and Spread of Nationalism* (London 1983).

5 Duncan Redford (ed.), *Maritime History and Identity: The Sea and Culture in the Modern World* (London, 2014), 3; Marion Gibson, 'Vikings and victories: sea-stories from the "Seafarer" to Skyfall and the future of British maritime culture', *Journal for Maritime Research* 17/1(2015), 1–2.

6 Jan Rüger, *The Great Naval Game. Britain and Germany in the Age of Empire* (Cambridge 2007).

7 Two exceptions are the essays by Henrik Arnstad, 'Havet och svenskheten' and 'Möten i monsunen' (unpub., Stockholm University 2016).

8 Bertil Åhlund, 'Sveriges flotta. Förening för sjöfart och sjöförsvar – en historik', *Forum Navale* 61 (2005), 19–20.

9 'Öfverstyrelns berättelse rörande "Föreningen Sveriges Flotta"', *Vår Flotta*, Apr. 1907, 91; 'Öfverstyrelns berättelse rörande "Föreningen Sveriges Flotta"', *Vår Flotta*, May 1913, 55.

10 Crister Strahl, *Nationalism och socialism* (Lund 1983), 9–10, 27–9; Billy Ehn, Jonas Frykman & Orvar Löfgren, *Försvenskningen av Sverige* (Stockholm 1993), 50–1.

11 Anders Berge, *Sakkunskap och politisk rationalitet: Den svenska flottan och pansarfartygs-frågan 1918–1939* (Stockholm 1987); Bo Stråth, *Sveriges historia 1830–1920* (Stockholm 2012), 192.

12 Arvid Svenske, 'Försvarsvilja och värnkraft', *Vår Flotta*, Jan. 1912, 4.

13 'Ett fosterländskt tal', *Vår Flotta*, Mar. 1910, 26.

14 'Var redo!', *Vår Flotta*, Oct. 1911, 111; 'Från allmänheten. Hvad är meningen?', *Vår Flotta*, Oct. 1907, 174; Arvid Svenske, 'Försvarsvilja och värnkraft', *Vår Flotta*, Jan. 1912, 4.

15 'Till amiral Saumarez' minne', *Vår Flotta*, Nov. 1910, 127.

16 'Industriellt uppsving och försvarsplikt', *Vår Flotta*, Nov. 1911, 127.

17 'Sjömaktens inverkan på världskriget', *Vår Flotta*, Nov. 1918, 108.

18 'Fakta som tala', *Vår Flotta*, Apr. 1914, 39.

19 H. Wrangel, 'Betydelsen af en stark örlogsflotta och tryggade sjöfartsförbindelser', *Vår Flotta*, Jan. 1908, 2.

20 'Vårt sjöförsvars betydelse', *Vår Flotta*, Feb. 1911, 20–1, original emphasis.

21 'Ett fosterländskt tal', *Vår Flotta*, Mar. 1910, 25–6; compare 'Den svenska handels-flottan just nu', *Vår Flotta*, Jan. 1920, 5.

22 'Från allmänheten: Hvad är meningen?', *Vår Flotta*, Oct. 1907, 174.

23 Arvid Svenske, 'Några synpunkter rörande vårt försvarsläge', *Vår Flotta*, Oct. 1912, 126.

24 'Ångfärjeförbindelsen Trelleborg-Sassnitz', *Vår Flotta*, Mar. 1908, 33.

25 'Från Göteborgs hamn', *Vår Flotta*, Apr. 1909, 47.

26 'Svenska handelsflottans nyförvärf 1910', *Vår Flotta*, Aug. 1911, 88; 'Sjöintressen', *Vår Flotta*, Apr. 1913, 42; 'Svenska handelsflottans tillväxt 1911, *Vår Flotta*, July 1912, 91; 'Nya svenska handelsfartyg under 1907', *Vår Flotta*, Apr. 1908, 37–9.

27 'Meddelande', *Vår Flotta*, Jan. 1907, 3; 'Fakta som tala', *Vår Flotta*, Apr. 1914, 39.

28 H. Wrangel, 'Betydelsen af en stark örlogsflotta och tryggade sjöfartsförbindelser', *Vår Flotta*, Feb. 1908, 17; 'Hvarför behöfver Sveriges flotta sjögående pansarbåtar?', *Vår Flotta*, Apr. 1909, 44.

29 'Den svenska handelsflottan just nu', *Vår Flotta*, Jan. 1920, 8.

30 S. Natt och Dag, 'Herraväldet på Östersjön', *Vår Flotta*, Mar. 1906, 31 & Apr. 1906, 46.

31 Otto Lybeck, 'Sveriges sjökrig i deras samband med den politiska historien', *Vår Flotta*, Aug. 1912, 102.

32 'Äntringen av "Styrbjörn" den 17 augusti 1808', *Vår Flotta*, Aug. 1908, 93.

33 'Till amiral Saumarez' minne', *Vår Flotta*, Nov. 1910, 127; 'Äntringen af "Styrbjörn" den 17 augusti 1808', *Vår Flotta*, Aug. 1908, 93.

34 'Flottans neutralitetsvakt: En redogörelse utarbetad inom Sjöförsvarsdepartementet', *Vår Flotta*, Apr. 1919, 26.

35 Inthorn 2007, 2; Wodak et al. 2009, 7–35.

36 'Yachtseglingen: Några ord om dess utveckling och nuvarande ståndpunkt', *Vår Flotta*, Mar. 1907, 51.

37 'Havet', *Vår Flotta*, Aug. 1920, 94.

38 'Yachtseglingen. Några ord om dess utveckling och nuvarande ståndpunkt', *Vår Flotta*, Mar. 1907, 51.

39 'Kanonbåten Svensksunds västkustvakt', *Vår Flotta*, May 1908, 50.

40 'Yachtseglingen. Några ord om dess utveckling och nuvarande ståndpunkt', *Vår Flotta*, Mar. 1907, 51.

41 'Havet', *Vår Flotta*, Aug. 1920, 94.

42 'En behjärtansvärd vädjan', *Vår Flotta*, Sept. 1913, 110; 'Från allmänheten: Gud först, sedan Sveriges flotta och så allt det öfriga', *Vår Flotta*, May 1908, 64; 'Huru Sverige förr en gång förstått att skydda sin neutralitet', Mar. 1917, 39.

43 'Äntringen av "Styrbjörn" den 17 augusti 1808', *Vår Flotta*, Aug. 1908, 93; 'En svensk sjöofficers bravur', *Vår Flotta*, Oct. 1905, 124; Ernst Holmberg, 'Ett sorgespel på hafvet', *Vår Flotta*, Aug. 1909, 94–5; Ernst Holmberg, 'För flaggans heder', *Vår Flotta*, Jan. 1911, 12.

44 'Nationalinsamling för försvaret', *Vår Flotta*, Jan. 1912, 10.

45 'En ekonomidag å en torpedbåtsdivision', *Vår Flotta*, Oct. 1908, 120.

46 'Från Sveriges minsta garnisonsort', *Vår Flotta*, Feb. 1911, 18; 'Hjälpminfartyget Gundhilds undergång', *Vår Flotta*, Oct. 1918, 102.

47 Arvid Svenske, 'Försvarsvilja och värnkraft', *Vår Flotta*, Jan. 1912, 6.

48 'Tandborstning efter "skaffningen"', *Vår Flotta*, Nov. 1915, 140; 'Sjömansdräktens historia', *Vår Flotta*, Mar. 1911, 32; 'Bilder från Kusteskadern', *Vår Flotta*, Aug. 1905, 90; 'En ekonomidag å en torpedbåtsdivision', *Vår Flotta*, Oct. 1908, 121.

49 'Idrotten vid 1909 års Kusteskader', *Vår Flotta*, Sept. 1910, 99.

50 'Ett öfningsföretag med lifbåten', *Vår Flotta*, Sept. 1911, 104.

51 'Ett hårdt lif', *Vår Flotta*, May 1915, 58.

52 'Från vinterkustflottans sjötåg', *Vår Flotta*, Apr. 1913, 41, original emphasis.

53 'Villomeningar', *Vår Flotta*, Mar. 1910, 34.

54 Stråth 2012.

55 Stråth 2012, 240; Torbjörn Nilsson, *Mellan arv och utopi: Moderata vägval under hundra år, 1904–2004* (Stockholm 2004), 82.

56 'Handling bättre än ord!', *Vår Flotta*, Oct. 1906, 121.

57 'Ur riksdagsprotokollen', *Vår Flotta*, Nov. 1911, 125.

58 Nilsson 2004, 80.

59 Claes-Göran Alvstam, 'Geopolitik och politisk geografi', in Bert Edström, Ragnar Björk & Thomas Lundén (eds.), *Rudolf Kjellén: Geopolitiken och konservatismen* (Stockholm 2014), 24–28.

60 Stråth 2012, 126; Bert Edström, 'Inledning', in Edström, Björk & Lundén (eds.), 8–19.

61 Nils Edling, *Det fosterländska hemmet: Egnahemspolitik småbruk och hemideologi kring sekelskiftet 1900* (Stockholm 1996), 198; Conny Mithander, '1905: Genombrottet för en ny konservativ nationalism', in Sven Eliaeson & Ragnar Björk (eds.), *Union och secession: Perspektiv på statsbildningsprocesser och riksupplösningar* (Stockholm 2000), 205.

62 Patrik Hall, *Den svenskaste historien: Nationalism i Sverige under sex sekler* (Stockholm 2000), 251.

63 Stråth 2012, 118, 494.

64 Ulf Larsson, 'Bilden av Sverige: Värner Rydéns bok om medborgarkunskap', in Alf W. Johansson (ed.), *Vad är Sverige? Röster om svensk nationell identitet* (Stockholm 2001), 139.

65 Ehn et al. 1993, 52, 140.

66 Ehn et al. 1993, 97; Henrik Berggren & Lars Trägårdh, *Är svensken människa? Gemenskap och oberoende i det moderna Sverige* (Stockholm 2006), 89; Hall 2000, 109.

67 Erik Örjan Emilsson, 'Recasting Swedish Historical Identity', in Mats Andrén (ed.), *Cultural Identities and National Borders* (Gothenburg 2009), 193–4; Fredrik Svanberg, 'Vikingar: Myt och verklighet', in Lotta Fernstål et al. (eds.), *Sverige i tiden: Historier om ett levande land* (Stockholm 2015), 36–37; Berggren & Trägårdh 2006, 185–7; Ehn et al. 1993, 139–40.

68 Richard J. Blakemore, 'The ship, the river and the ocean sea: concepts of space in the 17th century London maritime community', in Redford 2014, 102.

69 Women seldom wrote for the journal or figured in it with any agency. One exception was a speech by Anna Wallenberg, chairman of Women's League for Sweden's Naval Defence, printed in 1910: 'Ett fosterländskt tal', *Vår Flotta*, Mar. 1910, 26.

CHAPTER 8

Tommi the sea dog

Maritime collections and the material culture of Baltic boat children

Mirja Arnshav

In the Second World War a great number of teddy bears, dolls, and soft toys crossed the Baltic Sea as their young owners escaped by boat from occupied Estonia and Latvia to Sweden. The children's material culture associated with the Great Escape is forever soaked with memories of these sea journeys. As part of maritime history, they draw our attention to the children's representation, and call for a broader take on maritime museums' collecting.

His name is Tommi. He is roughly 10 centimetres tall and covered with fine, short fur, golden in colour. He has upright ears and a purple ribbon around his neck. His eyes are made of dark brown glass, while his nose is an ordinary round button. Originally he had a long red tongue sticking out of his mouth, but it was lost a long time ago. Tommi is a stuffed animal, a soft toy dog given to a young boy called Taavi back in 1943 and taken to Sweden one year later when the family fled westward in a tugboat. In 2020, the threadbare creature was documented by the Swedish National Maritime Museum as part of the project *The Materiality of the Great Escape.*[1]

Where does Tommi fit into the collections of the Maritime Museum, a museum traditionally dedicated to 'sea dogs' of a very different

kind? What are his story and his place in maritime history? Drawing on
Tommi's case, this essay discusses a battery of objects associated with
the children of the Great Escape – things that were once taken on board
the Estonian and Latvian refugee boats and that are now ready to form
part of the collections of the Maritime Museum. These objects bring
to the fore the absence of children's material culture from the existing
collections and illustrate how such acquisitions add to the Maritime
Museum's arsenal of maritime histories – and to some extent also pushes
the boundaries of maritime history (Fig. 8.1).

Assemblages from the Great Escape

In the Second World War, the Baltic countries suffered three occupations:
a short Soviet occupation (1940–1941) followed by a German occupation
(1941–1944), and lastly a second Soviet occupation which continued
long after the war (1944–1991). A few years after the German takeover,
refugees began to stream westward. At first it was mostly limited to
Coastal Swedes, a Swedish-speaking minority with enduring cultural
and historical bonds to Sweden who had lived on the Estonian coast
since the Middle Ages, and who now reacted against forced conscription
and distress. However, in the summer and autumn of 1944, as the Baltic
countries once again became battlefields and a Soviet takeover loomed,
people fled en masse. In order to avoid deportations and terror, about
30,000 people migrated to Sweden by boat. The refugees came from
all sorts of backgrounds: young and old, men and women, workers and
intellectuals, farmers and townspeople. Many of them were convinced
the situation was only temporary; that the Western world would not
leave the Baltic countries in the power of the Soviet Union and that
soon – within months – they would return (Fig. 8.2).

Since many migrants were hoping to return home soon, and since
the decision to leave was often postponed until the last moment, most
people travelled light. Much luggage was lost during the journey to the
coast or while hiding and waiting for a boat to arrive. Also, since there
was a great lack of boats, it was not unusual that bags and suitcases were
left on shore to make room for more people. Hence, while some boat

Figure 8.1. Tommi, a soft toy with a sea story. Photo: Anneli Karlsson, Swedish National Maritime Museum/SMTM.

owners and captains shipped a good deal of their household goods and belongings to Sweden, the vast majority arrived almost empty-handed, with only what they could carry.

To an archaeologist, the things packed and taken aboard the escape boats make a fascinating area of study, giving glimpses of people's hopes, precautions, and priorities and reflecting the material culture of ordinary Estonian and Latvian homes. But just as interesting are the somewhat surprising and largely unstudied material constellations and encounters formed in the course of a desperate escape. As often seems to be the case with migrant material culture, the general order of things was somewhat dissolved.[2] In the suitcases objects normally separated were temporarily brought together, and on board the boats traditional nautical objects such as nets, oars, compasses, and binoculars mingled with things with few maritime associations such as soft toys, tableware, sewing machines, and more.

In Tommi's case, too, escape brought with it new entanglements. In the wake of the sea journey, things from the family's former Estonian home and part of the equipment from the escape boat were settled in the new home. As a result, a ship portrait and the ship's clock along with some of the medical equipment, tableware, and navigational instruments shared a space with the family's packed belongings such as a torch, an Estonian table flag, a bundle of Reichsmark and some Estonian coins, a pair of cufflinks and a tiepin, a toy aircraft and a small pull-along toy duck, a manicure set and a hairslide, a darning mushroom, a pair of amber earrings, two watches, and another soft dog. And in time the items' association became stronger as part of the legacy of the escape and as valued memory objects.

How are we as maritime scholars to understand this somewhat peculiar mix of things and their dissonant maritimity? Is it wise to reserve a place in maritime history for the skipper, the boat, and its equipment, but not for the other people on board and all the things sharing the escape experience?

A viable point of departure for exploring the materiality of the Baltic refugee boats – and for that sake the materiality of the Maritime Museum and the framing of certain things as 'maritime' – is the assemblage theory, as developed by Gilles Deleuze, Felix Guattari, and others, according to which assemblages can be defined as a bundling or assembling, in which the elements so assembled do not belong to a pre-given list and are not fixed in shape. An assemblage is in constant flux, whether due to aggregation or disintegration processes, and is thus constructed as the elements are entangled together. Hence, the main point of assemblage theory is not to define the boundaries of what appears as a totality, but to stress how assemblages emerge, gather, and come into existence.[3]

In line with this approach, a broad, open-minded understanding of maritime material culture is encouraged. In documenting the now dispersed material assemblages that first took shape on the Baltic refugee boats, the documentation will add to another assemblage; the collections of the Maritime Museum.

Figure 8.2. A young boy carrying a teddy bear, leaving Haapsalu for Sweden in late August 1944. Photo: Harald Perten, National Archives of Estonia.

Tommi's story

Although Tommi's picture may stand out in the collections of the Swedish National Maritime Museum, he is not the only reference to a dog. On the contrary, there are several examples of dogs forming part of maritime history. A number of photos and items record the existence of seafaring dogs – there is even a proof of service detailing the efforts of the fox terrier Nicke, a ship's dog on the coastal battleship *Drottning Victoria*. Another example, interesting because they are among the most iconic items in maritime history, are the Staffordshire dog figurines – a pair of pottery dogs associated with the separation between sailors and their wives.

In a curious coincidence with the Staffordshire dog figurines, Tommi also used to be one of a pair. His companion was another soft dog of similar size and with a similar name: Sammi. And at the beginning of their story there was an even larger pack: there used to be another Tommi, and another Sammi too. The two soft toys were named for two real dogs at the family farm on the northern coast of Estonia, about 50 kilometres east of Tallinn. In the early 1940s, the soft dogs' owner Taavi used to spend time there during the Soviet bombing raids on Tallinn, close to where they lived.

In the autumn of 1944 Taavi's family decided to escape. The two soft dogs Tommi and Sammi were packed in their owner's only suitcase while their namesakes, the farm dogs, had to be left behind. On the 22 September, just as Tallinn was about to surrender to the Soviet forces, the two soft toys were taken aboard the tugboat *Loksa*, on which Taavi's father was appointed chief officer. The ship was part of a convoy to evacuate people from Tallinn to Liepaja in Latvia, from where they were to move on to Germany. They had left it to the last minute. As they prepared in the harbour, parts of the capital went up in flames in the final Soviet bombing raid. At sea, the evacuees witnessed the detonation of the remotely controlled mines laid by the Germans in Tallinn harbour, and later saw several ships in the convoy go down after being hit by Soviet air forces.

Having left the Gulf of Finland in calm weather they now faced a far older enemy – the weather. The boats were struck by a storm which left the convoy scattered and in disarray. *Loksa*, which as a tugboat was not built to carry passengers nor operate at sea, took in so much water that the bilge pumps could not keep up. The boat was allowed to turn back and seek the shelter of the island of Hiiumaa. From there, after the storm had subsided, the captain seized the opportunity to make for Sweden with all 50 passengers, mostly Estonian civilians. As the seas were still rough, Tommi's owner Taavi was badly seasick, just like many others in the crowded boat. He kept crying 'Mummy, sick', but there was nothing anyone could do.

On the morning of 24 September, *Loksa* reached the Swedish coast and Taavi and his soft dogs were carried ashore. The dogs were later installed in a new home, safe on a shelf in the living room. Sammi, the less pretty of the two so Taavi was allowed to play with him, was eventually so tatty he was thrown away, while Tommi remained more or less intact. Exile stretched on far longer than anyone had expected, and the family never got to see the real Tommi and Sammi again.

Figure 8.3. A machinist's drawing of *Loksa*, the tugboat on which Tommi and Sammi travelled to Sweden. Photo: Anneli Karlsson, Swedish National Maritime Museum/SMTM.

Of the original pack of dogs – the farm dogs and their namesakes – Tommi the soft dog is the only one left. The story of how Tommi the soft dog became a boat refugee, while the original Tommi remained in Estonia in many ways speaks volumes about the shared human experience of fleeing being an act of leaving behind. Just as much as the small dog draws our attention to things salvaged and saved by an escape, it also speaks of separation, and of loss.

Things on the move

The story of Tommi the soft dog and his and his owner's experiences on board *Loksa* is one of thousands of individual stories from the Great Escape over the Baltic Sea (Fig. 8.3). Tommi's owner Taavi was far from the only child to flee the Baltic States because of the war. Among the refugees who left in 1943 and 1944 were some 5,000 young children. The exact number is not known, since most estimates of refugee numbers rely on residence permits, which were not required for children under 16 living with adult relatives.[4] Today, those child refugees are the only ones left to remember, to speak from first-hand experience of the Great Escape, or to pass on fragments of knowledge picked up from older family members. Hence, the oral testimony documented by the Swedish National Maritime Museum and personal belongings from the time have a natural bearing on the children's experiences and understanding.

Drawing on childhood memories and associated objects when exploring migration by sea is thought-provoking and challenging. For example, it becomes apparent that from a child's perspective, things adults would normally consider to have few if any maritime connotations may well be seen differently. Take the small suitcase in which Tommi was packed when leaving his Estonian home. Taavi remembers that before he made any friends in Sweden his favourite game was to play being at sea again. Since there were not many toys in his new home, things the family had brought with them from Estonia stood in as a boat. Taavi recalls sitting in the old suitcase he had with him on *Loksa*, imagining it was a boat at sea. An elegant ashtray his parents had packed became a small boat he steered over the floor–sea. So did a boat-shaped nail file in a manicure set which had been in his mother's luggage. 'Ships and boats were everywhere in my imagination,' Taavi explains, adding that the escape over the sea, who went and who remained behind, was an ever-present topic of conversation in his family and the Estonian exile community (Fig. 8.4).

As is clear from the documentation, children's belongings were common, sometimes perhaps even prioritized, on many of the escape boats. For example, Tommi's owner Taavi finds it telling that of the total of three or four bags he and his parents carried, one was his own small suitcase containing clothes, but also 'unnecessary' things such as the two soft dogs Tommi and Sammi, a toy aeroplane, and a small duck toy. Reflecting on the heirlooms of the escape, other people make the same observation. 'As we speak it strikes me that almost everything we brought with us – like my favourite doll and several of my stuffed animals, photos of me as a child, my christening gown, baptismal font with its cloth, as well as a number of my christening gifts such as silver spoons and some paintings – were *my* things, or at least closely associated with me,' a woman who was the only child of the family concludes, and continues, 'I believe my parents must have thought it especially important to save those things, so I would feel comfortable and so that later I would be able to connect with my origins.' (Fig. 8.5).

Today, Anita, as she is called, has most of the things she and her parents escaped with to Sweden. Her own children were baptized in her old christening gown, and her soft toys – a rabbit originally a gift from her father to her mother, a bear she got for her first Christmas, another little teddy bear, and a small spotty dog – have always been around. Her much-loved doll Lisa, though, was unfortunately destroyed by Swedish medical staff after only a couple of months in Sweden, as there was a concern that its beautiful plaited hair would spread diphtheria (Anita had been infected when she was vaccinated on arrival in Sweden, and she had kept the doll close while she was ill on the diphtheria ward).

Anita's observation that her parents' care for her and the affection they felt for mementoes of her early childhood can be read from the selection of things they took as they escaped, is not unique. Many families seem to have left their homes carrying similar things in their luggage, including children's everyday clothes and Sunday best, christening gowns, baby photos, storybooks, and toys. There are also examples of children's material culture taken by their parents to Sweden for nostalgic reasons – like a six-year-old daughter's long since outgrown first shoes.

Children were not always the ones responsible for packing their own things. As Tommi's owner Taavi was only just over two when escaping, he reckons his parents must have packed his little suitcase. Anita, who is slightly older, reckons her parents arranged her packing for her, but remembers she did have a say when it came to choosing which of her toys and teddy bears to take. Seven-year-old Ulvi remembers her mother rushing to pack two suitcases with some of Ulvi's books, dressmaking fabric, and some other family belonging – a spontaneous selection that later appeared strange. Ulvi took her teddy bear and held it tight for

Figure 8.4. Taavi's 'boats' – maritime objects from a child's perspective. Photo: Anneli Karlsson, Swedish National Maritime Museum/SMTM.

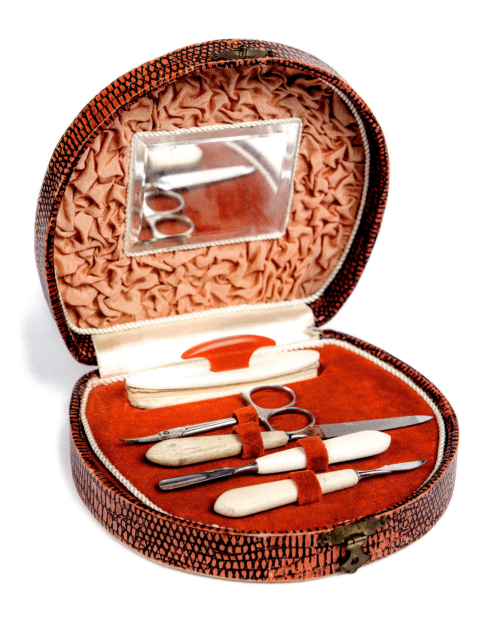

Figure 8.5. Anita's spotty dog and a photo of the two back in Riga, packed in the hope it would ease her transition to her new home country while retaining some ties to her past. Photo: Anneli Karlsson, Swedish National Maritime Museum/SMTM.

the whole crossing, as she and her sister shivered on deck, refusing to go downstairs into the crowded, stinking hold. Ulvi was heartbroken when it was taken from her on arrival to be fumigated, but she got it back and has kept it ever since.

Older children were sometimes entrusted with their own packing. Taimi, who was 14 at the time of the escape, took her teddy bear Mischka, some picture books, and her violin. Helju, the same age as Taimi, took her sketch pad and drew the unfamiliar coast while hoping the boat would show up. Mare, 9, packed her diary and a notebook with sketches and greetings from her friends, while slightly younger Ligita took her ABC and an illustrated book of Latvian folk songs.

Other things were apparently taken by children in secret or without being noticed by the adults. Helmi, who was 9, remembers them leaving in a hurry, and how she sneaked her most precious things – a picture card of the cute fawn Bambi from a newly released Walt Disney film and a box for gramophone needles (glittering treasure in Helmi's eyes) with Nipper the HMV dog from the painting *His Master's Voice* – into her dad's sack while her parents were hastily getting their things together.[5] On departure, 6-year-old Tiit had his pockets full of cartridges and hand grenade detonators he had found in the countryside and saved for fun. He remembers that when leaving Tallinn his father told him to empty his pockets and throw it all overboard, but that he disobeyed him – which caused a stir when they arrived in Sweden, as his clothes were disinfected with heat.

Needless to say, most belongings were never packed. In talking about her saved teddy bears, Anita recalls her favourite big brown bunny, which was probably too big, and in the end was left behind. Taimi, who valued the few books she owned highly, recalls not being allowed to take her German history books because they were too heavy. The further fate of these objects and all the other things that used to form part of the refugees' old lives are not known, but most probably they took a different path – one that did not involve a formative sea journey.

Maritime collections, missing children, allied artefacts

In explaining why he was not interested in merchant vessels, the famous wreck explorer and latest discoverer of the royal ship *Vasa*, Anders Franzén, once said that merchantmen did not really matter much in maritime history. Such ships primarily consisted of their cargo, he explained, adding that cereals, firewood, gold, tar, porcelain, and a thousand other goods did not qualify as maritime history just because they happened to be on ship.[6] Although it is easy to dismiss this conclusion as hasty and simplistic – there are copious amounts of porcelain and recovered goods from shipwrecked merchantmen in the storerooms of maritime museums – he did point to something interesting. 'Maritime' as a concept is not something fixed once and for all. Rather it is an assemblage in constant negotiation, underpinned and reproduced by institutions, scholars, and even heritage acts, but also challenged by new approaches and new definitions.[7]

Journeys of the kind associated with Tommi and other children have seldom gained much attention from scholars and curators in the field of maritime history. While the sea and the oceans are continually linked to shipping, cruising and leisure boats, fishing, piracy, naval warfare, and all their associated characters, they have less frequently been understood as spaces navigated by boat refugees. However, as recently stressed by several scholars and heritage institutions, migration by boat is a recurrent and significant phenomenon at sea, and ought to be acknowledged as maritime history.[8]

Like many other maritime museums around the world, the focus of the Swedish National Maritime Museum in Stockholm has always been shipping, sailors, and naval history, and more lately leisure craft. Being a national museum and authorized heritage institution, the museum is a leading national player when it comes to defining and maintaining a maritime canon, but also when pushing back its barriers. Its collections, which date to the early twentieth century, are central. While having a structuring effect on what narratives and episodes the museum mediates, they are also constantly evolving, partly due to continued collecting.[9] Every time an object is taken from a previous context to be added to the museum's collection – or assemblage, as it is conceptualized here – it gains new identities and joins new material alliances. Therefore, to some extent each new acquisition has the potential to affect parts of the collections' existing holdings and its general demarcations.[10] Accessioning an object or picture into the Maritime Museum's collection hence has an interesting twofold effect. On the one hand, the museum provides the object with a solid maritime identity; on the other hand, each new acquisition has the potential to push the boundaries and challenge our notions of the meaning of 'maritime'. So happens when Tommi the soft dog and the rest of the refugee children's belongings join the collections.

The overall picture when browsing the collection database of the Maritime Museum to find the likes of Tommi, or other examples of the Estonian and Latvian children's material culture, is one of absence.[11] Surprisingly few items testify to children's experiences of sea voyages. The search term 'leksak' ('toy') results in just three boat models, while 'dop' ('christening') – bearing in mind the many christening gowns and associated gifts the Baltic refugees took with them – without exception reflects the tradition of christening new ships. Keywords such as 'barn' ('children') result in little more than 300 photos and items, of which most are photos of children learning to sail or posing with their families on quays or ships. With a few exceptions – a photo of a small child playing in a rowing boat, and another of two kids reading comics in the forepeak of a leisure craft – there are almost no items relating to children playing, or of comfort and safety when at sea. An orange life jacket shows how kids of the 1950s or 1960s were sometimes equipped while going boating, but it is difficult to tell from the collections what other things they might have worn or packed before setting out on the boating holidays.

There are a few items in the collections that in a way echo some of Tommi's and his fellow soft toy's experiences, though – a small teddy bear and a little eagle wearing orange life jackets. Much like the comforting role of a teddy in the context of grief and safety, such soft toys are used by the Swedish Sea Rescue Society on missions where children are involved – for example, as when the society in 2015 assisted in saving migrants trying to cross the Mediterranean (Fig. 8.6).[12] Thus the only

Figure 8.6. Soft toys juxtaposed. A teddy bear in a life jacket, distributed by the Swedish Sea Rescue Society to young migrants crossing the Mediterranean, and a worn teddy bear comforting a 7-year-old girl during her escape to Sweden on *Salme* in 1944. Photo: Anneli Karlsson, Swedish National Maritime Museum/SMTM.

two previous soft toys in the collections both relate to experiences of fleeing, of dangerous sea crossings, and of comfort. Further, there are two inflatable life jackets worn by migrants crossing the Mediterranean, which in another context might have been considered children's toys – something which is underlined by the warnings printed inside stating 'This is not a life-saving device' and 'Will not protect against drowning'.[13]

To some extent, the soft dog Tommi, Anita's childhood teddy bears, and the rest of the Baltic refugee children's belongings bridge experiences separated by time and place. The warm knitted gloves and elegant christening gowns from 1944 are a sharp contrast to the multicoloured inflatable floating devices presently used in the Mediterranean, while the teddy bears distributed by Swedish rescuers and those carried by children escaping to Sweden form another sort of intersection. Together, they enrich our understanding of migration by boat, but also point to a general lack of representation of children in the collections, and perhaps also a tendency to confine the collecting and representation of children's material culture to areas closely linked to vulnerability.

Travelling memories and places in history

As pointed out by several scholars in the field of material culture, migration, and memory studies, memories are in constant motion, travelling not only across geographical borders and but also across media, social, political, and semantic boundaries. Memory travel thus involves a great variety of memory carriers, including material culture.[14] To escape by boat is to set out on a very special kind of sea voyage; one that will transform the life of all people on board. To some extent, this transition clings not only to humans, but also to things, which gain experiences and take on new meanings as they travel.[15]

Being such a profound turning point in life, the Great Escape across the Baltic Sea is nowadays part of all the objects that formed part of it. Although many of those things were never meant to go to sea, they did at some point find themselves in an escape boat in the middle of the Baltic. Hence Tommi, Mischka, Bambi, Lisa, and all the other soft toys and children's belongings of the Great Escape, like the ashtray, suitcase, and nail file Taavi later imagined to be his escape boats, have become imbued with memories of these sea journeys. Just as in the case of the many recovered artefacts from shipwrecks in museum warehouses, they tell us about the moments when the sea intervened in events in a way which stood out from everyday life – causing a shipwreck, dispersing a convoy, or offering itself as a route to freedom.

Besides being source material testifying to historic events, the artefacts of the Great Escape also have a unique ability to guide our historical interest and to make us move on from knowledge of the historical facts to a deeper understanding. Pay an interest in the luggage of former refugees setting out from Estonia and Latvia for Sweden at the end of the Second World War, and the children's presence on the refugee boats becomes apparent and understandable in a way that is beyond the written sources alone. Scrutinizing the material assemblages of the refugee boats, it is also evident that despite harsh and pressing circumstances, children's belongings and associated items were often prioritized at the expense of other kinds of artefacts when packing for hazardous sea voyages and an unknown future. As much as they reflect parental care and affection, they also speak of absences, whether lost homes or loved ones. And they illustrate that not everyone crossing the sea is an old sea hand, and that the sea not only takes lives, it also saves lives.

In adding these artefacts to the Swedish National Maritime Museum's collections – or assemblage, as it is better understood – the boat children step into maritime history, revealing new stories and reminding us of events not previously dealt with by the museum. What is more, they also point to far larger gaps in the collections; gaps as regards the overall representation of children's material culture and their experiences of the sea.

Who has a place in maritime history? From now on, Tommi the sea dog and his fellow Estonian and Latvian soft toy comrades do. In joining the collections of the Maritime Museum, their photographs, like their stories, illustrate the need to continually develop the collection, so setting the stage for future conversations, new narratives, and fresh perspectives on the many ways the sea intervenes in human life.

Notes

1 This essay draws on interviews and documentation carried out as part of the National Maritime Museum's project 'Flyktens materialitet' ('The Materiality of the Great Escape'), funded by the Swedish National Heritage Board's R&D grant ref. 4.2-2018-1234 for 2019–2021. The informants referred to in the text are Anita Nilsson, Ligita Legzdins, Riina Noodapera (daughter of Helju Kivisto), Taavi Kaaman, Taimi Wiburg, Tiit Tamme, Tiiu Valmet, and Ulvi Paff.

2 Jason De Léon, *The Land of Open Graves: Living and Dying on the Migrant Trail* (Oakland 2015).

3 Gilles Deleuze & Félix Guattari, *A Thousand Plateaus: Capitalism and Schizophrenia* (Minneapolis 1987); Manuel DeLanda, *Assemblage Theory* (Edinburgh 2016); see also Ben Jervis, *Assemblage Thought and Archaeology* (London 2019); Yannis Hamilakis & Andrew Meirion Jones, 'Archaeology and Assemblage', *Cambridge Archaeological Journal* 27/1 (2017), 77–84.

4 Sven Alur Reinans, 'Balterna i Sverige: Några demografiska aspekter', in Lars-Gunnar Eriksson (ed.), *De första båtflyktingarna: En antologi om balterna i Sverige* (Stockholm 1986).

5 Mirja Arnshav, *De små båtarna och den stora flykten* (Lund 2020), 70.

6 Anders Franzén, 'Varför forska i örlogsskepp?', *Meddelanden från Marinarkeologiska Sällskapet* 5/4 (1982), 6–9.

7 Christer Westerdahl, *Norrlandsleden*, 1: *Källor till det maritima kulturlandskapet: en handbok i marinarkeologisk inventering* (Härnösand 1989); Christer Westerdahl, 'Fish and Ships: Towards a Theory of Maritime Culture', *Deutsches Schiffahrtsarchiv Wissenschaftliches Jahrbuch des Deutschen Schiffahrtsmuseums* 30 (2008), 191–236; David Berg Tuddenham, 'Maritime Cultural Landscapes, Maritimity and Quasi Objects', *Journal of Maritime Archaeology* 5/1 (2010), 5–16.

8 Vinh Nguyen, 'Nước/Water: Oceanic Spatiality and the Vietnamese Diaspora', in Lydia Mannik (ed.), *Migration by Boat: Discourses of Trauma, Exclusion and Survival* (New York 2016), 65–79.

9 Fredrik Svanberg, *Museer och samlande* (Stockholm 2009), 9–11; Gösta Webe, 'Föreningen Sveriges Sjöfartsmuseum 75 år', in Anders Björklund (ed.), *Sjöhistoriska museet 50 år* (Stockholm 1988); Mirja Arnshav, '100 Years of Contemporary Collecting: Revisiting the Sailor Tattoos at the Maritime Museum, Stockholm', in Owain Rhys & Zelda Baveystock (eds.), *Collecting the Contemporary: A Handbook for Social History Museums* (Edinburgh 2014), 214–49.

10 Adriana Muñoz, *From Curiosa to World Culture: A History of the Latin American Collections at the Museum of World Culture in Sweden* (Gothenburg 2012); Barbara Kirshenblatt-Gimblett, 'Objects of ethnography', in Ivan Karp & Steven D. Lavine (ed.), *Exhibiting Cultures: The Poetics and Politics of Museum Display* (Washington 1991), 386–443; Chris Wingfield, 'Collection as (Re)assemblage: Refreshing Museum Archaeology', *World Archaeology* 49/2 (2018), 1–14; Lotten Gustafsson Reinius, 'Innanför branddörren: Etnografiska samlingar som medier och materialitet', in Solveig Jülich, Patrik Lundell, & Pelle Snickars (eds.), *Mediernas kulturhistoria* (Stockholm 2008), 73–7; Lotten Gustafsson Reinius, 'Ordna', in Marie Cronqvist (ed.), *Allt som tänkas kan: 29 ingångar till vetenskapens villkor* (Gothenburg 2010), 116–31.

11 Sjöhistoriska museet (Swedish Maritime Museum) at the website DigitaltMuseum, digitaltmuseum.se/owners/S-SMM-SM.

12 Maria Sturken, 'Historieturister: Souvenirer, arkitektur och minnets kitschifiering', in Johan Redin & Hans Ruin (eds.), *Mellan minne och glömska: Studier i det kulturella minnets förvandlingar* (Gothenburg 2016), 186–211.

13 DigitaltMuseum, s.v. 'Jag räddar liv', digitaltmuseum.se/.

14 Astrid Erll, 'Resande minnen', in Redin & Ruin 2016, 163–211; Baiba Bela, 'Complexities of Memory Travels: The Latvian Case', in Kirsti Jõesalu & Anu Kannike (eds.), *Cultural Patterns and Life Stories* (Tallinn 2016), 211–38; Maja Povrzanović Frykman, 'Sensitive Objects of Humanitarian Aid', in Jonas Frykman & Maja Povrzanović Frykman (eds.), *Sensitive Objects: Affect and Material Culture* (Lund 2016), 79–104.

15 Hans Peter Hahn & Hadas Weiss (eds.), *Mobility, Meaning and the Transformations of Things: Shifting Contexts of Material Culture through Time and Space* (Oxford 2013).

CHAPTER 9

How to break the rules just right

Åland smugglers, 1920–1950

Ida Hughes Tidlund

In the Baltic Sea, near several national borders and inhabited by a seafaring people, the Åland Islands became a hub for illicit trade early on. When Finland banned alcohol in the early twentieth century, the smuggling escalated to unforeseen levels, despite international collaborations and new border agreements. But parallel to these grand attempts, on a local level in Åland the game of smuggling continued according to its own complex rules.

My grandmother was a smuggler. Working on one of the passenger ships trafficking the route between Mariehamn in Åland and Stockholm in Sweden, she was given the fringe benefit of buying tobacco products at low prices in the ship's tax-free shop. When the ship moored in Stockholm, she walked down to the bars and restaurants in the old town, selling them tax-free cigarettes to sell on to their customers. A win–win situation, according to her. All involved – my grandmother, the restaurant owners, the smokers – made or saved a little money.

My grandmother lived in Åland, the island archipelago between Finland and Sweden. Working at sea and knowing how to take advantage of the many crossings between countries, she was a typical Ålander. As typical was her light-hearted attitude to the black market. True, avoiding detection was paramount as getting caught would cost her the job. But it was not anything to be ashamed of, as 'everyone' did it and no one was harmed by it.

In a recent study of smuggling, the historian Alan Karras agrees with this view. Smuggling, he argues, is a victimless crime. The large-enough profit for an individual is a tiny amount of lost revenue for the injured party, the state.[1] And, he continues, smuggling actually serves the state, as it eases the economic pressure on its citizens, making smuggling 'the perfect compromise' for everyone involved.[2] There are less positive sides to smuggling, though. Checking for contraband is expensive, and the money and effort spent chasing smugglers could be better used in other ways. Unrestricted business with harmful products can cause injuries. Smugglers often put themselves at risk when avoiding detection, making the activity not only illegal but dangerous. Smuggling can be unfair when those who trade legally make less profit than the criminals. But this essay does not intend to assess contraband per se. The aim is instead to explore the accepted rules associated with smuggling at a time and place where it was a standard practice.

The leading role is played by the maritime border between Åland and Sweden – the border that enabled the tax-free sales of tobacco products on the ferry on which my grandmother worked. Smuggling takes place not only near borders but because of them. Borders are essential for smuggling, as the act of crossing a border transforms an object into contraband.[3] Smuggling can be summarized as a breaking of borders; geographical, legal, commercial and perhaps social. The act of violating a limit is what defines smuggling.[4] Smuggling thus demonstrates that borders are not as watertight as they might seem; there are loopholes and gaps in their purportedly impermeable line, and these passages are sought out by those in the contraband business. This is particularly the case when it comes to borders in the sea, being harder to control. Åland's location near several maritime borders made the island province a prime spot for contraband activities in the first half of the last century, on all scales both large and small.

The essay considers the stories of three men, born in Åland at the turn of the twentieth century, and here called Jansson, Karlsson, and

Eriksson, which are among the commonest surnames in Åland. Their stories have been selected as centrepieces since they represent different positions in the local smuggling hierarchy. Jansson smuggled when the opportunity arose for a little extra cash. For Karlsson, smuggling was his main source of income, and he knew the rules of the game well. Eriksson knew the rules too, but from the other side of the law. He was a coastguard and supposed to prevent smuggling, but enforcing the law can be socially costly.

The men were interviewed by staff from the Åland Museum between thirty and sixty years after the events described. The interviews were not about smuggling per se, as the staff conducted interviews with around a thousand islanders, who were asked to talk about their lives – families, traditions, occupations, travel, and whatever else that they wanted to say about their long lives. The three stories were found among the many archived interviews as a part of a dissertation project about how the international borders around Åland have influenced a century of daily life in the region. The interviews and interviewees have been anonymized, if only because smuggling is illegal and the men's stories referred to actions of a possibly criminal nature. I say 'possibly', because an action is not proven criminal until it has been charged and prosecuted, and to my knowledge none of the men were ever tried for their smuggling activities.[5] Some short fragments from other islanders' stories occur in the text, too, and these are only referred to by their year of birth.[6]

Borders and contraband

The Åland Islands number up to 6,000 islands, rocks, and skerries, of which one in ten is inhabited. It is an insular landscape, as insular is the base of the word island, but not in the meaning of isolated. The islands' location in the middle of the Baltic Sea has made them a hub for the sea trade and traffic in which the archipelagic populations on both sides of the Baltic Sea were involved, originally called 'peasant sailing' (*bondeseglationen*).[7] Stockholm has long been the usual destination for peasants and fishermen from the islands. Although other cities such as Turku and Helsinki might be nearer, Stockholm was the preferred market, with larger demand there promising greater profits, which by extension saw the city grow.[8] Ålanders took food, livestock, wood, and sand there and brought other products home. It was not free trade, though. By the fifteenth century, Ålanders were paying a tax in kind – firewood – which had to be delivered to Stockholm. In 1624, 50 per cent of Stockholm's total tax revenue came from Ålanders.[9] Such border-based restrictions and regulations were important sources of income for the state. In 1809, when a new international border detached Finland from Sweden, ships from Åland and Finland had to pay custom duty on goods previously traded freely into Sweden.[10] Åland boats were so important to trade they were given various exceptions, but thirty years later the number of Åland ships registered in Stockholm harbours had plummeted.[11] It is possible that the number of boats arriving without registering was higher. As the historian Simon Harvey has shown, wherever a line was drawn and customs duty was payable, smuggling was bound to take place.[12] The increased taxes in the 1840s did indeed lead to increased smuggling between Åland and Stockholm.[13]

The border between Sweden and Finland determined the smuggling around Åland. But the smuggling actually determined the border, too. Harvey claims that the world as we know it has been materially transformed by smuggling in the past.[14] For example, the world would not be as it is now if trade along the Silk Road had not commenced.[15] By the same token, the territorial outline of Sweden and Finland was an explicit response to contraband, too. When the League of Nations became involved in the conflict between Sweden and Finland regarding the Åland Islands' future, smuggling was a theme of immense meaning. The League of Nations redrew several borders in Europe in the aftermath of the First World War, and the 'Åland Question' concerned where the border between Finland and Sweden should run since Finland had become independent in 1917; east or west of the Åland Islands. Both states claimed that the islands naturally belonged to them and presented arguments based on history, ethnicity, and language. After careful consideration, the League of Nations settled in 1921 that the islands were to belong to Finland. Counteracting smuggling was a decisive argument for the border's location, as 'To have [the eastern] water as a tax border, where the seafaring is hard to control, would to a high degree promote smuggling'.[16]

The waters between Åland and Finland could not be sufficiently controlled. It was deemed as too narrow, and having too many islands offering places to hide. Patrolling those waters would be difficult, too. The League of Nations posited how a custom control vessel chasing after a smuggler's boat would risk crossing the international border in pursuit, and how that would cause complaints.[17] As the relationship between the two states was already awkward, future tension should be avoided. Therefore, the decision was that the Sea of Åland was the 'natural' divide between Finland and Sweden. The correct border was in the end a border of expediency, heavily influenced by the desire to stop the smugglers. Smuggling was a dire enough problem to determine where the Sweden–Finland border would run.

A booze war in the Islands of Peace

It was not just any old smuggling that the League of Nations wanted to avert. The main product they had in mind (as had the smugglers) was alcohol. One of the first acts of the newly independent state of Finland had been to ban alcohol. Finland, like many other states, had tried to reduce alcohol consumption for a long time. In 1865, there were attempts to turn people to drinking beer instead of spirits, as it was assumed that if the regular consumer became a 'devotee of beer', the spirits problem would be solved. The strategy was a little too successful. Beer consumption exploded, leading the temperance movement to advocate complete abstinence, but bills on this were turned down by Finland's Russian rulers. The independent state of Finland went dry on 1 June 1919, meaning that manufacture, sale, and storage of anything stronger than 2 per cent was prohibited.[18]

Prohibition led to a rapid increase in smuggling. This was an expected problem, but it had been assumed that the smuggling would disappear once things had had a chance to settle down. But the opposite was the case. In 1919, just over 5,000 violations of the Prohibition Act were registered; in 1931 there were 30,000.[19] Of course, statistics on smuggling

Figure 9.1. The smuggling ship *Helmi* moored in Mariehamn, Åland. Photo: Åland's Museum.

are incoherent. Being a murky business, high numbers of confiscations do not necessarily mean more smuggling, but perhaps more control.[20] This was already known. In 1932, it was emphasized that attempts to determine the extent of smuggling had drawn a blank (Fig. 9.1). The illicit traffic was hidden, leaving the field open to guesses and specu-lation.[21] Either way, the historian John Wuorinen stated that alcohol prohibition was honoured more in the breach than in the observance.[22]

On the other side of the Baltic Sea, Sweden used a different system to control alcohol consumption. The 'Gothenburg system', established in 1865, involved the organization and supervision of alcohol use in the region. Forty years on, the system was introduced nationally. It was predicated on all profits from the sale of alcohol going to the state, which also compensated shops for lost revenue. Passbooks were issued

Figure 9.2. 'No! Is this to be our future?' A Swedish poster against the prohibition law, expecting a ban to lead to increased smuggling. Photo: Swedish Museum of Spirits.

in which all purchases of alcohol were registered, although only people who were old enough, had sufficient income, and lived a moderate life were eligible for a passbook. The allowed amount varied depending on gender, income, and marital status, and the passbook was withdrawn if there were signs of abuse or illicit trade.[23] The results of this system were deemed satisfactory enough for the majority of the Swedish population to vote against a prohibition law in 1922 (Fig. 9.2).

In the middle between the two countries was Åland. Caught between two diametrically opposite alcohol policies, the Islands of Peace as they were known became a main battlefield in the 'booze war' of the Baltic Sea. An Åland woman born in 1910 referred to prohibition between 1919 and 1932 as the 'work' years – the Finnish for smuggling is *joppaus*, derived from the Swedish word for 'work'.[24] Prohibition created the market for 'work' as smuggling met demand. The Åland Islands were far from dry during the state-appointed drought. Alcohol was cheap and plentiful. A litre of brandy cost as little as a packet of cigarettes. It had been assumed that alcoholism would decrease with prohibition, but instead it increased fourfold.[25] One reason for this was the growing consumption of spirits. Beer and wine were bulky items to smuggle and therefore rare. Spirits were preferred because of their smaller volume and greater value.[26] Hence, smugglers provided consumers with stronger alcohol. Booze was everywhere – 'you got a drink wherever you went, you could swim in it' – and people even fed the pigs with brandy 'and the pigs got so drunk'.[27] But alcohol was not the only smuggled product, as Jansson's story will show. After prohibition, and in particular during rationing in Finland in the Second World War, the common contraband was coffee, sugar, petrol, and other household goods. Such was the world in which Jansson, Karlsson, and Eriksson lived.

Jansson claims to eat a horse

In 1968, an old man was interviewed about his life.[28] The man, here called Jansson, was happy to share stories of his many dramatic sea crossings. One of them was in September 1922, when he and a friend sailed across the Åland Sea to Stockholm. Jansson had heard there was high demand for wood and decided to take a boatload over. The stormy weather and difficult crossing delayed them and they did not arrive in Stockholm harbour until late at night. The next morning, they slept late, only to be woken up by the footsteps on the deck. They realized that it was the customs officers boarding their sailing boat and leapt up as their load did not only consist of wood: they had brought plenty of cigarettes to sell. In the interview, Jansson claimed not to know it was contraband. Yet he had hidden his cigarettes under the firewood, indicating that he knew it was illegal. His partner had not hidden his own yet, so he 'flew up and threw his cigarettes under the mattress' and then pretended to be asleep. The customs officers entered and asked if they had any alcohol on board. The men truthfully replied that they had none. But the custom officers still searched the boat, and soon found the cigarettes. Jansson chuckled when he described what happened next:

> I said, 'I am a heavy smoker and the trip can be long in autumn, very stormy, so I made sure to be well-supplied'. And I gave the boys a carton [of cigarettes] each and they were happy. I got to keep the rest.

Besides cigarettes, Jansson had brought meat from a horse he had had slaughtered. That, too, was against the rules, as the restrictions on the sale of foodstuffs had been tightened. Another archived interview mentioned some of the implications. A man born in 1892 used to transport pike and meat to Stockholm to sell, but ceased when 'it got a bit fussy' in the late 1920s. Inspectors dressed in white coats had come down to the harbour to check on what was being sold, talking about hygiene and requiring all meat to be salted for at least a week before being sold.[29] Jansson was told that selling his horsemeat would require a licence, which he did not have. The custom officers put seals on the bags to make sure they were not opened. But Jansson found a way around this too:

> I said, 'I need a bag open, I must have some to eat'. And yeah, that was okay. But we did not eat much, no, I sold most of it and made good money. And when that bag was empty, I told customs, 'come and open up another bag, I'm out of food'. And they came, opened a bag, and removed the seal, and... yeah.

Figure 9.3. Unknown woman at the fish market in Stockholm to where many Ålanders were heading with their loads, 1938. Photo: Stockholm City Museum.

'So, it was a good trip', commented the interviewer. 'Yes. And we sold the wood too,' replied Jansson.

The markets were full of people there for a while to trade. Jansson and his friend were kept busy during their stay in Stockholm, selling the wood openly and the rest on the side (Fig. 9.3). They returned home a fortnight later from a successful trip, just in time to harvest the potatoes, and the interview continued with Jansson's accounting for how he made a living by shipping, hunting seals, and fishing. The main theme of the interview was Jansson's memories of the sea – sailing, boats, ice, waves, and wind – and selling contraband was one detailed story among many.

These were the stories of small-scale smuggling in the archived interviews: peripheral, both in the interviews and as a source of income. It could be a risky business, but safe enough for many to try it. When returning from Stockholm, they could bring back sugar, coffee, and petrol for personal consumption. Customs officials in Mariehamn checked the amounts. Sometimes, there was customs duty to pay on the goods, which ate up the profit. But mostly, officials were generous in their interpretation of the amounts brought back. 'You deserve some cheap sugar now you have travelled so far' is in one interview said to have been a common comment.[30] Some officials were stingy while others were more flexible in their interpretation of goods and amounts. The sailors knew whom to avoid, and tried to time their return to their home harbour. It could be worthwhile choosing a customs office further away, if a penny-pinching official was on duty in one's regular harbour. Small bribes were not uncommon either.

Smuggling could be profitable for everyone involved, if the limits were a little flexible on both sides. Illicit trade could be more or less prohibited, depending on the item and the intention. To understand the different scales of contraband, it is necessary to look at what was being smuggled.[31] When the intention was to make some pin money, many officials turned a blind eye, an approach the ethnologist Helena Ruotsala has observed in a study of smuggling in northern Finland.[32] As one participant in that study put it, smuggling did not 'even smell of sin' as long as it consisted of items for personal consumption.[33] But there were strict rules to adhere to in this unofficial agreement on how business could run smoothly, in a 'I'll look away if you pretend to be innocent' kind of way. Jansson's claim to have a voracious appetite and be in need of a great deal of horse meat for 'personal consumption' was incongruous. It was not Jansson's shrewd lying that saved his goods, but rather a matter of both sides playing according to certain rules. The customs officials most likely knew he was lying, and Jansson presumably knew they knew. But *because* he lied, they could pretend to believe him, a transaction lubricated by some cartons of cigarettes changing hands. According to Karras, such dealings are not a matter of individual state representatives acting in a corrupt manner, but the state itself turning a blind eye. Laws, he writes, are created with a specific aim in mind, but obedience is not necessarily one of them. National laws can be more about gaining legitimacy and authority by showing the population that the legal regime exists and is relevant.[34] Laws that restrict consumer behaviour are widely violated, and that outcome is not only generally understood – it is preferred. Karras calls laws about consumption restrictions a charade that each side had its own reasons to go along with. An eradication of smuggling would bottle up an economic pressure that contraband actions let flow. Instead of risking consumers revolting en masse, the state adopts a lax approach to illicit trading.[35]

This holds true for the small-scale smuggling Knutsson calls popular illegality. In her thesis about smuggling in Sweden in the eighteenth century, she suggests a division between popular and business illegality. Popular illegality, she argues, was conducted by the common people looking to bolster their income. Business illegality involved people higher on the social ladder who orchestrated smuggling to extend their trade.[36] Some have pointed out that smuggling is rarely seen as an immoral or serious offence, but rather a justifiable way of supporting oneself.[37] Jansson showed no signs of embarrassment when talking about his successful smuggling, nor did the interviewer, who commented on the journey being a 'good trip'. But the organized, business-like smuggling was an activity that one more warily admitted to having been involved in. That type of smuggling was usually described as taking place 'elsewhere', by 'others'. During prohibition, smuggling alcohol was lucrative business. The profits smugglers made, like the fact alcohol was not a household staple, meant the authorities were more inclined to intervene. But the alcohol business was not free from corruption. Alcohol was illegal for private consumption, but vets and doctors could prescribe it for medicinal purposes. One interviewee described how pharmacies in Åland had huge stores of alcohol. Blue prescriptions were for spirits, mostly prescribed by vets; doctors usually prescribed using yellow scripts, which were for 'nobler drinks'. There was 'everything. Wines, whiskey, brandy, liqueur… we had it all.' One day, continued the interviewee, a gentleman came in with 50 prescriptions for three-star brandy. 'Fifty bottles! Oh yes.' The interviewee was at pains to point out that he had been not much more than a helper at the pharmacy: he simply collected the bottles to be dispatched by the pharmacist. Perhaps the story would not have been offered with such carefree ease had he had a more central role. He also emphasized that the doctors and vets involved in the shady business were not local – 'The scripts were all from Helsinki. You could always buy a prescription from Turku or Helsinki' – elegantly locating the root of the problem somewhere other than in his own region.[38]

Karlsson broods over lost cognac

Like many others Karlsson was a jack of all trades.[39] He farmed, fished, and traded to both Sweden and mainland Finland. During prohibition, he was also active as a smuggling middleman. His job was to sail to international waters where the ships with alcohol in stock were anchored, purchase the booze, and get it safely to the customers without getting caught by patrolling coastguards.

As alcohol policies were national, international borders determined which type of restriction applied where. The same borders defined the area where authorities could intervene against smuggling. Beyond, in international waters, national law did not pertain, which was why the 'booze ships' could anchor there safely. Custom officers patrolled near the border, waiting for smugglers to cross back into national waters on their way home with their loads. The smugglers travelled at night, running as silently as possible and without lights to avoid being spotted. Being experienced, or taking someone who knew every inch of the sea, was paramount. People with local knowledge could make extra cash by piloting a smuggler's boat without being involved with the goods.[40] To limit the risk of being caught with evidence in the boat, the contraband was often hidden for later collection. Common hiding places were on islands or in the sea, often in canisters tied together and lowered to the seabed, where they waited 'like pearls in a pearl necklace', as Karlsson described it.

A few years into prohibition, countries with Baltic coastlines plus Norway joined forces to tackle smuggling. They met for a conference in Helsinki in 1925 and concluded that collaboration on international customs controls was required to thwart alcohol consumption, being 'a peril to general morals'.[41] The main problem for the custom officials was that they could only arrest smugglers in national waters, while the smugglers could seek protection in international waters. The authorities' inflexible approach to borders gave the smugglers too great an advantage, which was why the convention resulted in a new law that gave every nation the right to confiscate vessels within twelve nautical miles of the coast, rather than the existing three nautical miles: a 'radical replacement of the territorial border'.[42] Smugglers were not put out by this. In the early years of prohibition, one interviewee said, the booze ships were so close that the fishermen could easily sail between their fishing nets and the ships whenever they felt like a drink. After the change in the law, collecting alcohol took a little more planning, 'but there were no problems sailing twelve miles instead of three'.[43]

The adjustment of authorities' extended rights did not include international waters, however. The booze ships were still safe in maritime no-man's-land, and according to Karlsson they were like floating bars. They were staffed by sailors, who took care of the transport, and salesmen responsible for the business. When anchored, the sailors sat out on deck and played the accordion. 'There was no villainy atmosphere at all', remembered Karlsson. Local smugglers when they arrived were thrown a rope and boarded the booze ship. Some of the booze ships had a bar counter where smugglers could try the stuff on offer for free. 'You just had to point at what you wanted', described Karlsson, and the smell of alcohol was so strong 'you could get drunk from just breathing'. Sometimes, Karlsson was given bottles of wine for himself to keep: 'just cheap Spanish wine, but that's okay, too'. You paid on the spot. A bottle cost 3 or 4 marks to the supplier, plus a fee of around a quarter of a mark per bottle for transport if you had come in someone else's boat. The same bottle could be sold for 40 marks further up the Finnish coast, indicating that the business could be profitable.[44]

One night during prohibition, Karlsson had been out to international waters to collect a special order for a local restaurant: more than a hundred canisters of spirits plus six crates of the finest French cognac. The cognac was too valuable to be hidden, so Karlsson brought it all the way home. He was tired after the night's work, and tipsy after having been on the smuggler's boat, so he just stowed the crates in his boathouse and went to sleep, only to be woken up by his mother shortly after. She had been alerted by a glimpse of something green out at sea – the colour of the coastguard. Karlsson ran down to the shore and spotted a solitary figure in a rowing boat, who slowly rowed past the boathouse, where the doors were slightly ajar. (Patrolling coastguards often used rowing boats, as the islanders had learnt to recognize the sound of the patrol boat.) There was no time for Karlsson to hide the crates. The coastguard called for the patrol boat, which was waiting just out of sight. Karlsson described what happened next:

> They took the crates and raised all those bloody banderoles with stars and flags they used when they had confiscated something really good.

Losing so much of the cognac was going to cost Karlsson a great deal of money, but such were the rules of the game. But he had another reason to be bitter about their triumph. Karlsson saw that the patrol boat was making for the other side of the island, and followed to see what the coastguards would do. He hid in some bushes and watched as

> the steward came out with a tray of glasses, and he took a bucket of water and rinsed the glasses, and then he sniffed at all the glasses as if to check that the smell of alcohol was gone.

Bobbing in the water around the patrol boat were bits of the crates. It was far from the first time Karlsson had lost a load, but this time he was upset. He read the newspapers closely after the incident to see if the confiscation was reported, and was dismayed to find it was not. In the interview, he pointed out that customs officers were not known for stealing what they had confiscated and said it 'must have been an exception'. The rules of the game were strict: smuggling was a game with high returns and high risks. All involved were expected to respect the rules, and the customs officers stealing a load was an obvious breach. But Karlsson disliked customs officers who took their job too seriously almost as much. According to him, zealous officials did not play fair: 'they looked up every single bottle, just to mess with us'.

All stories considered here were told in retrospect. Perhaps the temporal distance helped the men talk about their law-breaking, and in a way that was rather brash and boastful. Besides complaining about the treacherous coastguards, Karlsson used the interview to brag about being

Figure 9.4. The 'King of Smuggling', Algoth Niska (1888–1954), author of an autobiography focusing on his career running contraband. Photo: Åland's Museum.

the type of smuggler the better sort of restaurant relied on to deliver nice cognac. Smuggling gave rise to many anecdotes, but the stories are more than that. According to Karras, smuggling stories are sources with which one can explore the relationship between state and consumers living within its authority.[45] The image of a smuggler as unyielding and independent, like Karlsson, is an important aspect of those anecdotes. As Harvey puts it, smuggling is an individual-oriented free-trade response to protectionism, and just as important a by-product are the stories of the smuggler as rebellious, resilient, surrounded by an air of romance.[46] The archived interviews have many stories of wily individuals making a fool of a customs officer or repeatedly dodging the plodding authorities. There is often bravado in the shape of a man who uses his wits to cunningly escape from customs officers, sometimes with the help of the locals acting as middlemen or helpers. The most popular stories were about the 'big sharks' – the organized smugglers in international networks. In the Baltic Sea, the biggest shark of all was Algoth Niska, who was active throughout prohibition and was already a legendary in Finland (Fig. 9.4). The stories about Niska were so popular that in 1931 he published a book called *Mina Äventyr* ('My adventures') describing the many occasions when he had outwitted the customs officers.[47] A former customs officer involved in chasing Niska said in an archived interview he 'was a real man', not without admiration. 'No one could ever catch him! He got away, every time'.[48] Niska himself put his success down to divine intervention, further emphasizing his achievements: 'God protects the smuggler.'[49] One interviewee remembered Niska as a regular visitor to her family home. He was a handsome and popular guest who brought 'sweets for the kids and booze for the grown-ups'. When Niska left, custom officers would come ashore to search for hidden contraband. She and her siblings used to play a trick on the officers. They placed large, empty tins in piles of branches and twigs, knowing that the officers looked for hidden alcohol by poking around with sticks. When the stick hit a tin, they thought they had found evidence. The children laughed when the custom officers had to move all the wood to find the tins, only to realize they had been tricked.[50] Niska's visits, and perhaps the stories of his escapades even more so, gave the children an opportunity to make a fool of the officers just as Niska had done.

The authorities made repeated attempts at catching Niska and eventually succeeded. Large-scale smuggling was not tolerated in the same way as Jansson's. But where did Karlsson fit in? He called himself a middleman, but from his stories it seems his smuggling escapades were numerous and stretched over decades. During prohibition, large-scale smuggling became so bad a problem in Finland that it was said to be 'a national shame'.[51] The state could not turn a blind eye at too conspicuous a smuggling operation, which was why business illegalism was treated differently from the popular illegalism of Jansson's type.

Eriksson fails to catch smugglers

The young Finnish state's resources for combating smuggling had proved insufficient in the first decade of independence. Smuggling threatened the very foundation of the state: booze ships were anchored just outside its borders, and the population near the coasts were said to be in danger. Something had to be done. In 1930, the Finnish coastguard was established as a special agency under the Finnish Border Guard.[52] Besides assisting vessels and people in difficulties at sea, their task was to patrol the areas where smuggling was worst and arrest the smugglers. That way, the push-back against the contraband business could be more efficient for a lower cost.

Åland was pointed out as a region of special concern and the Åland Sea as a high-risk smuggling area where patrolling was 'always justified'.[53] The coastguards were local Ålanders trained in mainland Finland by the military. Eriksson, our third interviewee, was one of those coastguards.[54] He patrolled a high-risk area in the 1950s when smuggling was still immense. It was not rare, he said in the interview, to find barrels of spirits floating in the sea. Nevertheless, Eriksson caught no one. Nor had his local colleagues. But he said that some patrol boats from Turku had caught a few. All through the interview, Eriksson seemed reluctant to discuss it and replied tersely to most questions regarding his work. The interviewer tried different approaches. To the question of whether Eriksson thought he and his colleagues made a difference by patrolling, he replied: 'I do not know what to say.' The interviewer altered the question slightly, and asked whether the coastguard found the night patrols motivating, and the coastguard replied, 'Well, we did not think so, but what could we say. If orders came – '.

Orders came from the central administration in mainland Finland, where Eriksson had trained. He spoke openly about his experiences there and the resentment he felt towards his employer, the Finnish Border

Guard, a military authority, although the coastguards were civil. Eriksson had had a tough time during training. Relations between the state of Finland and the autonomous minority of Åland were often tense, and the animosity was often apparent on an individual level. Eriksson had been 'bawled at' several times and 'terribly tormented' for being an Ålander: 'we were not worth a jot'. He had found comfort and assistance from some of the others, however, and that was lucky: food was dull and scarce, and 'I would have starved if they had not shared with me'. A contributing factor in the Ålanders being bullied was that they had difficulties understanding the military hierarchy, due to the demilitarization of autonomous Åland. Eriksson and other Ålanders who had little experience of rank badges often made mistakes, because 'we did not know when to leap up when a person entered the room, or when to remain seated'. When he returned to Åland as a coastguard having completed his training, he felt relief. He and his colleagues agreed to ignore the blind discipline, except when Finnish officers visited to review their work and the coastguards had to stand to attention in uniform again.

To understand smuggling, one must understand the intentions of the smuggler.[55] Why do people resist the law and put themselves at risk? According to Harvey, profit is always at the root of it.[56] But it is equally important to understand the intention of the people working against it. How could a coastguard fail to catch smugglers in an area where smuggling was rife? People's approaches to the law, wrote Clifford Geertz in 1983, are fine-tuned to every nuance, resulting in a local sensibility of legality that might be different from that of the central authorities.[57] And this opens up for a more open-ended understanding of 'profit'. A marine pilot who worked in the area around Åland described in an interview how he regularly found contraband floating in the sea. Sometimes, he took it home. Other times, he handed it in to the coastguards for the reward, and other times again, he warned the smugglers.[58] His decision was based on what he would benefit most from, and the most suitable 'profit' could vary. A coastguard who worked in Åland in the 1930s explained that when he caught smugglers they often lied about their names.[59] The interviewer did not ask how he could know they were lying, or how he did not know the names of people he caught patrolling

Figure 9.5. Confiscated alcohol, 1950s. Photo: Swedish Customs Museum.

an area near his home. Like Jansson claiming to be hungry enough to eat a horse, even an obvious lie can be productive.

Later in the interview with Eriksson, the focus shifted to a ship's bell. Eriksson explained that the bell was loot. The coastguards had the job of rescuing sailors when boats capsized. First, Eriksson said, they saved the sailors, just as they were supposed to. That done, they would loot the boat – generally alongside the villagers, who were often quick to turn up. According to the official regulations, the coastguards were supposed to protect the ship from looters, but they thought it was only fair to remove 'all that was loose' according to tradition. On the occasion when Eriksson took the ship's bell, he also took home some cooking utensils and enough bread to last him a year. They also took 'loads and loads of brandy, contraband probably' to the coastguard station. The next day, they talked about returning to the ship to protect it as they knew the villagers would be back, but with that much brandy to drink they spent the day at the station instead (Fig. 9.5).

With this in mind, Eriksson's tight-lipped replies to the questions about him failing to catch smugglers should be seen in a different light. Perhaps he did encounter smugglers, but never reported them, whether because the contraband could benefit him financially, or because a report would come at a social price. It cannot have been easy, representing an often-scorned government agency in a local setting, in particular as relations between the autonomous region of Åland and the sovereign state of Finland were often tense. Against that backdrop, one can imagine that Eriksson was more loyal to his fellow Ålanders than to a resented employer. Orders from Finland were followed to a point: when told to, they did patrol at night. And they did assist seamen in distress. But having done so, they followed the unwritten rule and looted the ship of everything that could be easily removed.

Need versus greed

My grandmother did not smoke. She just bought cigarettes in bulk. And when walking from the quay down to the old town in Stockholm with a bag full of cigarettes, she was in the company of several colleagues – women with their own regular customers to deliver to. It is unlikely that the staff at the tax-free shop thought the women who regularly bought in such quantities did so for their own personal use. But why put a stop to an activity that meant a good profit? It was good business for their employer too. If my grandmother had read this, I suspect she would have objected to the first sentence, saying she was not a smuggler, she just smuggled a little bit like everyone else – certainly this was the general way of speaking about smuggling in the archived interviews.

The three cases illustrate there were rules for everyone involved. For business to run smoothly, those rules had to be adhered to by both sides. Law is black and white; praxis is not. But the smugglers had more leeway in their actions than the customs officers, who had to be stricter in their approach because they were supposed not only to follow the law, but to represent it. In the case of Jansson, the customs officers turned a blind eye to his small-scale smuggling. His main trade was respectable enough, and his habit of selling a little something on the side was useful for the people working in the harbour, who could buy food and cigarettes for a decent price. And it was equally useful for the customs officers, who could point out that they knew what was going on to gain a little something themselves. In contrast, the big shark Algoth Niska was not allowed to continue his business undisturbed. Smuggling to that degree was actively prevented. The distinction can be phrased as the difference between need and greed. To smuggle due to need is to simply increase the margins of one's income in a context where scarcity was common – so common that the customs officers themselves could relate to it. A greedy smuggler, on the other hand, was involved in a game where the possible profit by far outweighed profits considered to be 'decent'. Tolerance of that kind of smuggler was decisively lower. The line between activities that vexed the authorities and those they turned a blind eye to could be thin. Smugglers should avoid being caught red-handed, or over-reaching, or becoming too rich from it. Perhaps the customs officers who stole Karlsson's load reckoned he had crossed the line from smuggling from need to smuggling from greed when he became involved moving such high-quality French cognac, and that he had hence entered a game in which different rules applied. But as the case of Eriksson clarifies, the value of the smuggled goods was not the only condition customs officers considered. One's morals and social position could be more influential in deciding one's course of action than the law one was supposed to adhere to, or even represent.

Notes

1 Alan L. Karras, *Smuggling: Contraband and Corruption in World History* (Lanham 2010), 68.

2 Karras 2010, 67, 111.

3 Cf. Johan Lundin & Fredrik Nilsson, *Spritsmuggling på Östersjön: En kulturhistorisk studie av nätverk i tillblivelse* (Göteborg 2015), 18 .

4 Karras 2010, 7.

5 Cf. Karras 2010, 6.

6 I wish to thank Staffan Beijar of the Åland Museum for the generous access to the archived interviews.

7 Lars G. Soldéus, *Fiskköpare och sumpskeppare i Ålands och Åbolands skärgårdar* (Saltsjöbaden 2017).

8 Soldéus 2017, 12.

9 Lars G. Soldéus, *En skärgårdsskuta kommer lastad: Bondeseglationen till Stockholm* (Saltsjöbaden 2020), 15.

10 Kerstin G:son Berg, *Redare i Roslagen: Segelfartygsrederier och deras verksamhet i Gamla Vätö socken* (Stockholm 1984), 104.

11 Berg 1984, 149.

12 Simon Harvey, *Smuggling: Seven Centuries of Contraband* (London 2016), 16.

13 Soldéus 2020, 136.

14 Harvey 2016, 202.

15 Harvey 2016, 11.

16 *Ålandsfrågan inför Nationernas Förbund*, ii: *Den Av Nationernas Förbunds råd tillsatta rapportörkommissionens utlåtande = Rapport présenté au Conseil de la société des nations par la Commission des rapporteurs* (Stockholm: 1921), 107.

17 Ålandsfrågan 1921, 107.

18 John H. Wuorinen, 'Finland's prohibition experiment', *Annals of the American Academy of Political & Social Science* 163/1 (1932), 216–18.

19 Wuorinen 1932, 221.

20 Karras 2010, 49.

21 E. P. Sanford, 'The Illegal Liquor Traffic', *Annals of the American Academy of Political & Social Science* 163/1 (1932), 40.

22 Wuorinen 1932, 221.

23 Olov Kinberg, 'Temperance Legislation in Sweden', *Annals of the American Academy of Political & Social Science* 163/1 (1932), 208–209.

24 Helena Ruotsala, 'From Crime to Cultural Heritage: Cross-Border Activities and Relationships in the Tornio River Valley', *Anthropological Journal of European Cultures* 18/1 (2009), 30–49.

25 Wuorinen 1932, 222.

26 Sanford 1932, 39.

27 As recounted by one man born in 1910 and one man born in 1898 respectively.

28 Born around 1900, interviewed in 1968.

29 Man born in 1892.

30 Man born around 1920.

31 Anna Maria Knutsson, *Smuggling in the North: Globalisation and the Consolidation of Economic Borders in Sweden, 1766–1806* (Florence 2019), 25.

32 Ruotsala 2009

33 Ruotsala 2009, 38.

34 Karras 2010, 110.

35 Karras 2010, 67.

36 Knutsson 2019, 18.

37 Boris Ersson et al., *Smuggling: Berättelser om lurendrejeri och varusmuggling* (Stockholm 1994); Anssi Paasi & Eeva-Kaisa Prokkola, 'Territorial Dynamics, Cross-Border Work and Everyday Life in the Finnish–Swedish Border Area', *Space & Polity* 12/1 (2008), 13–29; Péter Balogh, *Perpetual Borders: German–Polish Cross-Border Contacts in the Szczecin Area* (Stockholm 2014), 45; Knutsson 2019, 21.

38 Man born in 1912.

39 Born around 1910, interviewed in 2000.

40 In interviews with men born in 1910, 1910, and 1920 respectively.

41 Statens offentliga utredningar (SOU) (Swedish Government Official Reports), SOU 1927:34 *Betänkande med förslag till åtgärder gentemot spritsmuggling från fartyg, som uppehålla trafik med utlandet m.m.* (Stockholm 1927).

42 Lundin & Nilsson 2015, 16.

43 Man born in 1910.

44 Man born in 1910.

45 Karras 2010, 49.

46 Harvey 2016, 11–12.

47 Algoth Niska, *Mina Äventyr* (Helsinki 1931).

48 Man born in 1897 and interviewed in 1988.

49 Algoth Niska, *Över gröna gränser* (Helsinki 1953).

50 Woman born in 1924.

51 *Rajamme Vartijat* 80/1 (2014), 40.

52 *Rajamme Vartijat* 80/1 (2014), 80.

53 SOU 1935/24 *Betänkande med förslag till ändrad organisation av den statliga verksamheten för bekämpande av olovlig införsel av spritdrycker m.m.* (Stockholm 1935), 27, 53.

54 Born around 1920, interviewed in 2009.

55 Karras 2010, 49.

56 Harvey 2016, 16.

57 Clifford Geertz, *Local Knowledge: Further Essays in Interpretive Anthropology* (New York 1983), 187.

58 Man born in 1915.

59 Man born in 1897.

CHAPTER 10

Here, there and everywhere
Ash disposal at sea and the construction of a maritime memory landscape
Hanna Jansson

Ash disposal at sea is a rapidly growing phenomenon in Sweden. To scatter the ashes of a loved one over water may appear particularly appealing if the deceased had had a strong connection to the sea. It may also give rise to private sites of memory in the maritime landscape as the mourners attribute new meanings to the sea.

We took him aboard our boat. And his wife had brought along some of his personal things. We played some music by Evert Taube, and then she went to the stern… (voice breaks) and poured the ashes into the sea. And we laid down our roses and watched them drift away and we threw his belongings into the sea. Then we had a drink from a bottle they had brought home from their last trip (voice breaks). And the weather was so grey, the entire day, but just as we poured the ashes in the water, the clouds open up, a piece of blue, and the sun came out.

Ingalill's friend Sven lived in the Stockholm archipelago and was an avid sailor. He loved the sea and when he passed away his family considered no other option than scattering his ashes there. Together with Sven's widow, Ingalill and her husband tried to make the scattering act reflect Sven's personality and life history. They chose a site where they had often sailed together, close to where he had lived. The personal items his wife took with her on the boat were then scattered at sea with his cremated remains.

This essay discusses how people who have scattered the ashes of a loved one at sea describe and interpret this form of burial. Why did they scatter ashes at sea or on a lake? What meaning is ascribed to the sea in the lives of the now deceased and their surviving relatives? In particular I focus on a recurring ambiguous approach to the sea as a grave – where the deceased are believed to remain both at the specific scattering site and wherever water is found. This raises questions about how water is established as a burial site, and how memorial sites are created in the maritime landscape.

In my research project on ash disposal at sea, I study how the sea is constructed as a resting place and memorial site through stories, rituals, and practices. This essay is based on interviews with nine relatives who have scattered ashes over water, one woman who envisions a future scattering of her own remains, and three undertakers and a priest who in various ways have come into contact with the phenomenon.[1] In addition, ten interviews from a previous Swedish study on ash disposal and information and documents from the public authorities in charge are used as reference material.[2]

Ash disposal in Sweden

The cremation rate in Sweden has reached 80 per cent, the majority either buried in cemeteries or scattered in memorial groves.[3] Ash disposal outside cemeteries has been permitted in Sweden since 1957, but for a long time there were only some 100 cases per year. Over the past two decades however, the number of ash disposals has tripled and now corresponds to nearly 3,000 burials a year, representing almost 3 per cent of all deaths in the country.[4] Unsurprisingly, ash disposals over water are most common in the coastal areas and where the country's larger lakes are located. As we will see, the choice is often motivated by the deceased's strong biographical or emotional connection to the sea or a particular lake, from which follows this is a rare, albeit increasing, option in the inland regions.

In Sweden, ash disposal outside cemeteries and memorial groves is strictly regulated and, according to the Funeral Act and the authorities, should be allowed only in exceptional cases. An application to the county administrative board must be filed after death, and one may not apply for one's own future disposal. Ashes should be scattered at least 300 metres from land or any settlement, in locations where there is little movement. Urns must not be stored at home, but are to be collected from the crematorium or undertaker in conjunction with the burial.[5] After the burial, a certificate must be signed and sent to the county administrative board to attest that the disposal has been realized in accordance with the application.[6] It is easier to obtain a permit for disposals over water than land.[7] This is mainly due to the authorities' stated goal of keeping the living and the dead physically separated from one another – a conception that characterizes many Western societies in modern times.[8] Accordingly, large mountain and forest areas are considered appropriate, while ash disposal is not allowed in densely populated areas, hiking trails, national parks and nature reserves, or on beaches. The county administrative boards' guidelines for ash disposal also emphasize that it is desirable to avoid multiple scatterings in the same place, as this could give rise to perceived cemetery-like areas or family graves, which is believed to cause changed behaviour in the area and inflict negatively on activities such as hiking or mushroom picking.[9]

'I want you to scatter my ashes at sea'

What motivates the choice of the sea or a lake as a resting place after death? As my study and previous research show, one recurrent intention is to avoid a traditional grave left unvisited and untended.[10] Margret has recently retired and lives in a small town by one of Sweden's largest lakes. Every morning she looks out over the water from her window. When she dies she wants to be scattered out there, she says, nodding towards the lake. Born and raised in another part of the country, she feels no strong attachment to her town. Her son and grandchildren live in a different city and would not be able to visit her grave if she were buried in the local cemetery, she says. Increased mobility complicates grave maintenance and tending. The relatives I speak to recurrently make parallels to their troubled conscience over neglected family graves in distant parts of the country. Bengt has scattered both his parents' ashes at sea, and reflects on his own and their view on the matter:

> They [the parents] said that it was more a burden for the survivors to attend to a burial site that would disappear anyway. My grandparents' grave in [city] had without our knowledge been removed quite a short time before. And now I realize that my grandparents' grave in [city] is also gone. So that was one reason. That we siblings… perhaps not directly supported, we said that we would be perfectly prepared to ensure that a grave would be maintained and pay for it and so on. But we also saw the benefits of scattering at sea so we had no objections.

Those with whom I have spoken have also been attracted to the thought of the sea as a resting place. Margret may feel she lacks a sense of belonging to her town's past and future, but she loves the lake. It is a constant aspect of her everyday life, and she swims in it every morning from early spring to late autumn. In several of the cases a disposal at sea appears as an almost obvious choice; a choice that with one interviewee's wording is 'in line' with the deceased's previous life.

Even before his death, Maria's father was clear about what he wanted done with his remains. He was an atheist and did not want a Christian funeral. However both he and his wife were, as Maria calls it, outdoorsy. 'So when dad got sicker and sicker, he made it more and more clear that "the day I don't exist anymore, I want you to scatter my ashes at sea." My dad worked at sea. My mother's family is from the archipelago so we have a pretty strong connection to water' (Fig. 10.1). Maria's sister objected and instead wished for a grave on land – a fixed point to relate to and visit. But Maria regarded a burial at sea as an affirmation of her father's life story and professional and retired life, and his atheist stance.

Ash disposal in nature can be seen as an example of the increasingly individualized practices and rituals of death in recent decades. According to these ideals, dying and death should be adapted to the individual

Figure 10.1. Sweden's archipelagos are frequently framed as places the deceased cherished, and therefore as logical resting places. Photo: Hanna Jansson.

and his or her person or concerns, and to the perceived needs of the surviving relatives. Death has become increasingly life-centred.[11] Obituaries, funeral ceremonies, and gravestones are now modelled with the deceased person's personality, interests, and life history in mind. The markings and rituals of death come to reflect the life that preceded it. This also applies to ash disposals where, as we shall see below, not only the choice of this form of burial but also the actual scattering sites and the outline of the ceremonies are often chosen based on the personality of the deceased. First, however, we will familiarize ourselves with how ash disposal may be done.

Water, ashes and roses

Most scatterings described in the research material were preceded by church funerals or secular memorials, usually held months or up to a year before the scattering.[12] The scatterings can be described as loosely formed rituals; as special occasions characterized by distinct moods and where everyday reality is temporarily bracketed.[13] Whether religious or secular, rituals are generally said to include established and fixed orders, making them recognizable and predictable to the participants. Yet the burials in question here lack such pre-existing orders, as the relatives are free to outline the occasion to suit their own preferences, without the assistance of professionals such as undertakers, priests, or cemetery staff workers.[14]

The described scatterings both resemble one another and show great variety in details and dominant mood. At the beginning of the essay, Ingalill described how she, her husband, and her friend's widow scattered her friend's ashes at sea, together with personal items and flowers. Her story bears many similarities to the following description from Eva, whose husband's ashes were scattered on the coast near their holiday home:

> We chose a cliff by the sea with an offshore breeze, which would be best to get the ashes out. And all of us went down there, with the urn. And we had rice paper lanterns with us. We never got them up in the air, though, as it started to rain. But Anders' brother had brought rose buds with him. So our son emptied the urn. In the sea. And then Anders' brother laid down the roses, and it was as if they followed the ashes. We stood there, all of us, and watched the roses drift out. It was very beautiful. And we had Gammel Dansk [bitters] with us, for that was Anders' thing. And we had photos of him. There on that rock. So it was very beautiful.

Eva appreciates that day, but it was still marked by great sorrow. Her husband passed away shortly after they had both retired and they were about to move permanently to their house by the sea. Her grief is still apparent as we talk about her memories some years later. Hedvig, who partook in the simultaneous scattering of both her grandparents, instead recalls that day with joy. The context was very different to Eva's husband's burial. Hedvig's grandfather had been dead for some two years when they scattered his ashes, and the family's worst grief had subsided. As her grandmother had suffered from Alzheimer's for many years, Hedvig says they had already grieved for her too. When her grandfather died they knew that his wife had little time left, and decided to wait until her death before burying them together. In the meantime, the grandfather's ashes were kept in a family member's home.[15] After her grandmother's death the family chartered a boat and headed out into the archipelago, to the waters by her grandparents' beloved holiday home. For once the entire family was gathered, it was a warm and sunny day, and they were served lunch on board. They made a stop on an island where they went ashore, basked in the sun, and had a swim. The urns stood together on a table until the scattering:

> Someone poured the ashes out. And we had brought a wreath of roses that we laid down in the water. And my cousin had as a child wood-worked a small boat and given it to grandma and grandpa, and it was also laid down. It sank immediately. So it got to follow them down, with the ashes.

Here, too, personal belongings and flowers followed the ashes into the sea, during a scattering that appears to have been a pleasant and merry family outing. Other scatterings appear more toned down. When Bengt, as he says, 'launched' his parents' ashes, there were no flowers and no music was played. At his father's scattering his mother was present. Four months later her remains were scattered at the same site: a navigation mark that the spouses had seen from their window and which they them-selves had chosen as their resting place. Twice then the family went out by boat with flags at half mast, an urn, and picnic baskets (Fig. 10.2). A relative who is a priest said a prayer or sang a song – Bengt cannot recall which – while he lowered the water-soluble urn into the water by rope.[16] His brother hoisted the flag before they headed back to land and

Figure 10.2. Artist's impression of Bengt with his father's urn.
Image: Hanna Jansson.

drank the coffee they had brought along. At his mother's burial, Bengt
notes with a reference to a quote from Swedish writer and cartoonist
Albert Engström, it was 'the corpse herself who had baked the cookies'.

The surviving relatives construct individualized burial rituals through
improvisation and inspiration from established traditions of funerals
and death. For despite their individual differences, the described ash
disposals include elements easily recognizable from Christian or secular
funerals, memorials, burials, and graveyard visits. Flowers, prayers or
poetry readings, photographs of the dead, memorabilia, favourite music
or much-loved songs by for example the singer Evert Taube appear as
traditional resources for relatives who take full responsibility for the
burial, without support from professionals.[17]

In the right place

Maria often thinks of the bay where they scattered her father's ashes with a sense of joy and satisfaction. It was the boat's captain, she explains, who chose the scattering site and turned off the engine. 'This captain, he did not know anything about us. And the story is that my dad read a lot and was very interested in history. Amazingly, he knew *everything* about [history]!' she explains. 'And then this captain takes us out, and he says, "This is a good place".' Before the actual scattering, the captain told them the name of the bay, which Maria appreciated. 'It felt good, because then you have a place. You see? It was not just the sea, but 'my dad is by [the bay's name]. And there was a big battle there in the eighteenth century.'

Enthusiastically, Maria describes the great battle: 'And it was big warships and it was like Russians and Swedes and Danes and lots of sailors. And then I just felt like this, I get the chills just talking about it!' She interrupts herself and rubs her arms before continuing with a laugh: 'Yes, but of course my dad should be right *here*. He's got a great deal of friends here now! And then you felt like this, "How did the captain know this?" Everything has a meaning.' Later, Maria again returns to the idea of her father now being with his 'friends' from the past. Surely it is terrible that they, with Maria's words, died an agonizing death. 'But for me it was like "How nice! Then my dad gets to meet them there," you know? Then they can talk about the cannon balls or their chalk pipes or whatever.'

When Maria talks about the difficult choice of what to do with her father's ashes, her voice is still warm and cheerful. As discussed above, funerals and burial sites have become increasingly life-centred. Her father's resting place feels right to Maria, as she believes it fits well with his great interest in history. She imagines the other dead, whose remains may already be at the bottom, as his companions and company; a comforting thought that supports her in her grief. Therefore, she also rejoices in her mother's wish to once be scattered in the same place – then her father will be joined by her as well.[18]

A special place is not any place. A place can be said to arise when environments and landscapes are attributed meaning; when something catches our eye or piques our interest, or when spaces are associated with events, memories, or references – our own or those of others.[19] In a previous study on cruising sailors' online travel writing, I showed how they perceived place-like spatialities on long Atlantic crossings, created by every change in the weather.[20] Similarly, for relatives the scattering of ashes make places crystallize on the large bodies of water, as they tell me about the scatterings through memory practices, which we will return to below.

Tove, too, ascribes strong meaning to where they scattered her mother's remains, as she is confident that her mother herself intervened to choose the specific spot. Her mother grew up by a mountain lake and before her death stated that she wanted her ashes scattered there. She loved the lake where she used to swim as a child and where the women of the village washed clothes and carpets. When she passed away they first arranged a large church funeral for her, before fulfilling her wish the following summer. Tove and three other relatives, along with the captain of a borrowed boat, went out on the lake towards the point which Tove had specified in her permit application. 'And then we hear the engine malfunction', she says. 'And then the captain says that "Hang on, it says engine stop; that has never happened before. So, is it okay here?" "Sure, we don't care".' Tove emptied the ashes out of the urn where the boat had happened to stop, and her daughter sprinkled the red rose petals they had prepared. 'And it was really beautiful. The grey water and the sky and then these red petals, it was actually really nice.' Afterwards, the company returned to land and ate waffles together. Then they drove to a house above the lake where Tove and her mother had spent two summers together a few years before, and where their relatives now lived. The relatives explained that they had watched the boat stop, and Tove realized that the scattering site was in the line of sight from the house. 'From their window, where we had also been those summers. That's where it had stopped. I just "Okay! She's the one who... this is where it should be." So they had lit a candle and watched us, and grieved. It is kind of cool. … She stopped the boat. Where she wanted it done.'

In a similar albeit somewhat more humorous way, Ingalill describes how Sven also made sure to end up at least partly where he wanted to be. After they scattered his ashes, they returned by boat to the island where Sven and his wife lived. As they docked, they discovered a fine dust on the tiller. It took them a few seconds before they realized what it was. 'So he went along with us. He hitchhiked a bit. It felt good.' Later in our conversation I return to the matter of the ashes on the tiller, and Ingalill develops her view on it. 'He ended up at the home bridge. A little bit of him.' I ask her how it felt seeing the ashes on the tiller, as human ashes are a substance that can be perceived as emotionally difficult or possibly even revolting. Her reply comes with emphasis and surprises me. 'I was *so* happy! It was him in a nutshell.' As is often the case during our conversation, her voice fails – the grief is still strong. 'It was beautiful. He found his way home in his own way.'

A private memory landscape

Unlike when remains are buried in memory groves, those who scatter ashes outside cemeteries often know the precise scattering site, making this form of burial resemble those in traditional graves.[21] Hence, the scattering sites may become important places of remembrance for surviving relatives. For Eva's children and grandchildren, the rock from which they scattered Anders' ashes has become a recurring picnic spot – a place for coffee, chatting, and the children's evening swims in summer. In their case, the ashes were scattered from land, which of course facilitates this.

Memorial sites are often tangible and official, such as war memorials or plaques. They inform or remind passers-by of past events that should be remembered and recognized as a cultural heritage. But memorials can also be temporary and unsanctioned, as when flowers are left and candles lit at the scene of a traffic accident, a murder, or a terrorist attack. When it comes to the cases in this study, the memorial sites are private, away from built-up areas, and most often unrecognizable and unknown to others.

Ellen sends me a photograph of a flower wreath floating on the water; an image from this year's memorial tour. Some ten years previously they scattered her grandfather's ashes at sea on Midsummer's Eve, and every year they go out to the scattering site on that day to fish there. They also fished during the actual scattering, but that time to disguise their task for other nearby boats. Since they did not have the permit from the responsible authority the disposal had to be done surreptitiously; a challenge on a sunny day by the coast when many weekenders were out in their boats. The place itself is unrecognizable to her when she returns there, Ellen says, and the urn and flowers are for obvious reasons long gone. Instead, it is the memories of that day that make the anniversary excursions special.

What Ellen notes – that burial sites at sea are not obvious to the eye – is one of the aspects of ash disposal over water that first attracted me to study this phenomenon. In contrast to cemeteries, there are no headstones, bouquets, flowerbeds, or lanterns that signal to passers-by that this is indeed a burial site. Memory markings must instead be accomplished through other means than by a traditional grave, a memorial grove, or an accident site. One such way is recurring boat trips and temporary markings that sink, float away or dissolve. Ingalill and her husband have sailed past the place where they scattered Sven's ashes often and 'said hello'. Only they and Sven's widow know the exact place, as his wife wished to keep that information to herself. Ingalill and her husband had also a few years before lost a friend who drowned when sailing in the archipelago, and whose body was never found. For several anniversaries of his disappearance, they sailed with his family to the spot where he was believed to have fallen overboard. They always took flowers from their garden which they placed in the water there. Only for a short moment, when flowers or memorabilia are still floating on the surface, is the remarkability of the specific spot visible to the eye. As a result, the maritime landscape becomes a meaningful memorial and burial site only for the initiated, through place-bound experiences, stories, memories, and shared reference points.[22]

Figure 10.3. A memorial plaque and flowers by the lake. Photo: Hanna Jansson.

Still, there might be permanent memorials ashore that indicate the sea is a burial site and a place of mourning or remembrance. With the ashes in the urn lies a small metal or ceramic badge with the deceased's name and personal identity number. Louise, an undertaker who has scattered her father's ashes in the archipelago, kept her father's badge. She then buried it under her mother's gravestone in the cemetery where she was already interred. To the stone was added an inscription stating that their father had been scattered at sea. Louise was not as pleased with him being scattered as other family members, and wanted something more tangible of him to remain. 'The badge is just a symbol, but for me it is really important. For me he is there, in mum's grave. For my sister he is in the sea.'

A willow tree grows on the shore of Lake Vättern, near a popular path where people stroll and walk their dogs. A metal plaque is attached onto the tree's root, with an inscribed name, nickname, an image of an angel, and the date of birth and death of a woman whose ashes were scattered on the lake's water. The high grass hides it from view and it is easy to miss if one does not know of its existence. One Midsummer

Figure 10.4. The willow with the memorial plaque at its base. Photo: Hanna Jansson.

Eve, I find a small bouquet of hand-picked flowers tied with string on the plaque (Fig. 10.3 & 10.4). Some fifteen years after the woman's death someone clearly still visits the memorial site. And just a few metres away from it, my children and I wade into the lake to swim.

A molecule finds its way

For many interviewees, it is apparently important that the ashes were scattered in a specific place. There is also a strong conviction these are the places where the deceased can now be said to rest; that it is where they are or even want to be. At the same time, the materiality of the ashes and the chosen form of burial speak against this, a fact that the interviewees are well aware of. They have with their own eyes seen the ashes sprinkled on the water or flowers floating away, and imagined that the ashes followed them. Scattering ashes over land or water means precisely that: the remains are dispersed over a larger area. Therefore, many of the relatives also say their loved ones now, to some extent, can be anywhere and everywhere.

Only once has Bengt sailed past the navigation mark where they scattered his parents' ashes. He lives in another part of the country and it has therefore not become a recurring memorial site for him. Still, he marks anniversaries related to his parents several times a year: birthdays, their wedding day, and days of death, by taking a flower to whatever water he is currently closest to. He shows a photograph of a lilac branch floating in the water by one of Stockholm's many quays. 'This was the latest, it is on my dad's day of death. And it has been in the Mediterranean. It has been in the Oslo fjord. It has been in Lake Mälaren sometimes. It has been in the Hudson River at some point and so on. And we certainly see that as a point. With this.' He usually photographs the flowers and sends the pictures to family members with a greeting: 'Now it is on its way to the mark.'

What Bengt expresses, what his regular memory rituals show, is a recurring notion among the interviewees; namely that all the waters of the world are interconnected, which is why one can visit any sea or lake to think of one's dead, and place a flower or a keepsake to celebrate their memory.[23] Not only the site of the scattering, but also other waters, can function in the same way as a traditional gravestone, and above all a memorial grove. Eva's children and grandchildren have in a similar manner used Stockholm's water to remember Anders. They have thrown cinnamon buns and shots of spirits into the water, and a grandchild once trudged down to the quay after pickup from preschool 'to visit grandpa' (Fig. 10.5). Such practices make the water an active aspect of the family's mourning and memory work, and also incorporate the deceased into the family's continued everyday life.[24]

The flowers, buns, and drinks seem intended, if only metaphorically, to travel to the scattering site. In these cases, the water acts as a link to the burial place – all the way from Stockholm's inner city, New York, or the Mediterranean. But the reverse may also be the case, as survivors imagine that some small piece of the ashes may have travelled to them. Ingalill tells of a friend who moved to Spain and later died there: 'And then they scattered his ashes in a river. For it would flow into the Mediterranean and further up, well, across all the seas. His wife told me.' She falls silent, as so often in our conversation about her two other close friends who have, voluntarily and by tragic accident, found their resting places in the archipelago. The grief is palpable and her voice often breaks, she speaks slowly and with many pauses. But she laughs when she talks about the friend whose ashes were scattered in that Spanish river: 'The water moves on. It can get as far as you want. His wife said to us: "He comes up to you, a little bit of him comes up to you. A small molecule somewhere, maybe."' Her voice becomes serious again: 'So, that's a nice thought with funerals and burials in water.'

Tove is onto something similar. On the one hand, she would like to go back to the mountain lake, dip her toes in, and think 'Well, she's maybe partly still here.' At the same time, she thinks that now, some five years later, her mother may be somewhere else. 'Where is she? One wonders which way the water *runs*? Is there anything left there or is it spreading? Is she in Denmark or is she only in Åland? I do not know. It does not matter, but you play with the thought anyway like that, where her ashes are *at*. What's left? Maybe she's down here, maybe I do not have to go up there, if you're thinking about particles.'

Figure 10.5. Stockholm's many quays have become places to commemorate loved ones scattered elsewhere. Photo: Hanna Jansson.

Here, there and everywhere

A contradictory image of the notions of the sea as a burial site thus arises from the interviews. The contradiction is expressed by different interviewees, but sometimes even by the same person. The question concerns where the person whose ashes were scattered can actually be said to be – at the scattering site or wherever there is water? Are they here, there, or everywhere?

The stories of ash disposal at sea tell of the great importance of the sea and lakes for people in their lives and in death, and for their surviving relatives. As a constant and loved feature of life, the sea seems to these people and their interviewed relatives as a natural resting place, in a double sense, confirming and consolidating their social identity. The scatterings at least partially change the meaning of that water, though, and perhaps all bodies of water, rendering it a fluid memorial site for the surviving relatives.

For some of the relatives I have spoken to, it is not given that still living spouses once will be similarly scattered. Anna, who scattered her father's ashes, finds it hard to see this would suit her mother's personality as well. 'And that means I'm considering separating them,' she says. In such cases, the choice of ash disposal at sea may later mean further and perhaps more difficult choices for the mourners. For other interviewees, though, it is tempting to imagine an own future resting place at sea. 'Infinity and the sea and that… everything changes and the sea too… The rocks and the nature in the archipelago and all that. It stands for a continuity of sorts. Which is appealing' says Ingalill. 'So yes, absolutely. I would have no worries about it whatsoever.' Her husband has made it clear that he wants to be scattered in the same place as they scattered Sven's ashes, and where the two couples used to sail together. 'His wife, I have not talked to her about it but I can almost guarantee she has written it somewhere, that she wants to come to her Sven. So maybe we'll end up all four of us again!' Her voice breaks as she concludes, 'It is not a bad idea!'

Notes

1 Talking about experiences of death and grief can be emotional for both interviewee and interviewer. All respondents have been anonymized, as have all places, and when requested other details have been omitted or changed. All quotations are translated from Swedish and in places have been edited for clarity.

2 Curt Dahlgren & Jan Hermanson, '"Här ska min aska vila": Nya platser och riter för gravsättning av aska på andra platser än begravningsplats', in Curt Dahlgren & Göran Gustafsson (eds.), *Kring begravningar i nutid: Tre studier* (Lund 2006), 7–56. I wish to thank Curt Dahlgren for the generous offer to consult the material.

3 Sveriges Kyrkogårds- och Krematorieförbund (SKKF), 'Kremationsstatistik 2019' (2020), skkf.se.

4 SKKF 2020. For a detailed review of ash disposal in Sweden, see Dahlgren & Hermanson 2006; Elfrida Klacka, 'Sprida aska, var och varför? Om gravskicket askspridning och dess plats(er) i landskapet' (Swedish University of Agricultural Sciences 2017).

5 Länsstyrelserna, 'Gemensamma riktlinjer för askspridning' 2019, document via e-mail. Previously the required distance in Stockholm County was 600 metres from land or residence, and before that it had been 1,000 metres.

6 Approaches in Scandinavia and northern Europe vary. In Denmark ash can only be scattered at sea (www.borger.dk/sundhed-og-sygdom/doedsfald-og-begravelse/begravelse). Norway's rules are similar to Sweden's, albeit somewhat less strict (www.regjeringen.no/no/tema/tro-og-livssyn/gravferd/innsiktsartikler/om-askespredning/id445138/). On Åland (www.nyan.ax/notiser/aska-far-spridas-fritt/) and in Finland (www.metsa.fi/web/sv/spridandeavaskanefterenavliden) only a landowner's permit is required, which means the authorities have little control over where human remains are placed. In the UK relatives can store the urn at home, bury it in the garden, or (with permission) scatter it on the home turf of a favourite soccer team or similar. In the Netherlands a market has emerged for ash objects: jewellery or ornaments containing small amounts of a relative's or pet's ashes, which can be worn or displayed in the home. Leonie Kellaher, Jenny Hockey & David Prendergast, 'Wandering Lines and Cul-de-sacs: Trajectories of Ashes in the United Kingdom', in Jenny Hockey, Carol Komaromy & Kate Woodthorpe (eds.), *The Matter of Death: Space, Place and Materiality* (London 2010), 133–147; Brenda Mathijssen, 'The Ambiguity of Human Ashes: Exploring Encounters with Cremated Remains in the Netherlands', *Death Studies* 41/1 (2017), 34–41.

7 Dahlgren & Hermanson 2006; Klacka 2017.

8 Hanna Jansson, 'Ashes, Law and (Dis)Order. Negotiating Authority in Ash Scattering Rituals,' *Ethnologia Scandinavica* 51 (2021); Länsstyrelserna 2019; Eva Åhrén Snickare, *Döden, kroppen och moderniteten* (Stockholm 2002), 234; David Prendergast, Jenny Hockey & Leonie Kellaher, 'Blowing in the Wind? Identity, Materiality, and the Destinations of Human Ashes', *Journal of the Royal Anthropological Institute* 12/4 (2006), 883; Tony Walter, 'The Pervasive Dead', *Mortality* 24/4 (2019), 389–404.

9 Jansson 2021.

10 Dahlgren & Hermanson 2006; Kellaher et al. 2005, 2010; Klacka 2017; Prendergast et al. 2006.

11 Tony Walter, *The Revival of Death* (London 1994), 24, 33–4; Ingeborg Svensson, *Liket i garderoben: En studie av sexualitet, livsstil och begravning* (Stockholm 2007).

12 In law a dead body must be buried or cremated no later than one month after death, and ashes must be buried no later than one year after the cremation.

13 Barbro Klein (ed.), *Gatan är vår! Ritualer på offentliga platser* (Stockholm 1995); Barbro Blehr, 'Working, moving, visiting: On the quality of eveyday rituals', *Journal of Nordic Archaeological Science* 16 (2009), 33–38; Ove Ronström, 'Ritual och ritualisering', in Jenny Gunnarsson Payne & Magnus Öhlander (eds.), *Tillämpad kulturteori* (Lund 2017), 231–50.

14 The only condition is that the scattering is done in a reverent way, providing the dignity of the deceased. Jansson 2021; Länsstyrelserna 2019; for the independence of surviving relatives, see Lynn Åkesson, *Mellan levande och döda: Föreställningar om kropp och ritual* (Stockholm 1997); Walter 1994.

15 This is against current regulations and might be illegal under the Funeral Act and/or laws about desecration of graves (Jansson 2021).

16 In Sweden the sinking of water-soluble urns was not permitted until 2021: ashes should before then be scattered on the surface. For long the authorities chose to interpret the legal text which allows ashes to be scattered literally. However, relatives (like Bengt) reportedly did not know about the ban and therefore sank urns in good faith.

17 Barbara G. Myerhoff, 'We Do not Wrap Herring in a Printed Page: Fusion, Fictions and Continuity in Secular Ritual', in Sally F. Moore & Barbara G. Myerhoff (eds.), *Secular Ritual* (Assen 1977), 199–224.

18 Cf. Mathijssen 2017, 39.

19 Yi-Fu Tuan, *Space and Place: the Perspective of Experience* (London 1977), 6, 161; Lars-Eric Jönsson, 'Tidsgeograferna: Om jakt, landskap och situerade berättelser', in Katarina Ek-Nilsson, Lina Midholm, Annika Nordström, Katarina Saltzman & Göran Sjögård (eds.), *Naturen för mig: Nutida röster och kulturella perspektiv* (Gothenburg 2014).

20 Hanna Jansson, *Drömmen om äventyret: Långfärdsseglares reseberättelser på internet* (Stockholm 2017); 'Resans mikrodramer: Långfärdsseglares berättelser från Atlantöverfarter', in Simon Ekström & Leos Müller (eds.), *Angöringar: Berättelser och kunskap från havet* (Gothenburg 2017), 42–61.

21 Cf. Dahlgren & Hermanson 2006, 21; cf. Kellaher et al. 2005.

22 Jönsson 2014.

23 Kellaher et al. 2005, 246; Kellaher et al. 2010, 138.

24 In recent decades, the idea of 'continuing bonds' has become an increasingly common model of mourning. The idea is survivors should find new ways to maintain and nurture the relationship with their loved one. It is presented as an alternative to another well-known model where mourning is said to consist of different phases, and mourners should learn to 'move on' and put their grief behind them. The continuing bonds model recognizes grief as an admittedly changing yet continuous feeling in life and also considers memory and mourning practices as common, healthy parts of life (see Prendergast et al. 2006, 887).

About the authors

Mirja Arnshav is a postdoctoral researcher at the Centre for Maritime Studies at Stockholm University and the research coordinator at the Swedish National Maritime Museum in Stockholm. She received her PhD in Archaeology from Stockholm University. Her research interests centre on maritime heritage and contemporary archaeology. Her recent publications include her thesis, *De små båtarna och den stora flykten: Arkeologi i spåren av andra världskrigets baltiska flyktbåtar* (2020), and '"The sea shall have our weapons": Small arms and forced migration across the Baltic Sea during the Second World War', *Journal of Conflict Archaeology* (2019). She is co-editor (with Andreas Linderoth) of the Swedish Maritime Museum's anthology *Sverige och första världskriget: Maritima perspektiv* (2017).

Henrik Arnstad is a science journalist and author. He has an MA in History from Stockholm University. His research interests include ideology and its analysis, democracy, racism, fascism, and nationalism. He is also founder and captain of the Stockholm Company of Longbow Archers, the Sagittarii Holmiae. Among his recent publications are *Älskade fascism: De svartbruna rörelsernas ideologi och historia* (2013) and *Hatade demokrati: De inkluderande rörelsernas ideologi och historia* (2018).

Simon Ekström is Professor of Ethnology at Stockholm University, where he is also a researcher at the Centre for Maritime Studies. In the maritime field he has published *Humrarna och evigheten: Kulturhistoriska essäer om konsumtion, begär och död* (2017). He is co-editor (with Leos Müller) of CEMAS's recent collaborative volume *Angöringar: Berättelser* *och kunskap från havet* (2017). He is currently researching how objects and stories related to human death are given space in museum collections and exhibitions, with a focus on maritime museums and comparative views of other museums and presentations.

Niklas Eriksson is Associate Professor of Archaeology at Stockholm University and a researcher at the Centre for Maritime Studies. His research interests include maritime archaeology and naval architecture. His recent publications include *Urbanism Under Sail: An archaeology of fluit ships in Early Modern Everyday Life* (2014), *Riksäpplet: Arkeologiska perspektiv på ett bortglömt regalskepp* (2017), and *Stormaktsskärgård: Marin landskapsarkeologi utmed farlederna mot Stockholm* (2021).

Anna Maria Forssberg is Associate Professor of History and researcher at the Vasa Museum in Stockholm. She specializes in European domestic war propaganda in the early modern period, on which she has published *The Story of War: Church and Propaganda in France and Sweden 1610–1710* (2017). She works at the nexus of museums and academia, promoting collaborations and combining the two research traditions of museum objects and archive studies, for example as co-editor (with Karin Sennefelt) of *Fråga föremålen: Handbok till historiska studier av materiell kultur* (2014). Her latest publication is the edited volume, *The Sculptures of Vasa: A Story of Power* (2021) and she is currently researching the people on and around the ship *Vasa*.

Ida Hughes Tidlund is a postgraduate research student in Ethnology at Stockholm University. Her thesis, to be completed in late 2021, concerns the nature of the maritime borders of the Åland Islands since their establishment. Her research interests include islands, borders, and historical sources. Her recent publications include *Märket. The makings and meanings of a border in the Baltic Sea* (2019), and *Och ålänningarna började sköta sig själva. Ålänningar i historisk vardag berättar om sin plats och sin tid* (2021).

Hanna Jansson is a postgraduate researcher in Ethnology at Stockholm University and at the Centre for Maritime Studies. Her research interests include rituals, storytelling, and digital folklore. Among her recent publications are her thesis, *Drömmen om äventyret: Långfärdsseglares reseberättelser på internet* (2017), 'Ashes, Law and (Dis)Order: Negotiating Authority in Ash Scattering Rituals', *Ethnologia Scandinavica* (2021), 'At the Times of Writing: Expectation and Experience in Cruising Sailors' Online Travelogues', *Western Folklore* (2020), and 'Med tanke på läsarna: Resebloggandets narrativa och sociala balansgång', *Tidskrift for Kulturforskning* (2019).

Fredrik Kämpe is a postgraduate research student in History at the Centre for Maritime Studies at Stockholm University. His thesis will address the protection of Swedish long-distance shipping in the second half of the eighteenth century, and especially the role of the Konvojkommissariatet, Sweden's Convoy Office, but his interests extend to maritime and naval history of all kinds. He also works at the Swedish Naval Museum in Karlskrona.

Andreas Linderoth is the research coordinator at the Swedish Naval Museum in Karlskrona and has a PhD in History from Lund University. His research interests include Swedish naval history of the nineteenth and twentieth centuries and Sweden in the Cold War. He is the editor of several books, the latest being *Fredrik Henrik af Chapman: Myt och verklighet* (2020). He has also published on Swedish naval officers and the introduction of torpedo boats and submarines in the Swedish navy.

Leos Müller is Professor of History and Director of the Centre for Maritime Studies at Stockholm University. His research interests include Sweden's maritime history, early modern neutrality, and Sweden's place in global history. His publications include *Consuls, Corsairs and Commerce: The Swedish Consular Service and Long-Distance Shipping, 1720–1815* (2004), *Sveriges första globala århundrade: En 1700-tals historia* (2018), and *Neutrality in World History: Themes in World History* (2019). He is co-editor (with Simon Ekström) of CEMAS's recent collaborative volume *Angöringar: Berättelser och kunskap från havet* (2017).

Abigail Christine Parkes is a postgraduate research student at the school of engineering at the University of Southampton. Her research focus is the use of the longbow aboard *Mary Rose*, integrating material science techniques into archaeology to better understand the weapon itself. Her other research interests include medieval England, blackness in medieval and Tudor society, early seafaring, and Ancient Egypt. She is also working with the Nautical Archaeological Society to catalogue a collection of international, traditional watercraft records to make them accessible.

About the Centre for Maritime Studies

The Centre for Maritime Studies (CEMAS), founded in 2010, is an interdisciplinary research initiative for maritime studies and a collaborative effort between Stockholm University and the Swedish National Maritime and Transport Museums (SMTM). CEMAS brings together researchers of maritime studies, primarily in ethnology, archaeology, and history, and coordinates international networks and contacts in order to strengthen ties between researchers in the maritime research area. CEMAS offers a PhD programme of internationally high standards.

Who are we?

The current members of the CEMAS Steering Board are Göran Blomqvist (Chairperson), Anna Götlind (Stockholm University), Sarah Holst Kjaer (Stockholm University), Nanouschka Myrberg Burström (Stockholm University), Anna Maria Forssberg (SMTM), Andreas Linderoth (SMTM), Fredrik Svanberg (SMTM), and Fredrik Kämpe (PhD student representative).

The researchers currently associated with CEMAS are Leos Müller (Professor of History and head of CEMAS), Simon Ekström (Professor of Ethnology), Hanna Jansson (postdoc in ethnology, 2019–2021), Mirja Arnshav (postdoc in archaeology, 2021–), Ida Hughes Tidlund, (PhD student in ethnology, 2016–), and Fredrik Kämpe (PhD student in history, 2017–).

A selection of CEMAS publications, 2010–2021

2010

Ekström, Simon, 'Begrepp i bur: Om kulturbruk och kulturbråk', *Kulturella perspektiv* 3 (2010), 5–17.

Lundblad, Stefan & Leos Müller, 'Centre for Maritime Studies (CEMAS): A New Hub of Maritime Historical Research in Sweden', *International Journal of Maritime History*, 22/1 (2010), 279–81.

Müller, Leos, 'Swedish Shipping in Southern Europe and Peace Treaties with North African States: An Economic Security Perspective', *Historical Social Research* 35/4 (2010), 194–209.

Müller, Leos, 'The Swedish–Norwegian consular services in the nineteenth century (1814–1905)', Jörg Ulbert (ed.), *European Consular Services 1800–1900* (Rennes 2010), 261–270.

Müller, Leos, Göran Rydén & Holger Weiss (eds.), *Globalhistoria från periferin: Norden 1600–1850* (Lund 2010).

2011

Müller, Leos, 'Sweden's neutral trade under Gustav III: The ideal of commercial independence under the predicament of political isolation', in Koen Stapelbroek (ed.), *Trade and War: The Neutrality of Commerce in the Inter-State System* (Helsinki 2011), 143–60.

Müller, Leos, 'The Swedish Convoy Office and Shipping Protection Costs', in Anna Maria Forssberg, Mats Hallenberg, Orsi Husz & Jonas Nordin (eds.), *Organizing History: Studies in Honour of Jan Glete* (Lund 2011), 255–75.

Müller, Leos, 'The Swedish East India Company: Strategies and Functions of an Interloper', in Markus A. Denzel, Jan de Vries & Philipp Robinson Rössner (eds.), *Small is Beautiful? Interlopers and Smaller Trading Nations in the Pre-Industrial Period* (Stuttgart 2011), 73–93.

Müller, Leos, Philipp Robinson Rössner & Toshiaki Tamaki (eds.), *The Rise of the Atlantic Economy and the North Sea/Baltic Trades, 1500–1800* (Stuttgart 2011) published with the support of CEMAS.

2012

Müller, Leos, 'Svensk sjöfart, neutralitet och det väpnade neutralitetsförbundet 1780–1783', *Sjuttonhundratal: Nordic Yearbook for Eighteenth-Century Studies* (2012), 39–58.

Müller, Leos, 'The Forgotten Age of Swedish Shipping: The Eighteenth Century', *International Journal of Maritime History*, 24/2 (2012), 1–18.

Müller, Leos, 'The League of Armed Neutrality and Sweden's Policy in the Late Eighteenth Century', *Revue d'Histoire Nordique* 14 (2012), 131–50.

2013

Ekström, Simon, 'Följa hummer', *Rig* 3 (2013), 65–79.

Müller, Leos, 'Peace: Sweden's Neutrality and the Eighteenth-Century Inter-State System', in Göran Rydén (ed.), *Sweden in the Eighteenth-Century World: Provincial Cosmopolitans* (Farnham 2013), 201–21.

Svensson, Harry R:son, '"Det är märkvärdigt hur 10 á 12 personer, hvilka en gång har varit tillsammans kan spridas ut öfver jordytan": Svenska örlogsofficerare i utrikes tjänst under 1800-talet', *Militärhistorisk Tidskrift* (2013), 87–104.

Svensson, Harry R:son, 'Svenska örlogsofficerare i utrikes tjänst under 1800-talet', *Marinmusei Vänners Årsbok* (2013), 19–39.

2014

Arnshav, Mirja (ed.), *Svenska Sjömanstatueringar* (Stockholm 2014) with contributions by CEMAS researchers Simon Ekström and Lisa Hellman.

Ekström, Simon, 'Var slutar en hummer? Om familjehistorier, hummerfiske och platsskapanden', in Katarina Ek-Nilsson, Lina Midholm, Annika Nordström, Katarina Saltzman & Göran Sjögård (eds.), *Naturen för mig: Nutida röster och kulturella perspektiv* (Gothenburg 2014), 77–90.

Hellman, Lisa, 'Espaces d'intersection: Les relations sociales des employés de la Compagnie Suédoise des Indes Orientales à Canton au XVIIIe siècle', in Gérard Le Bouedëc (ed.), *L'Asie, la mer, le monde: Le temps des compagnies des Indes* (Rennes 2014), 117–134.

Hellman, Lisa, 'Ett ensamt skepp på öppet hav? Kopplingar, kontakter och utbyten ombord på svenska ostindiefarare', *Historisk Tidskrift* 3 (2014), 357–84.

Hellman, Lisa, 'Using China at Home: Knowledge Production and Gender in the Swedish East India Company, 1730–1800', *Itinerario* 1 (2014), 35–55.

Makko, Aryo, 'I Imperialismens kölvatten? Ett maritimt perspektiv på stormaktsspelet, kolonialism utan kolonier och den svensk-norska konsulsstaten, 1875–1905', *Historisk Tidskrift* 3 (2014), 499–523.

Müller, Leos & Stefan Eklöf Amirell (eds.), *Persistent Piracy: Historical Perspectives on Maritime Violence and State Formation* (Houndmills 2014).

Müller, Leos & Stefan Lundblad (eds.), special issue on maritime history, *Historisk tidskrift* 3 (2014).

Svensson, Harry R:son, 'The Case of Fabian Philip, Karlskrona's First Jewish Entrepreneur: A Swedish Example of the Port Jews Phenomenon?', *Sjuttonhundratal: Nordic Yearbook for Eighteenth-Century Studies* (2014), 69–89.

2015

Arnshav, Mirja, *Medeltidsbåtarna från kvarteret Svalan: En dokumentationsrapport baserad på båtfynden från undersökningarna 1991* (Stockholm 2015).Frihammar, Mattias, 'Vrak och övergivna båtar: En armada i minnets marginaler', in Helena Hörnfeldt, Lars-Eric Jönsson, Marianne Larsson & Anneli Palmsköld (eds.), *I utkanter och marginaler: En vänbok till professor Birgitta Svensson* (Stockholm 2015), 165–76.

Hellman, Lisa, *Navigating the foreign quarters: Everyday life of the Swedish East India Company employees in Canton and Macao 1730–1830* (PhD thesis, Stockholm University; Stockholm 2015).

Makko, Aryo & Leos Müller (eds.), *I främmande hamn: Den svenska och svensk-norska konsulstjänsten ca 1700–1985* (Malmö 2015).

Müller, Leos & Hanna Hodacs, 'Chests, Tubs, and Lots of Tea: The European Market for Chinese Tea and the Swedish East India Company, *c.*1730–1760', in Felicia Gottman, Hanna Hodacs, Chris Nierstrasz & Maxine Berg (eds.), *Goods from the East, 1600–1800: Trading Eurasia* (Houndmills 2015), 277–93.

2016

Ekström, Simon, Leos Müller & Tomas Nilson (eds.), *Sjövägen till Sverige: Från 1500-talet till våra dagar* (Malmö 2016).

Frihammar, Mattias, 'Maritimt minnesland: Om båtar, fritid och nostalgi', in Kerstin Gunnemark (eds.), *Sommarliv i Norden: Om minnen, drömmar och materialitet* (Gothenburg 2016), 301–324.

Marzagalli, Silvia & Leos Müller, '"In apparent disagreement with all law of nations in the world": Negotiating neutrality for shipping and trade during the French Revolutionary and Napoleonic Wars', *International Journal of Maritime History* (2016), 108–117.

Müller, Leos, 'Swedish merchant shipping in troubled times: The French Revolutionary Wars and Sweden's neutrality 1793–1801', *International Journal of Maritime History* (2016), 147–64.

Müller, Leos, 'Trading with Asia without a Colonial Empire in Asia: Swedish Merchant Networks and Chartered Company Trade, 1760–1790', in Cátia Antunes & Amélia Polónia (eds.), *Beyond Empires: Global, Self-Organizing, Cross-Imperial Networks, 1500–1800* (Leiden 2016), 235–52.

Pålsson, Ale, *Our Side of the Water: Political Culture in the Swedish Colony of St Barthélemy 1800–1825* (PhD thesis, Stockholm University; Stockholm 2016).

Svensson, Harry R:son, 'The Cultural Impact of Swedish Royal Navy Officers' Foreign Duty on Karlskrona Society', *Marinmusei Vänners Årsbok* (2016), 97–112.

2017

Arnshav, Mirja & Anna McWilliams, 'Submarines in the Silent World: Exploring Films as an Archaeological Record', *Journal of Contemporary Archaeology*, vol 4, no 1. (2017), 19–37.

Ekström, Simon & Leos Müller (eds.), *Angöringar: Berättelser och kunskap från havet* (Gothenburg 2017) (edited volume with contributions by CEMAS researchers).

Ekström, Simon, 'Långt bort och förunderligt nära: Den arkivaliska serien som kulturvetenskaplig källa och vetenskaplig metod', Lars-Eric Jönsson & Fredrik Nilsson (eds.), *Kulturhistoria: En etnologisk metodbok* (Lund 2017), 23–40.

Ekström, Simon, *Humrarna och evigheten: Kulturhistoriska essäer om konsumtion, begär och död* (Gothenburg 2017).

Hammar, AnnaSara, 'Att klara livhanken i en främmande stad: Om båtsmansfamiljer i Stockholm på 1670-talet', in Marko Lamberg & Anna Götlind (eds.), *Tillfälliga stockholmare: Människor och möten under 600 år* (Stockholm 2017).

Jansson, Hanna, *Drömmen om äventyret: Långfärdsseglares reseberättelser på internet* (PhD thesis, Stockholm University; Stockholm 2017).

Kämpe, Fredrik, 'Neutralitetens pris: Handelsflottan och folkförsörjningen', in Mirja Arnshav & Andreas Linderoth (eds.), *Sverige och första världskriget: Maritima perspektiv* (Lund 2017), 97–112.

Müller, Leos, 'Under svensk flagg i Medelhavet: Algeriska sjöpass 1770–1800', in Marie Lennersand & Leos Müller (eds.), *Från Afrikakompaniet till Tokyo: En vänbok till György Nováky* (Stockholm 2017), 38–63.

Svensson, Harry R:son, *Fabian Philip, familjen Ruben och örlogsstaden: Entreprenörs-familjen som grundade Mosaiska församlingen i Karlskrona 1780–1945* (PhD thesis, Stockholm University; Stockholm 2017).

2018

Eriksson, Niklas, 'A New View of the "Edesö Wreck": Identifying the Swedish naval vessel *Bodekull*, built 1659–1661 and sunk 1678 from written sources', *International Journal of Nautical Archaeology* 47 (2018), 391–404.

Eriksson, Niklas, 'Trupptransporten som blev en mjölskuta: identifieringen av "Dalarövraket" som flottans fartyg *Bodekull* (1661–1678)', *Forum Navale* 74 (2018), 12–52.

Hellman, Lisa, 'The Life and Loves of Michael Grubb: A Swedish Trader in Eighteenth-Century Canton and Macao', in Paul van Dyke & Susan Schopp (eds.), *Private Side of the Canton Trade 1700–1840* (Hong Kong 2018).

Müller, Leos, 'The Forgotten History of Maritime Neutrality, 1500–1800', in Pascal Lottaz & Herbert Reginbogin (eds.), *Notions of Neutrality* (Lanham 2018), 67–86.

Müller, Leos, Peter G. Maxwell-Stuart & Steve Murdoch (eds.), *Unimpeded Sailing: A Critical Edition of Johann Gröning's Navigatio Libera* (Leiden 2018), extended 1698 edition.

Müller, Leos, *Sveriges första globala århundrade: En 1700-talshistoria* (Stockholm 2018).

2019

Arnshav, Mirja, 'En familjetragedi i Ulvens kölvatten', *Fynd: Tidskrift för Göteborgs Arkeologiska Museum och Fornminnesföreningen i Göteborg* (2018).

Arnshav, Mirja, 'Pälshandlare, flyktingsmugglare och ingermanländare: Tre gåtfulla båtvrak utmed den bottniska kusten', in Marcus Lindholm, Staffan Beijar & Kenneth Gustavsson (eds.), *Bottnisk Kontakt XIX* (Mariehamn 2019), 104–23.

Ekström, Simon, 'Grymma skämt: Humrar, svart humor och existentiell ångest', in Simon Ekström & Lars Kaijser (eds.), *Djur: Berörande möten och kulturella smärtpunkter* (Stockholm 2019), 173–98.

Eriksson, Niklas, 'Gribshunden – det sista drakskeppet?', *Gränslös* 10, Centrum för öresundsstudier, Lunds universitet, (2019), 11–27.

Eriksson, Niklas, 'Gribshunden: Vraget af kong Hans skib', *Skalk*, nr 2 (2019), 612.

Eriksson, Niklas, 'How large was Mars? An investigation of the dimensions of a legendary Swedish warship, 1563–1564', *Mariner's Mirror* 105/3 (2019), 260–74.

Eriksson, Niklas, 'Skeppsvrak i Haninge skärgård', in Anna Röst (ed.), *Haninge: Kulturhistorisk översikt* (Haninge 2018), 30–4.

Eriksson, Niklas, et al., 'Gribshunden – medeltidens modernaste skepp', *Gribshunden 1495: medeltidens modernaste skepp*, Blekingeboken 97, (2019), 11–40.

Jansson, Hanna 'Med tanke på läsarna: Resebloggandets narrativa och sociala balansgång', *Tidskrift for Kulturforskning* 1 (2019), 5–22.

Müller, Leos, *Neutrality in World History: Themes in World History* (New York 2019).

Tidlund, Ida Hughes, 'Märket: The makings and meanings of a border in the Baltic Sea', in Anna Källén (ed.), *Heritage and Borders* (Stockholm 2019), 61–82.

2020

Arnshav, Mirja, '"The sea shall have our weapons": Small arms and forced migration across the Baltic Sea during the Second World War', *Journal of Conflict Archaeology* 19/2–3 (2020), 126–42.

Arnshav, Mirja, 'Flyktingkällan i Katthammarsvik: Om fördrivning av tid och människor', *META: Medeltidsarkeologisk Tidskrift* (2020), 89–109.

Arnshav, Mirja, *De små båtarna och den stora flykten: Arkeologi i spåren av andra världskrigets baltiska flyktingbåtar* (PhD thesis, Stockholm University; Lund 2020).

Ekström, Simon, 'From Excerpt to Cosplay. Paths of Knowledge in the Archive', *Culture Unbound*, nr 1, 2020, 116–40.

Ekström, Simon, 'Hummer på bordet: Hundra år av publika måltider och kommunikativa råvaror', Charlotte Birnbaum & Stephan Rössner (eds.), *Alla tiders råvaror: Från skämt kött till gotländsk tryffel*, Gastronomisk kalender. Gastronomiska akademiens årsbok (Stockholm 2020), 122–33.

Jansson, Hanna, 'At the Times of Writing: Experience and Expectation in Cruising Sailors' Online Travelogues', *Western Folklore* 79/2–3 (2020), 251–83.

Kämpe, Fredrik, 'Chapmans mångsidiga fregatter: Nya perspektiv på Bellonatypen', in Andreas Linderoth (ed.), *Fredrik Henrik af Chapman: Myt & verklighet* (Karlskrona 2020), 191–211.

Müller, Leos & Klas Rönnbäck, 'Swedish East India trade in a value-added analysis, c.1730–1800', *Scandinavian Economic History Review* (2020), 1–18.

Müller, Leos, 'Scandinavian Trade in Canton and "Borrowed Bengal Money": The Global Role of Minor European Companies Trading in Asia, 1760–1786', *Journal of World History* 31/3 (2020), 597–619.

2021

Ekström, Simon, 'Döden efter döden: Om museer som dödslandskap', in Emilie Reinhold & Oscar Vandery (eds.), *På tal om döden: Essäer* (Gothenburg 2021), 167–92.

Ekström, Simon, *Sjödränkt: Spektakulär materialitet från havet* (Gothenburg 2021).

Eriksson, Niklas, *Stormaktsskärgård: Marin landskapsarkeologi utmed farlederna mot Stockholm* (forthcoming Lund 2021).